Ebony Magazine and Lerone Bennett Jr.

Ebony Magazine and Lerone Bennett Jr.

Popular Black History in Postwar America

E. JAMES WEST

UNIVERSITY OF
ILLINOIS PRESS
Urbana, Chicago, and Springfield

Frontispiece: Lerone Bennett Jr. in his office at the Johnson
Publishing Company in Chicago, 1973. Photo courtesy of the
National Archives, Environmental Protection Agency.

Library of Congress Cataloging-in-Publication Data
Names: West, E. James, author.
Title: Ebony magazine and Lerone Bennett Jr. : popular black
    history in postwar America / E. James West.
Description: Urbana : University of Illinois Press, 2020. | Includes
    bibliographical references and index.
Identifiers: LCCN 2019032960 (print) | LCCN 2019032961 (ebook)
    | ISBN 9780252043116 (cloth) | ISBN 9780252084980
    (paperback) | ISBN 9780252051999 (ebook)
Subjects: LCSH: Ebony (Chicago, Ill.)—History. | Bennett, Lerone,
    Jr., 1928-2018. | Journalists—United States—Biography. |
    African American journalists—Biography. | Historians—
    United States—Biography. | African American historians—
    Biography.
Classification: LCC PN4900.E34 W47 2020 (print) | LCC PN4900.
    E34 (ebook) | DDC 051—dc23
LC record available at https://lccn.loc.gov/2019032960
LC ebook record available at https://lccn.loc.gov/2019032961

To Candi

Contents

Acknowledgments

Thanks to Dawn Durante, the University of Illinois Press, and my anonymous readers for dragging this project toward a semblance of respectability.

Thanks to the inimitable Eithne Quinn.

Thanks to the Arts and Humanities Research Council, the British Association of American Studies, Duke University, the Eccles Center for American Studies at the British Library, Emory University, the Fulbright Commission, the Hagley Museum and Library, Historians of the Twentieth Century United States, the Leverhulme Trust, the Library of Congress, Northumbria University, the United States Embassy in London, the University of Chicago, the University of Manchester, and other institutions and organizations which have financially supported this project.

Thanks to friends, colleagues, and correspondents Joy Bennett, Tom Bishop, Timuel Black, Simeon and Carol Booker, Onyema Bright, David Brown, Nathan Cardon, Rod Clare, Beverly Cook, Alex Cooke, Julie Devonald, Andrew Fearnley, Doug Field, Cynthia Fife-Townsel, Raquel Flores-Clemons, Marnia Gardner, Nick Grant, Josh Gulam, Aaisha Haykal, Laretta Henderson, Barbara Karant, Sam and Emma Kulabowila, Colin Lago, Carol Lockman, Katie McGettigan, Anita Mechler, Shayna Mehas, Ethan Michaeli, E. Ethelbert Miller, Amani Morrison, Saima Nasar, Robert and Susie Newton, Jackie Ould, Hannah Parker, Hannah Proctor, Lori Ramos, Ben Reed, Mary-Lou Reker, Will Riddington, Sarah El Sheikh, Ruth Tait, Amy Tobin, Mark Walmsley, Brian Ward,

Christine White, Janine Wilson, Nick Witham, Annie "Nonya" Wonsey, and John Woodford.

Thanks to my family.

Thanks to Skye for keeping me company. You're the worst, but you're ok.

Thanks to Candice Gregory-Thomas, my partner in crime and everything else.

Portions of chapters 2, 3, and 6 were previously published as "The Books You've Waited For: *Ebony* Magazine, the Johnson Book Division, and Black History in Print," in *Against a Sharp White Background: Infrastructures of African American Print*, edited by Brigitte Fielder and Jonathan Senchyne (Madison: University of Wisconsin Press, 2019), 62–82; "Power Is 100 Years Old: Lerone Bennett, Jr., *Ebony* Magazine and the Roots of Black Power." *The Sixties: A Journal of History, Politics and Culture* 9 (2016): 165–88; "A Hero to Be Remembered: *Ebony* Magazine, Critical Memory and the 'Real Meaning' of the King Holiday," *Journal of American Studies* 52 (2018): 503–27.

An overview of Bennett's career addressing some of the main themes and ideas of this book was published as "Lerone Bennett, Jr.: A Life in Popular Black History," *The Black Scholar* 47 (2017): 3–17.

Ebony Magazine and Lerone Bennett Jr.

Introduction

In the June 1969 issue of *Ebony*, its editors used the popular "Backstage" feature to invite readers on a literary tour through the Chicago offices of parent company Johnson Publishing.[1] The magazine's audience was introduced to the circulation team, whose state-of-the-art IBM computers printed mailing lists for close to one million monthly subscribers, as well as other departments housed at the company's imposing headquarters on South Michigan Avenue.[2] Such sojourns were typical of *Ebony*'s "Backstage" column, which, as its title suggests, offered a glimpse into the internal workings of the nation's largest black periodical. A highlight of the tour came in the Promotions Department, where readers were introduced to "a jewel of a mailing piece" that was being distributed to prospective subscribers. The centerpiece was an illustrated brochure titled "Buried Afro-American History." Echoing the title of black bibliophile Arthur Schomburg's seminal 1925 essay in *Survey Graphic*, its editors praised the brochure's effectiveness in enlightening potential subscribers as to why the magazine "digs up the black past."[3] Indeed, "Backstage" declared that the brochure was "so interestingly written and so well illustrated," it would be a shame for existing subscribers to miss out, and invited black history enthusiasts among its audience to request a copy of their own.[4]

When read in isolation, the "Buried Afro-American History" brochure could be dismissed as one of many marketing ploys used by publisher John H. Johnson to reinforce *Ebony*'s status as the most widely read black magazine in the world.[5]

However, when placed in its rightful context, the brochure represents just one small part of a vast and deeply rooted editorial, activist, and educational project. Opening any issue of *Ebony* from the early 1960s onward, readers could find a new installment in one of the magazine's black history series, a commemorative article on a "Negro pioneer" such as Frederick Douglass, news of a black history text marketed through the company's mail order service or reviewed on the "*Ebony* Book Shelf," or a letter to the editor praising its historical coverage. In a publisher's column written in 1968, Johnson noted that an increasing percentage of the magazine's content was geared toward rectifying "how little black people know of their own history." He declared that "from the yellowed pages of forgotten newspapers and from the writings of black historians who have themselves compiled volumes of black history, we have become one of the most authoritative sources of black history in the world today."[6]

Such statements were foregrounded in the writing of senior editor Lerone Bennett Jr., who oversaw the development of *Ebony*'s historical content following his arrival at the magazine during the mid-1950s. As the company's in-house historian, Bennett authored scores of articles, series, and special features on black history for *Ebony*. His copy fed directly into more than a dozen books on black history and culture that were published between the early 1960s and the end of the twentieth century—including texts such as *The Challenge of Blackness* and *The Shaping of Black America*, which sought to articulate a "new conceptual envelope for black American history," and wildly popular studies such as *Before the Mayflower*, which remains one of the bestselling black history books of all time.[7] *Ebony* provided Bennett with a readership of millions and the scope to become arguably the most well-known black historian in postwar America.[8] Conversely, Bennett's public standing helped to legitimate *Ebony*'s role as an "authoritative source" for black history education.[9]

Despite its massive circulation, the breadth and depth of its black history content, and the mandate established by its publisher and expanded by its editors, *Ebony*'s enormous influence as a "history book" has been largely overlooked. In turn, notwithstanding his enduring popularity and influence, Bennett's own career both inside and outside of Johnson Publishing has been routinely ignored. This book contributes to a correction of these scholarly oversights, presenting the first substantive analysis of *Ebony*'s historical content, as well as the first in-depth examination of Bennett's career at Johnson Publishing and his emergence as a popular black historian. I focus here on the 1960s, 1970s, and 1980s, a period that scholars such as Pero Dagbovie and Robert Harris Jr. have contended marked black history's "coming of age."[10] In doing so, I place *Ebony* and its contributors within a broader revival of writing on, and interest in, the African American past, one that helped to shift black history from the margins to the mainstream of American historical and cultural thought during the decades following World War II.[11]

Ebony and the Rise of Popular Black History

Since it first appeared on newsstands in November 1945, *Ebony* has endured as a voice and a symbol of African American upward mobility. Based on cash orders for its second issue, *Ebony*'s editors already felt confident enough to anoint it as "the biggest Negro magazine in the world in both size and circulation."[12] By its first anniversary, the periodical had announced an advertising circulation guarantee of four hundred thousand copies per month.[13] An eclectic blend of sports, entertainment, celebrity gossip, and fashion, mixed with a hearty dose of middle-class consumerism and topped with an upbeat promise to "mirror the happier side of Negro life," *Ebony*'s standing as a black counterpart to *Life* magazine carried widespread appeal for an increasingly prosperous and predominantly urban black audience.[14] However, *Ebony* was less well received by black academics such as sociologist E. Franklin Frazier, who accused the magazine of catering to the "make-believe world" of the black bourgeoise—an opinion that would remain in vogue for much of the twentieth century.[15]

Over the past few decades, however, a diverse range of scholars have aimed to complicate the sentiments expressed by Frazier and other early critics of *Ebony*. While new studies acknowledge the limitations of the magazine's middle-class consumerism and its celebration of celebrity culture, they have also noted its role in providing a counternarrative to negative black stereotypes in popular and political culture, and in championing the rise of the black consumer market. As Adam Green rightly observes in his 2007 study, *Selling the Race*, *Ebony*'s classed politics of racial respectability did not negate, although certainly served to shape, its impact as an outlet for new visions of black urban modernity and group identity. Similarly, in *Madison Avenue and the Color Line*, Jason Chambers has emphasized the magazine's role in establishing commercial power as a vital part of the ongoing struggle for civil, social, and political rights during the years following World War II.[16] Such work can be placed alongside that of Lizabeth Cohen, Robert Weems, and other scholars who have reevaluated the role of consumer activism in the modern black freedom struggle.[17]

Scholars have also looked to move away from the myopic focus on publisher Johnson that has characterized much of the public debate around *Ebony*'s significance. A pioneering black corporate executive, entrepreneur, and publisher, Johnson is rightfully regarded as a titan of twentieth-century black business.

Unfortunately, a reluctance to deviate from a heavily curated corporate narrative, compounded by the historiographical influence of Johnson's hagiographic memoir *Succeeding against the Odds*, has left us with a popular version of *Ebony*'s history that is both uneven and incomplete. Thankfully, researchers have increasingly challenged this narrative to position Johnson's accomplishments as, in Green's formulation, the "shared accomplishment of an eclectically diverse and talented staff: one whose varied experiences and social orientation equipped it to represent postwar black life in uniquely ambitious ways."[18] Aided by access to new archival material and digital resources, scholars such as Jonathan Fenderson and Siobhan Carter-David are continuing to expand our understanding of Johnson Publishing Company's magazines: their local, national, and international significance, their cultural, political, and economic legacy, and the editorial and ideological diversity of their collaborators and consumers.[19]

Among such rich debates, one facet of *Ebony*'s content remains curiously underexplored—its role as an outlet for information about black history. That is not to say this role has been completely ignored. Indeed, black scholars such as Vincent Harding and Molefi Kete Asante have long called for a reconsideration of *Ebony*'s value as a history text. In a 1987 article published in *The Black Scholar*, Harding made an enthusiastic case for *Ebony*'s importance as a source of historically oriented content and its significance as "a kind of running contemporary history of [the] black struggle in America."[20] Similarly, Benjamin Quarles has argued that *Ebony*'s content "left a deep imprint on hundreds of thousands of readers hitherto unresponsive to the call of the past."[21] More recent figures such as Laretta Henderson and Margena Christian have also discussed the role of *Ebony* and other Johnson publications as vehicles for African American youth and adult education.[22]

However, no scholar has effectively considered the development of *Ebony*'s role as a "history book": as what communications scholar Carolyn Kitch describes as a "disseminator of information about history (and explainer of history's significance) to African Americans."[23] Arguably, Kitch has come closest to fulfilling this brief through her own work, which has deftly grappled with the intersections of history, American journalism, and public memory. In her 2005 study, *Pages from the Past*, Kitch explores the underappreciated role of American magazines as "public historians" in supplementing and at times supplanting the work of more recognizable historical institutions. Basing one chapter around case studies of *Ebony* and *American Legacy*, a quarterly black periodical focusing on black history and culture which was founded in 1995, the author details the role of black magazines in helping to construct a form of countermemory that challenges white-authored historical perspectives.[24] Yet the starting point for Kitch's analysis is the mid-1980s, a point which—as this book demonstrates—is less a moment of departure than the culmination of a project begun in earnest several decades earlier.

Why should we care about *Ebony*'s engagement with and dissemination of black history content? What lessons can be wrung from focusing on a specific element of an individual periodical, albeit over a relatively long period? Perhaps the easiest argument for our attention can be made on the grounds of *Ebony*'s extraordinary penetration into the homes, beauty salons, and barbershops of black America. As the first chapter of this study illustrates, *Ebony* was hardly the first black periodical to promote black history for a popular audience, nor was its coverage as consistent as that of more educational or historically oriented outlets such as *The Crisis* or the *Negro History Bulletin*. However, the magazine's vast circulation, pass-on readership, and public visibility helped it to surpass these periodicals to emerge as one of the nation's most powerful disseminators of popular black history throughout the period examined in this book.

By its fortieth anniversary in 1985, *Ebony*'s monthly circulation guarantee for advertisers was 1.7 million copies, double the circulation of its closest competitor and weekly sister publication, *Jet*. Based on a pass-on readership of more than five people per copy, magazine statistics firm Media Mark suggested that more than 40 percent of black adults read the magazine every month, the "highest market penetration of any general-interest magazine in the nation."[25] Based on sheer popularity alone, we can argue that the magazine's content is worthy of further interrogation by periodical scholars and students of African American print culture. A renewed focus on *Ebony* also helps to complicate established narratives of black periodical decline during the post–World War II decades. A tendency to equate discussions of the "black press" with the fortunes of black legacy newspapers such as the *Chicago Defender* has meant that the growing influence and readership of black consumer magazines during the later decades of the twentieth century has been largely overlooked.[26]

More broadly, the expansion and evolution of *Ebony*'s historical content reflected the magazine's position at the forefront of a "black history revival" that gathered speed during the years following World War II.[27] Just as the context of *Ebony*'s broader engagement with black history helps us to understand the appeal of its "Buried Afro-American History" brochure, so too does this engagement take on added significance when placed within the postwar transformation of black history's production, reception, and consumption. *Ebony*'s historical content was catalyzed by, contributed to, and served to complement the struggle for black-centered education and the black independent school movement, the institutionalization of black studies within American higher education, the growth of black history programming on commercial television, the embrace of black history by corporate advertisers, the federal recognition of Black History Month, and the movement to establish a national holiday for Dr. Martin Luther King Jr.—all important parts of black history's "coming of age" and its transition from the margins to the center of American cultural, historical, and political representation.[28]

Lerone Bennett Jr. and the Role of the "Popular Black Historian"

While *Ebony* as an organ provides us with a window into this broader shift, we must also acknowledge the figure at the heart of its efforts to promote and disseminate black history. As *Ebony*'s senior editor and in-house historian, Lerone Bennett Jr. was the driving force behind much of its historically oriented content. Following his arrival at the magazine during the 1950s, Bennett wasted little time in carving out a unique niche for himself as a journalist-historian par excellence. The editor used *Ebony* as a platform to establish himself as a nationally recognized expert in black history. This platform became a springboard to participate in a diverse range of black intellectual, educational, and political projects, including the development at Northwestern University of the college's first Afro-American Studies Department and the formation of the Institute of the Black World in Atlanta, Ga. By the 1980s, Bennett had established himself as one of the nation's leading African American historians, with his role at *Ebony* remaining central to his efforts to probe "the deeper meanings of black history."[29]

It is remarkable how little scholarly attention has been afforded Bennett. In a paper at the 2003 annual meeting of the Association for the Study of African American Life and History, Nell Irvin Painter positioned the editor as "one of the most influential historians in the United States," yet with the notable exception of colleagues such as Vincent Harding, as well as the more recent contributions of historians such as Pero Dagbovie and Christopher Tinson, Bennett's work has been largely overlooked.[30] This apathy is indicative of the broader neglect of black intellectual history within the academy, something that organizations such as the African American Intellectual History Society are attempting to address.[31] In Bennett's case, his recent passing in February 2018 at age eighty-nine provided an opportunity for media outlets and the American public to at least partially address this imbalance. Former colleague A. Peter Bailey described Bennett in the *Pittsburgh Courier* as a "master journalist, master historian [and] master teacher."[32] Mainstream outlets such as the *New York Times* and the *Boston Globe* eulogized Bennett as a "leading scholarly voice" who was a pillar of the black community and "essential in the formation of *Ebony*'s historic trajectory."[33]

Yet such eulogies provide relatively little insight into the complexities of Bennett's role and reception as a "popular historian." Variations of this term are used throughout this book to describe scholars who have established their reputation as historians largely or completely in the absence of professional training and, for the most part, outside of the academy. Summarizing the prevailing tone of dismissal, Stefan Berger contends that the popular historian is popular "in the sense of consciously popularizing the results of professional historical research."[34] For Bennett and other black popular historians, the term has been used to both implicitly and explicitly separate their work from that of professionally trained black academics, with Daryl Michael Scott valuing Bennett's contributions "only as a motivational tool or as a means of counting grievances."[35] These intellectual hierarchies have been enforced by scholars such as August Meier and Elliott Rudwick, whose landmark 1986 study *Black History and the Historical Profession* focused on the "professionalization" of black history through figures such as Carter G. Woodson and largely dismissed the important contributions of "amateur" black historians.[36] Bennett himself was keenly aware of such criticisms, noting in later interviews how the label of "popular historian" was often used to marginalize his work.[37]

This study builds on the more recent work of figures such as Stephen Hall, Ian Rocksborough-Smith, and Jeffrey Snyder to reconsider Bennett's place within the black intellectual and historical canon.[38] As Painter noted in her 2003 tribute to Bennett, the cultural meanings of black history "interest all Americans, not just professional historians," and different authors and historiographical traditions are necessary in the task of deconstructing and reconstructing American history.[39] Aiming to avoid pigeonholing Bennett's scholarly interventions, I offer a reading of his work that is sympathetic to what Hall describes as the "complexities of black historical production and the myriad ways in which black writers craft a historical discourse."[40] In turn, I join Snyder in advocating for an inclusive, rather than exclusive, view of black history work that includes outlets such as *Ebony* as well as "lay historians, scholars in other disciplines, schoolteachers, schoolchildren, bibliophiles, librarians, archivists, "race women," "race men," journalists, and artists."[41]

In short, I set out to answer the following questions: What can we gain by treating Bennett's writing in *Ebony* as significant historical scholarship, rather than assuming its subservience to the work of professionally trained historians? What might we learn by taking *Ebony* seriously as a "history book," based on the strength of its voice, the sincerity of its editors, and the reception of its audience? How was the magazine's developing black history voice shaped and reshaped by a diverse and often competing array of internal and external forces? And what can a closer examination of *Ebony*'s historical content tell us about the broader trajectory and impact of the "black history revival" that fed into and back out of the postwar black freedom struggle?

Outline, Archives, and Intervention

To address these and other pertinent questions, I have divided this study into six broadly chronological chapters. Chapter 1 connects the early development of, and reception to, *Ebony*'s historical content with the longstanding role of black periodicals as outlets for the dissemination and popularization of black history. As this chapter demonstrates, an emphasis on the differences between "popular" and "professional" black historians or historical texts can often obscure the complex, collaborative, and highly contested evolution of black history as a field of study throughout the nineteenth and early twentieth century. From the content of *Freedom's Journal* and other antebellum black newspapers to the impact of nationally syndicated African American periodicals such as the *Pittsburgh Courier*, journalists, scholars, and activists strategically employed black periodicals as a tool to help advance black history education and to disseminate information about the African American past.

Chapters 2 and 3 focus on the consolidation of *Ebony*'s role as a "history text" during the 1960s and the connected emergence of Bennett as a nationally recognized popular historian and black public intellectual. In chapter 2 I analyze the close connections between Bennett's first "Negro History" series, which was published in *Ebony* during 1961 and 1962, and the release of his first book-length study, *Before the Mayflower*, which had its roots in the magazine's black history series. The relationship between these texts and the response to them from *Ebony*'s audience and external critics help illuminate the deeply contested nature of *Ebony*'s role as an outlet for black history education. In chapter 3, the role of black history as a both a blueprint for and a medium to help direct and decipher contemporary social and political struggles is brought into sharper focus, most notably through an exploration of *Ebony*'s 1965 special issue on "The WHITE Problem in America" and the publication of Bennett's "Black Power" series. Against the backdrop of Black Power's emergence as a national slogan during 1967, Bennett's efforts to examine the impact of "Black Power" during Reconstruction helped to counteract mainstream media attempts to paint Black Power as an apolitical and ahistorical phenomenon.

Chapter 4 situates the evolution of *Ebony*'s historical content during the late 1960s and early 1970s within the broader struggle for black-centered education and the impact of the black campus movement. Taking aim at textbook bias and white American "heroes" such as Abraham Lincoln helped to consolidate *Ebony*'s "legitimacy" as a black-authored historical text, while special issues such as "The Black Revolution" reinforced the connections between black radical protest in the past and present. On an individual level, Bennett's deepening relationship with organizations such as the Institute of the Black World and Northwestern University helped to enrich his understanding of black history as a scholarly discipline and political philosophy. However, such connections also underscored the uniqueness of his role at *Ebony* as well as the complexities of combining his position at Johnson Publishing with his burgeoning reputation as a militant black historian and activist-intellectual.

Chapters 5 and 6 focus on *Ebony*'s response to the "mainstreaming" of black history in American popular and political culture during the 1970s and 1980s. For much of the first four chapters, *Ebony*'s importance as an outlet for black history education can be measured against the broader neglect of the African American past within American society. However, the assassination of Dr. Martin Luther King Jr. in 1968 and the widespread rioting that followed his death were symptoms of increasing racial tensions that forced American media companies, politicians, and educational institutions to at least partially address the black community's enduring demands for greater cultural and historical representation. For the purposes of this study, the most significant fallout from the riot and revolt of the 1960s was the "turn" toward black history, perhaps most clearly seen through the development of Black Studies as a scholarly discipline, the willingness of white politicians to use "black heritage" as a means to court African American voters, and the tremendous impact of Alex Haley's *Roots* saga and its subsequent miniseries adaptation by the American Broadcasting Company during the 1970s.

Centered on public commemoration of the American bicentennial and the movement to establish a national holiday for Dr. Martin Luther King Jr., these chapters interrogate how *Ebony*'s editors and readers negotiated the magazine's continued importance as a "history book" in a changing literary, cultural, and political climate. *Ebony*'s discussion of these landmarks and events revealed growing tensions between a broader retreat from an activist-oriented discussion of black history and Bennett's continued emphasis on the radical potential of the African American past. *Ebony*'s senior editor rejected the commodification and commercialization of black heritage during the bicentennial as "an affront to truth and freedom," putting him at odds with the magazine's dogged support of capitalism as a route to racial equality.[42] In turn, while *Ebony*'s coverage of the King holiday movement revealed generational anxieties over the future of black history participation, Bennett seized it as an opportunity to remind readers that black history was a political philosophy that "organizes our world and valorizes our projects."[43]

This project would not have been possible without two important new collections of archival material. Bennett's partially processed papers at Emory University, which include a wealth of correspondence, personal papers, photographs, and audiovisual material, proved vital in helping me to flesh out the connections between Bennett's own writing and the broader development and impact of *Ebony*'s role as a black history text. Serendipitous circumstances also conspired to provide me with access to an unseen collection of Bennett's papers at Chicago State University Archives and Special Collections, where, as part of a fellowship with the Black Metropolis Research Consortium, I was able to explore this vast trove of material and contributed to its early processing and organization. In addition to Bennett's papers at Emory and Chicago State, I have mined dozens of other archival collections at institutions, including, but not limited to, Atlanta University Center, Chicago History Museum, Chicago Public Library, Duke University, Howard University, the Library of Congress, New York Public Library, Northwestern University, the University of Chicago, and the University of Illinois.

Despite such rich archival engagement, it is important to note the limitations of this study and to clarify the extent of my ambitions for this work. My access to the Bennett papers at Emory University came before his death, and much of the embargoed material that became available after his passing has not made its way into this book. Similarly, while I was afforded the unique opportunity to examine Bennett's papers at Chicago State, this access was truncated by copyright complications that placed an embargo on the collection and have severely limited subsequent explorations.[44] Perhaps most frustrating has been the continuing reluctance of Johnson Publishing Company to allow researchers access to its corporate archives, something that has been compounded by the company's increasingly precarious financial position, culminating in the sale of *Ebony* and *Jet* in May 2016 and its subsequent filing for bankruptcy liquidation less than three years later.[45] Let me be clear: this book is not and does not claim to be a comprehensive account of *Ebony*'s role as a black history text. Rather, I hope that this intervention provides both insight and inspiration for subsequent scholars to probe deeper into the tremendous cultural, historical, and sociopolitical impact of *Ebony* and Johnson Publishing Company.

Bennett's recent passing, which has brought his career and legacy back into the spotlight, has also prompted me to think seriously about the organization and focus of this study. As this manuscript has developed, it has oscillated between an attempt to write an account of Bennett's scholarly interventions through the lens of his role at *Ebony* and an effort to construct a history of *Ebony*'s role as a "history book" in which Bennett plays a central role. Given his remarkable productivity and popularity, Bennett remains a strikingly under-studied figure, and it is my hope that his collections at Emory, as well as a speedy resolution to his embargoed papers at Chicago State, will foster a new wave of critical scholarship. Certainly, there is much more to be said about Bennett as an individual: his personal and interpersonal relationships, his early childhood and college years, his eclectic range of book-length studies, his outspoken sup-port of reparations, his participation in landmark gatherings such as the Sixth Pan African Congress in 1974 and the Second World Black and African Festi-val of Arts and Culture in 1977, and his contributions to and participation in a tremendous range of black intellectual and activist networks on a local and international scale.[46] One day soon, someone—perhaps even this author—will write a critical intellectual biography of Bennett's life that will be a timely and important contribution to our understanding of modern American cultural and political history.[47]

This is not that book. However, it would be impossible to write a history of *Ebony*'s historical content without placing Bennett at the center. Bennett—both individually and editorially—was the nexus through which much of *Ebony*'s historical content developed. His reputation as a historian and public intel-lectual was vital to legitimating *Ebony*'s role as an outlet for black history. It is perhaps unsurprising, then, that the chapters collected here are in many cases bracketed by important moments in Bennett's professional career, such as the introduction of his first "Negro History" series or the publication of and public response to key essays, such as "Was Abe Lincoln a White Supremacist?" In turn, the chronological focus and boundaries of this study—stretching from the mid-1950s to the mid-1980s—overlap with landmark moments in Ben-nett's own career. I begin my discussion of the magazine's historical content in earnest following Bennett's arrival at *Ebony* during the mid-1950s and end my analysis with his promotion to executive editor in the late-1980s, a moment that consolidated a dramatic decline in his creation of original historical material as he assumed a more much active role in *Ebony*'s day-to-day operations.[48]

Given this overlap, I am conscious that shifting the focus from Johnson to rest just as squarely on Bennett risks replacing one "great man" narrative with another. Certainly, Bennett's role as *Ebony*'s in-house historian elevated him above many of his colleagues.[49] Yet it also true that *Ebony*'s function as an important outlet for black history did not begin, or end, with its senior editor. As this book illustrates, editors such as Allan Morrison, Era Bell Thompson, Alex Poinsett, and Hoyt Fuller, alongside an array of external contributors and an army of engaged readers, all played a significant role in pushing *Ebony* and Johnson Publishing toward a more sustained engagement with black history and the black freedom struggle. In one of his most instructive essays, "A Living History," Bennett contended that black history was a "perpetual conversation" that saw different voices "blending together into a mighty chorus that contrasts and combines different themes."[50] We might use this same analogy to think about the development of *Ebony*'s role as an outlet for popular black history. Bennett's voice was undoubtedly one of the loudest and most eloquent in the choir. However, it was also one in a chorus of many that came to influence all elements of the magazine's production and reception.

CHAPTER 1

An Abundance of Outright Untruths

From its inception in 1945, *Ebony*'s mandate to "mirror the happier side of Negro life" appeared to offer an alternative editorial philosophy than the one familiar to many readers of the black press. Over the previous century black periodicals had developed a reputation as a "crusading press" that campaigned tirelessly against racial injustice. The names of newspapers such the *Chicago Defender* aptly reflected a steadfast mission to protect black lives and, as Langston Hughes argued, provide "the journalistic voice of a largely voiceless people."[1] By contrast, *Ebony*'s aspirational vision of black middle-class living seemed at best a half-hearted attempt to soft-pedal civil rights. For critics such as E. Franklin Frazier, it was unclear how the magazine's enthusiastic embrace of conspicuous consumption or its exposés of "why Negroes buy Cadillacs" contributed to the ongoing struggle for racial equality.[2] Reflecting on his own childhood memories of the magazine, historian Jonathan Scott Holloway recalls that *Ebony*'s "editorial agenda was strikingly consistent: share local black success stories; visit movie stars or athletes or musicians at their homes; emphasize glamour and entrepreneurship; and above all, make sure everyone is smiling and has beautiful skin, hair, and teeth."[3]

However, if we choose to center other aspects of the periodical's coverage—most notably its efforts to promote black history—we can see how *Ebony*'s content marked not a departure from but an extension of an enduring black print tradition. While the magazine's content was mediated by its broader focus on consumerism and celebrity culture, *Ebony*'s black history and historically oriented content expanded the black press's long-standing role as a conduit for "black cultural heritage, moral values and educational knowledge."[4] Articles profiling the historical contributions of black pioneers maintained the magazine's promise to "mirror the happier side of Negro life" and expanded its preoccupation with "black firsts" to offer a celebratory engagement with the African American past. Intersecting with its developing coverage of the postwar black freedom movement, Vincent Harding has suggested that such content solidified its status as "a kind of running contemporary history of [the] black struggle in America."[5]

As this chapter demonstrates, Johnson's own interest in black heritage can be seen to have helped underpin an admirable, if uneven, push to promote African American history during the magazine's formative years. This was encouraged by early editors such as Allan Morrison and Era Bell Thompson, who agitated to see their own interests in black history and the black diaspora represented on the magazine's pages. The addition of Lerone Bennett Jr. to *Ebony*'s editorial team during the mid-1950s, coupled with the impact of the growing civil rights movement, provided further impetus for new historical articles and exciting public history projects such as the "*Ebony* Hall of Fame." Housed at the magazine's Chicago headquarters, this "unique historical gallery" encouraged reader participation in the construction and commemoration of the African American past.[6] While such projects were often short lived, they helped to lay the groundwork for a more comprehensive editorial engagement with black history, which took root from the beginning of the 1960s.

Black History and the Black Press

In late 1826 a group of activists and freemen gathered at the home of M. Boston Crummell, a former slave and prominent spokesman within New York's black community. The meeting had been arranged to combat the abject racism of the city's white-owned newspapers and their continued attacks on its black residents. Against such woeful misrepresentation, it seemed vital for the black community to formulate its own paper.[7] On March 16, 1827, the first issue of *Freedom's Journal* was released, marking the origins of the black press in America. In its inaugural edition, the *Journal*'s editors, John Russwurm and Samuel Cornish, addressed their readers directly, declaring, "We wish to plead our own cause. Too long have others spoken for us. Too long has the public been deceived by misrepresentations, in things which concern us dearly."[8] In the pursuit of civil rights and emancipation for all, the newspaper emphasized the importance of education in matters pertaining to both the present and the past. This extended beyond the black experience in the United States to include the ancestral homeland, with its editors contending that "useful knowledge of every kind, and everything that relates to Africa, shall find a ready admission into our columns."[9]

Such statements enunciated the desire of African American people to be seen and understood on their own terms. More specifically, Russwurm and Cornish's words powerfully articulated the role of black history and a shared African past in establishing a sense of community for both antebellum free blacks and the enslaved majority. For the *Journal's* editors, education was an "object of the highest importance" and a critical weapon in the battle for mental and physical emancipation. As such, Russwurm and Cornish strove to advertise black schools, celebrate black history, and draw connections between individual enlightenment and the collective advancement of the race.[10] While *Freedom's Journal* would fold after just two years, it was followed by dozens of black newspapers in the decades leading up to the Civil War. As scholars such as Eric Gardner and Elizabeth McHenry have noted, these pioneering publications continued to emphasize cultural and historical literacy as a way for enslaved Africans and free blacks to achieve respectability and join "the enviable ranks of virtuous, intelligent and useful men."[11]

Black periodicals continued to function as key outlets for black historical education during the postbellum era, a role necessitated by the desperate state of black history within the American educational system and the academy. In the aftermath of the Civil War, African American efforts to promote a more representative account of American history were hindered by the entrenchment of institutional racism within the nation's fledgling public-school system.[12] School textbooks became a key tool for the dissemination of racial hatred and the distortion of black history.[13] In the preface to his 1890 study *A School History of the Negro Race in America*, black educator Edward A. Johnson attacked the biases of school textbooks that appeared to have been "written exclusively for white children, and studiously left out the many creditable deeds of the Negro."[14] A similar scene emerged within American academia, where antipathy of black equality during the late nineteenth and early twentieth centuries would manifest itself through the work of the Dunning School and other apologists for white supremacy.[15]

Despite such opposition, African Americans remained committed to the recovery and preservation of their own heritage. In coming to terms with what Orlando Patterson has described as the "social death of slavery," emancipated black Americans placed increasing faith in the historical record as a tool to help construct a "legitimate social identity."[16] Such efforts often manifested themselves through African American literary history, with literature becoming a means to complicate and reformulate black popular memory.[17] Black scholars and historical enthusiasts also looked to create a range of learned societies, libraries, and reading rooms, which were pointed toward the dual goals of "increasing literacy and historical knowledge of the race."[18] Black periodicals played an important role in this process, both in helping to promote the activities of fledgling black history organizations and in functioning themselves as alternative spaces for black history education.

Given the role of black periodicals as outlets for popular black history, as well as the myriad interests of a burgeoning black elite, it is unsurprising that many figures straddled the line between journalism and historical scholarship during the nineteenth and early twentieth centuries.[19] In 1875, civil war veteran and Baptist minister George Washington Williams founded a short-lived black newspaper titled *The Commoner* in Washington, D.C., which he used to publish a number of black history columns.[20] Seven years later, Williams published his two-volume *History of the Negro Race in America*, which John Hope Franklin has contended marked the beginning of the "first generation of scholarship . . . in Afro-American history."[21] Williams was followed by figures such as Booker T. Washington, another renaissance man who, prior to the publication of his 1909 book *The Story of the Negro*, was able to cultivate a significant degree of influence over the black press. An impressively ambitious text, *The Story of the Negro* attempted "to sketch the history of the Negro people in America" in a way that mimicked the bootstraps rhetoric of Washington's influential memoir *Up from Slavery*.[22]

The links between journalism and black history scholarship remained strong into the "second generation" identified by Franklin, which was characterized by professionalization and an increasingly scientific approach to the study of the African American past.[23] Perhaps the most famous member of this generation was W. E. B. Du Bois, who became the first African American to earn a doctorate from Harvard in 1895. Du Bois would later parlay his academic training into an illustrious journalism career, most notably as the editor of *The Crisis*, the monthly magazine of the National Association for the Advancement of Colored People.[24] He envisioned *The Crisis* as a complementary vehicle for scholarly treatises such as his 1915 survey text *The Negro*, with early issues including features on African civilization, black soldiers in the American Civil War, and the Underground Railroad.[25] Other scholars who straddled this divide included William H. Ferris, who balanced his role as the literary editor of Marcus Garvey's *Negro World* with the production of a two-volume history of black life in the New World, titled *The African Abroad*.[26]

At the same time, the increasing professionalization of black historians threatened to create an intellectual hierarchy between black scholars trained by the academy and the continuing work of black journalists, lay historians, and bibliophiles.[27] This apparent bifurcation has tempted scholars to contrast the "scientific methods" of the second generation with the lack of formal training and academic credentials, which "remained the Achilles heel of the Afro-American popular historians."[28] Certainly, the institutionalization of the black history profession created new challenges for self-taught and self-trained "outsider" historians such as Joel Augustus Rogers, described by *The Crisis* in his 1966 obituary as "one of the great popularizers of Negro history."[29] For these figures, the black press remained a key tool for circulating historical material—most clearly seen through Rogers's long-running illustrated series "Your History," which was serialized in the *Pittsburgh Courier*, one of the nation's most widely circulating black periodicals.[30]

Yet this narrative framing risks creating a rigid binary between "professional" and "popular" black historians, and between "reputable" black history outlets (such as academic books and journals) and mass market alternatives (such as the black press). To discuss black historiography in these terms detracts from the myriad overlaps and intersections between a growing but still relatively small cohort of academically trained historians and a much larger pool of lay historians and black bibliophiles. As Stephen Hall has argued, the "wide variety of theoretical, methodological, and ideological tools" used by this diverse cohort of activists, academics, and intellectuals helped to build a "faithful account of the race."[31] Despite its limitations, the work of Rogers and other "lay" historians would have a telling influence on later generations of academically trained but increasingly nationalist-oriented historians.[32]

In turn, professional black historians such as Carter G. Woodson were not averse to using "popular" outlets in spreading the gospel of black history to a wider audience. Often described as the "father" of the black history movement, Woodson was an academically trained historian par excellence who, through his individual scholarship and his role in establishing the Association for the Study of Negro Life and History, arguably did more than any other figure to help professionalize black history as a scholarly discipline. He was also a passionate advocate for the promotion of popular black history and consistently utilized the black press to spread his message. Many of Woodson's book-length contributions were rooted in articles printed in black newspapers, while the black press helped to build mass support for his black history campaign.[33] Woodson would go on to create his own magazine, the *Negro History Bulletin*, which aimed to "reach the masses with authentic historical information."[34]

The *Bulletin* and other black periodicals continued to play an important role in promoting black history during the 1930s, even as support for black history education diminished within public-school systems across the country.[35] More broadly, the World War II era proved to be a pivotal moment for the black press in America. Frustrated by the contradictions between a "war for democracy" abroad and the entrenchment of Jim Crow at home, black newspapers orchestrated the "Double V" campaign, characterized by the *Courier* as a "two-pronged attack against our enslavers at home and those abroad who will enslave us."[36] The campaign brought retribution from the federal government by way of mailing restrictions and indictments for sedition. However, it also served to galvanize black communities across the country and helped lay the groundwork for the postwar civil rights movement.[37]

From a different perspective, the war years saw a new wave of black periodicals emerge that struck a different editorial tone from that of "crusading" black newspapers such as the *Courier*. As the average black reader became more educated and urbane, they looked for periodicals that were "less an initiator of protest than . . . a reflection of the tastes and habits" of the black community.[38] Among the new periodicals created in an attempt to meet this demand were *Color* magazine, published out of Charleston, West Virginia, by I. J. K. Wells, the first state supervisor of Negro education in the country.[39] Other periodicals included *Negro Story*, created by Chicago schoolteacher Alice Browning and social worker Fern Gayden, and *Our World*, the brainchild of John P. Davis, a former *Crisis* editor and a founder of the National Negro Congress.[40] At the forefront of this trend was the *Negro Digest*, which was created in 1942 by an ambitious young entrepreneur named John H. Johnson, with the help of his wife Eunice Johnson and *Defender* contributors Ben Burns and Jay Jackson.[41]

Adam Green has contended that *Negro Digest* was a periodical "unlike any preceding it in black journalism."[42] Adopting an altogether more moderate tone than the one espoused by "race periodicals" such as the *Defender*, the *Digest* introduced itself to readers with the claim that it was "dedicated to the development of interracial understanding and the promotion of national unity."[43] Envisioning his new publication as a black equivalent to *Reader's Digest*, Johnson gambled that the magazine would prove to be a hit with a growing black middle class "desperate for news about itself that existed beyond what was printed in the weekly police blotter or crime column."[44] This gamble proved to be a wise one: within eight months of its initial release the *Digest* was selling around fifty thousand copies a month. A little more than two years after its first publication, the periodical accounted for 20 percent of all black magazine sales in the country.[45]

The *Digest* initially stuck closely to the format its name implied, compiling existing articles on "racial issues, black history, and black identity" from other sources.[46] However, as its influence and popularity increased, the magazine became more ambitious, inviting original contributions that assessed black culture and history within and beyond the borders of the United States. Pero Dagbovie has argued that the *Digest* "served as an important outlet for black historians to share their philosophies of black history."[47] The magazine also printed articles from influential activists such as Eslanda Robeson, whose January 1945 article "Old Country for Thirteen Million" criticized the teaching of black history in American schools and encouraged readers to engage with their own heritage.[48] By this date, Johnson had already set his eyes on an ambitious new project—a glossy black photo-editorial magazine that would champion black middle-class respectability and the power of the "Negro Market."[49]

An Abundance of Outright Untruths

The publisher's vision came to fruition with the release of *Ebony* in November 1945. If *Negro Digest* had been modeled on *Reader's Digest*, *Ebony* took its inspiration from *Life*, the country's leading photo-editorial magazine. The similarities between the two were not lost on the editors of *Life*, which described Johnson's periodical as a "frank imitation."[50] *Ebony* offered black America's "best foot forward" through depictions of a high-functioning, aspirational, and predominantly middle-class black world.[51] Johnson was not the first black publisher to attempt such an ambitious project. Perhaps the most notable previous effort had been *Abbott's Monthly*, an eclectic mix of news, fiction, poetry, and photography issued by *Defender* publisher Robert Abbott during the early 1930s.[52] However, whereas Abbott's magazine struggled in the shadow of the Wall Street Crash, *Ebony* was able to tap into the economic and social gains made by black Americans during World War II. With "almost no fanfare or promotion, minimal advertising in black weeklies, and very little publicity," the magazine's first press run of twenty-five thousand copies immediately sold out.[53]

Ebony's aspirational content was rooted in celebrating black achievements in the present and imagining a better future that promised full participation in American democratic capitalism. However, Johnson's own interest in the black past, which had flowered during his adolescence, can be argued to have encouraged the development of historically oriented content. Mary Herrick, a white civics teacher at DuSable High School, was one important early influence, sneaking Johnson black history books and teaching her students to "be proud of our heritage."[54] The publisher also recalled countless afternoons spent learning about black pioneers, such as Booker T. Washington and Frederick Douglass, under the watchful eye of Vivian Harsh at the Hall Branch of Chicago Public Library. Harsh was the first black librarian to work for the Chicago library system and a prominent local organizer of black history events and book clubs.[55] Johnson's interest in black heritage would endure into adulthood, becoming part of *Ebony*'s mission to celebrate individual black achievement and champion African Americans who had "succeeded against the odds."[56]

These goals were reflected through early historical features such as "Great Negro Thinkers of History" in October 1946, which decried the "abundance of outright untruths about the Negro" espoused by American textbooks. The feature championed the role of pioneering black scientists, mathematicians, poets, and artists "who have given most to the rise of American civilization."[57] Like so much black history writing of the period, *Ebony*'s discussion of historical firsts was heavily gendered, with the magazine predominantly focusing on the contributions of "race men" such as Du Bois and George Washington Carver.[58] The editorial also adopted a meritocratic and reconciliatory tone, arguing that black achievements provided evidence that "intelligence knows no color line."[59] This approach to African American history, described as "contributionism" by Russell Rickford, presented black historical landmarks as "the product of industriousness and self-discipline in an increasingly meritocratic society."[60] Despite its limitations, the feature offers an instructive example of *Ebony*'s efforts to critique textbook bias, something that would become a prominent feature of its content during subsequent decades.

As *Ebony*'s coverage of black history developed, it provided a blend of entertainment and education that mixed recognition of black "firsts" with subtle critiques of American society. In its handling of California's centennial celebrations, *Ebony* denounced the California Centennial Commission's failure to recognize any of the state's "outstanding Negro pioneers" through official commemorations or events. This responsibility fell to the Golden State Mutual Life Insurance Company, which had installed two expansive murals in its new headquarters that "portrayed in strong dynamic colors the Negro's contribution to the history of California."[61] In related features, the magazine regaled readers with tales of black cowboys and traders who had helped shape the American West. Notable figures included James Beckwourth, whose discovery of a pass across the Sierra Nevada helped to instigate the California Gold Rush, and Biddy Mason, who arrived in California as a slave but would go on to become a real estate mogul and one of the richest women in the state.[62]

At the same time, *Ebony* utilized history to maintain an upbeat and deeply patriotic defense of black life in the United States. Perhaps the strongest example of its conciliatory historical tone came through a 1948 photo-editorial titled "Was Lincoln Anti-Negro?" Staunchly defending Lincoln's legacy, the magazine criticized attacks on Lincoln by "Negroes who should know better" and declared the sixteenth president to be "the greatest white friend the Negro ever had."[63] While *Ebony* acknowledged that black life in the United States was far from perfect, it impressed upon its audience that "being a Negro American is not so much of a handicap as a privilege . . . as patriotic Americans, we can truly count our blessings."[64] Such features offered a reminder that Johnson was unwilling to let his staff deviate too far from established historical norms and that the magazine remained primarily concerned with "promoting healthy race relations as well as showing a profit in the bookkeeping department."[65] This position was reinforced by readers such as Irene Cooper, who applauded the article and reiterated its contention that Lincoln was "the truest friend the Negro race has ever known."[66]

Two editors who played a major role in the early development of *Ebony*'s historical content were Allan Morrison and Era Bell Thompson. Morrison had been drafted into the magazine's editorial team shortly after it began publication in 1945. Blessed with an extraordinary memory and insatiable curiosity, Morrison was a journalist seen to echo "the vitality and the spirit" of early black press pioneers such as John Russwurm.[67] Prior to joining *Ebony* he had worked on the short-lived *Negro World Digest* (a precursor to Johnson's own *Negro Digest*) that he had started with friend and associate George Norford.[68] One of the magazine's notable accomplishments during its brief existence was the partial serialization of Earl Conrad's biography of the pioneering abolitionist and political activist Harriet Tubman, a move which ultimately helped Conrad secure a book contract with Associated Publishers in 1943.[69] Seventy years later, Jean Humez argued that Conrad's text remained the "standard biography" of Tubman and applauded its role in transforming her public image into that of "a militant, an African American woman warrior."[70]

Described by Johnson as a "zealous New Yorker who believed civilization stopped at the Hudson River," Morrison did not care for the Midwest and returned to New York in early 1947 to work as the editor of Adam Clayton Powell's *People's Voice*.[71] However, shortly after his return to the East Coast, Johnson opened an *Ebony* office in Manhattan, and Morrison accepted a position as the magazine's New York editor. He would remain with the company up until his premature death at age fifty-two in 1968.[72] While Morrison's colleagues described him as a "fierce Marxist" in private correspondence, Johnson was more concerned with his reputation as an "elegant and eloquent writer."[73] Morrison also found support from other leftists in the magazine's early hierarchy, most notably Ben Burns, a white Jewish editor and lapsed Community Party member, who described his colleague as "one of the most gifted and conscientious black journalists" in the country.[74] Despite such collegiality, Morrison's attempts to develop *Ebony*'s historical content were not always successful, with Jean Blackwell Hutson noting that his efforts to develop more *Ebony* features based on his research into black history and culture at the Schomburg Center in New York were repeatedly frustrated.[75]

Era Bell Thompson was arguably the magazine's strongest advocate for a more diasporic representation of black history and culture.[76] Born and raised in the overwhelmingly white world of small-town North Dakota, Thompson burst onto the literary scene with the publication of *American Daughter* in 1946.[77] Part memoir and part social commentary, the success of *American Daughter* led to a position as an associate editor of *Ebony*, and by the early 1950s Thompson had been promoted to co-managing editor.[78] Possessing a bravado that defied her diminutive stature, Thompson immediately made her presence felt within the male-dominated hierarchy of *Ebony*'s editorial team.[79] Johnson was a huge admirer of Thompson's—later describing the decision to hire her as the proudest of his professional career—and provided considerable latitude for her to take on ambitious travel assignments.[80] In 1953 the editor embarked on a four-month, eighteen-country tour of Africa to report on the growing push for decolonization and to explore the interconnected history of black America and the diaspora.[81] This experience provided extensive material for *Ebony* and fed into the publication of Thompson's second book, *Africa: Land of My Fathers*.[82]

Befitting his reputation as a pioneering black corporate executive, Johnson's ability to utilize black history as a marketing device would also play a pivotal role in the magazine's early development. Indeed, it was arguably the shared appeal of black history that saved *Ebony* from cancellation. The magazine's immediate popularity and high production costs quickly became a major headache for Johnson, who initially ran the magazine at a loss and subsidized its production with the revenue of sister publication *Negro Digest*.[83] Advertising executives were reluctant to chance recommending a black-oriented consumer magazine to their clients, particularly one with such a young publisher at the helm. Despite limited success with advertisers such as Chesterfield cigarettes, the income generated by *Ebony*'s advertising could not keep up with rising production costs. In a rare moment of vulnerability, the November 1947 issue of "Backstage" admitted that "this magazine has proved the most costly publication ever issued in the Negro field, and there have been times when red ink threatened to wipe out the black on our ledgers."[84]

Johnson's salvation came through a meeting with Eugene McDonald, the founder and CEO of the Zenith Radio Corporation. Through background research, Johnson discovered that McDonald was an experienced outdoorsman who had taken part in and underwritten an artic expedition in 1925. Eager to gain McDonald's support, Johnson decided to track down Matthew Alexander Henson, a pioneering black explorer who was believed to have been one of the first men to reach the North Pole.[85] With the help of Morrison, Johnson was able to locate Henson in New York and persuaded the explorer to sign a copy of his 1912 autobiography.[86] Johnson also inserted a profile of Henson into the July 1947 issue of *Ebony*, which adopted its familiar strategy of applauding Henson's achievements and denouncing public neglect of historical significance. The feature pointed readers in the direction of a new biography of Henson by Bradley Robinson that portrayed him as "a hero in the battle against the raging blizzard and sub-zero cold of the Artic."[87] Impressed by Johnson's efforts, McDonald agreed to advertise in *Ebony* and connected Johnson to other businesses, including Swift Packing and Quaker Oats.[88]

The encounter between Johnson and McDonald has been identified by publisher and scholars alike as a pivotal moment in *Ebony*'s development, and it is fitting that black history played a major role in its outcome.[89] Since making the decision to accept advertisements in *Ebony* from May 1946 onward, Johnson had sought to attract the backing of white businesses in almost every conceivable way.[90] He used *Ebony* as a bully pulpit to extol the potential of the "Negro Market" for prospective backers.[91] He enthusiastically courted office secretaries and bombarded advertising agencies by letter and phone, spending "almost every waking hour selling advertising."[92] Yet Johnson's efforts failed, in part because he was selling a model of black success based on himself. When the publisher met McDonald, he was selling something else: the historic achievements of black pioneers like Henson "who'd demonstrated that excellence would break down all barriers."[93] By situating *Ebony*'s role within a broader narrative of racial uplift and historical commemoration, Johnson was able to frame the patronage of white advertisers in a heroic and historically transcendent light.

Despite *Ebony* being perceived as a less scholastic enterprise than periodicals such as the *Negro History Bulletin*, Johnson's ability to harness the market potential of black history was not so different from many of the discipline's more learned practitioners. The efforts of Woodson and the ASNLH to popularize black history were frequently predicated on an ability to "sell" the past through book drives and fundraising campaigns.[94] In time, black historians themselves would became arbiters of black respectability and good taste that carried considerable appeal for advertisers. Joel Rogers was one notable black historian who became an advertising spokesman, featuring in the Seagram Company's "Men of Distinction" campaign that appeared in *Ebony* during the early 1950s. More substantial collaborations between black historians, historical organizations, and American businesses would follow during the 1960s, setting the groundwork for an embrace of black history by corporate America.[95] While largely beyond the scope of this study, it is important to recognize the impact of black history advertising as an integral component of the postwar black history "revival." As the nation's most popular black consumer magazine, *Ebony* would become a key vehicle for the dissemination of such advertising projects.[96]

Lerone Bennett Jr. and the Turn toward Black History

By the early 1950s, *Ebony* was publishing articles on black history and heritage at a relatively consistent pace. Features such as "The 15 Outstanding Events in Negro History" provided readers with a broad summary of the black experience in America, while human-interest pieces on historic black communities such as Gouldtown, New Jersey, celebrated locations where "Negro townsfolk still preserve their unique heritage and identity and are quietly proud of their past."[97] Many of its historical features were printed in February to coincide with Negro History Week, and the magazine applauded the efforts of its founder Carter G. Woodson to "teach America the glories of the Negro's past."[98] Black history would also become a recurrent part of other Johnson periodicals, most notably *Jet*, which was launched in November 1951 as "the first weekly Negro magazine in the country" and which included a feature titled "This Week in Negro History" in every issue.[99]

The majority of *Ebony*'s black history content reinforced its editorial prerogative to "mirror the happier side of Negro life" and would occasionally retain some of the more sensational overtones of its entertainment sections. A 1950 feature by Edward Clayton that promised to unveil some of the "famous Negro sons of white fathers" who lurked in the "dark recesses of America's ancestral history" echoed the scandalous tone of articles on racial passing and exposés on "5 Million U.S. White Negroes."[100] This emphasis on salacious rumor and scandal had become a recurrent feature of *Ebony*'s content by the early 1950s, while the launch of new publications such as *Tan Confessions* reflected Johnson's desire to establish a foothold in the lucrative "confessional" magazine market.[101] However, there were signs that the magazine's coverage of black history was changing, something that was connected to both short-term economic pressures and long-term sociopolitical forces.

In the first instance, an unexpected, if relatively temporary, decline in circulation prompted Johnson to reassess his circulation model. *Ebony*'s audience during its early years was largely composed of newsstand readers who were more responsive to the magazine's sensational content but less reliable than repeat subscribers. During the 1953–54 recession a sudden drop-off in newsstand sales led to *Ebony*'s circulation decreasing from five hundred thousand to four hundred thousand in just a single issue, providing a stark reminder as to the volatility of the newsstand market.[102] In response, Johnson pushed to increase subscriptions and to make *Ebony* less vulnerable to fluctuations in newsstand readership, developing a series of direct-mail campaigns and establishing collaborations with churches and schools to sell the magazine. Such efforts required a more family-friendly approach, with Johnson contending that his new target audience "wanted us to move away from the sensationalism that characterized some of our early articles."[103]

The highest-profile casualty of this period was Burns, the white Chicagoan who had steered much of *Ebony*'s early development. Despite Johnson's efforts to minimize Burns's contributions, more recent scholars such as Adam Green have looked to recover Burns's reputation as an editor "of universally recognized brilliance within black journalism."[104] The relationship between editor and publisher was complex: Burns was left frustrated by Johnson's lack of racial militancy but was happy to reap the prestige and financial rewards his role within the company generated. Johnson relied on Burns's talents as an editor but was not against using his white editor as a convenient scapegoat for editorial or philosophical criticisms of *Ebony*. In September 1954 Johnson abruptly fired Burns, citing an "overemphasis on sex, mixed marriage and other similar stories."[105] In his own memoirs, Burns provided a radically different interpretation of their parting, describing himself as the victim of a "raw deal" and one of the many figures who had been "used, abused, and then cast aside" by the publisher.[106]

Irrespective of the reasons behind Burns's dismissal, growing civil rights activism and mounting reader frustrations over *Ebony*'s conciliatory tone had undoubtedly put pressure on Johnson to develop a more fully rounded publication. Through photo-editorials such as "Is the Negro Happy?" in December 1953, *Ebony* had offered a go-slow approach to civil rights, suggesting that "although the common conception that all Negroes are happy is a preposterous one, the saying that it takes very little to make them happy is quite true."[107] However, the impact of the *Brown v. Board of Education* decision in 1954, the outrage generated by the brutal murder of Emmett Till, and the beginning of the Montgomery bus boycott in 1955 all helped to force Johnson's hand.[108] Simeon Booker, whose coverage of Till's murder for *Jet* magazine helped to establish him as one of the country's foremost black investigative reporters, suggested that such developments prompted the company's magazines to shift from "primarily entertainment/sports/society tidbits and gossip, to a hard-hitting source of news about black progress on all fronts."[109]

Less than two years after the publication of "Is the Negro Happy?" *Ebony*'s coverage of "The New Fighting South" spoke to the emergence of "a new militant Negro. He is a fearless, fighting man who openly campaigns for his civil rights."[110] This shift toward what Gene Roberts and Hank Klibanoff designated as a "more thoughtful and sober portrayal" of black life, alongside an increased engagement with civil rights activism, helped *Ebony* to distance itself from the salacious tone of black confessional magazines that had gained popularity during the early 1950s—a number of which had been produced under the Johnson Publishing umbrella—and to position itself alongside more "serious" black journals and newspapers as an important mouthpiece for the movement.[111] Furthermore, as the magazine's coverage matured, it became clear that its engagement with black history and the struggle for civil rights were intimately connected. In 1954 the arrival of a new editor helped to expand the magazine's historical coverage further.

It is unclear exactly what Lerone Bennett Jr.'s first impressions of *Ebony*'s content were upon joining the magazine. His archival collections offer little in the way of editorial correspondence during his formative years at the company, although they provide rich detail regarding his early life and intellectual development. Like Johnson, Bennett was a son of the South; born in Clarksdale, Mississippi, less than sixty miles from the publisher's hometown of Arkansas City.[112] Bennett's parents separated when he was a young child, and he relocated to the state capital of Jackson to live with his mother and her extended family.[113] As an African American growing up in Mississippi during the 1930s, Bennett was forced to deal with racism and the threat of violence on a regular basis. The editor recalled "a climate of total violence" that imperiled the lives of black folk on a daily basis. He would later describe the Delta as "the worst place in the world, bar none, for a black boy or black girl" to grow up, comparing it to the black experience in South Africa under apartheid.[114]

While Johnson had moved from Arkansas to Chicago as a teenager, Bennett remained in the South to complete his high school education, combining a role as the school newspaper editor with a writing gig for the *Mississippi Enterprise*, a local black weekly.[115] He would subsequently enroll at Morehouse College in Atlanta, the South's premier institution of higher education for black men. When Bennett arrived on campus, the university was in the midst of a revival led by its enigmatic president Benjamin Mays, a "preacher-prophet-teacher-disturber of the peace."[116] Bennett excelled in Atlanta, serving on the student council as sophomore- and junior-class president, becoming president of the Delta Phi

Delta Journalistic Society, and editing the *Maroon Tiger*, the college's renowned student newspaper.[117] In recognition of his achievements, Morehouse elected him to appear in the 1948–49 edition of *Who's Who among Students in American Universities and Colleges*.[118] After graduating, Bennett joined the *Atlanta Daily World*, rising to a position as city editor before being lured to Chicago by Johnson to join *Jet* as an associate editor in 1953.[119] One year later Bennett moved to a comparative position at *Ebony*—he would remain on the periodical's editorial team for more than half a century.[120]

Johnson may well have decided to remove Ben Burns prior to Bennett's appointment, and the two editors worked together only briefly before Burns's dismissal. Nevertheless, Bennett left a lasting impression on the beleaguered Burns prior to his contentious departure from Johnson Publishing. In later material, Burns eviscerated colleagues such as Herbert Nipson for their "turgid copy, lack of fresh ideas, and uninspired editorial style." By contrast, he spoke highly of the "soft-spoken, genteel, but highly militant" Bennett and noted his immediate entrenchment as the company's resident history buff following his arrival from Atlanta.[121] Even before Burns's dismissal, *Ebony*'s historical coverage had shown signs of more explicitly linking black history education and awareness to the coalescing struggle for civil rights in the present, with a February 1953 editorial informing readers that the roots of newfound "Negro militance" could be discovered "in the spirit of Negro History Week and the still-living words of Negro greats."[122] The arrival of Bennett, alongside more outspoken writers such as Booker and Robert Johnson, added to the formidable journalistic talents of Thompson and other JPC staffers who were eager to push the editorial envelope of *Ebony* and other Johnson magazines.[123]

In turn, Bennett exerted an immediate influence over the magazine's historical content, employing an understanding of black history as a "living history" that would come to underpin much of his later work. In "Dred Scott's Children," the magazine tracked down descendants of Scott still living in St. Louis close to the Missouri courthouse where their ancestor had first attempted to sue for his freedom in 1847, a precursor to the landmark 1857 Supreme Court case of *Dredd Scott v. Sandford*.[124] More consequential still was a 1954 article titled "Thomas Jefferson's Negro Grandchildren," which traced the histories of Jefferson's black progeny but avoided the salacious tone of earlier features such as "Famous Negro Sons of White Fathers."[125] In addressing the handful of black Americans "who can trace their ancestry back to the most illustrious of American founding fathers," Bennett was arguably the first journalist to seriously profile the relationship between Jefferson and Sally Hemings for a popular audience.[126] Bennett also focused on the impact of black political representatives during

Reconstruction, a theme that would be expanded into a full-length black history series during the mid-1960s.[127]

Perhaps the most significant new element of *Ebony*'s historical coverage during the 1950s was the introduction of the *Ebony* Hall of Fame. Unveiled to readers as part of the magazine's tenth-anniversary celebrations in November 1955, the Hall of Fame was described as a "unique historical gallery" that would be permanently housed at the Johnson Publishing Headquarters at 1820 South Michigan Avenue.[128] Johnson was immensely proud of the offices, which he had acquired for $52,000 in 1949 with trademark ingenuity. After the building's owner refused to sell the plot to a black-owned company, Johnson used white lawyer Louis Wilson as an intermediary buyer, with Wilson pretending to be acting on the interests of an East Coast publishing house. Johnson was able to inspect the building disguised as a janitor and after finalizing the purchase spent a further $200,000 renovating it for publishing purposes.[129] As the public front for Johnson's publishing empire, 1820 South Michigan welcomed hundreds of visitors a month, ranging from black schoolchildren and college students to international heads of state, such as Haitian president Paul Magloire and Liberian premier William Tubman.[130]

The Hall of Fame ably complemented *Ebony*'s expanding role as an outlet for black history education, with the induction of each subsequent black pioneer marked by a special feature in the publication.[131] The project's apparent popularity can be situated within a fledgling black public history movement that had taken root in Chicago during the 1930s, 1940s, and 1950s and had been promoted by other black publications such as the *Chicago Defender* and the *Chicago Bee*.[132] Such efforts were complemented by attempts to address educational inequities within the public school system, with activists pressuring the Chicago School Board to approve *Supplementary Units for the Course of Instruction in Social Studies*, one of the first black history texts to be used in the public schools of a major American City.[133] As Ian Rocksborough-Smith has noted, efforts toward curricular reform, the celebration of Negro History Week, and the publication of history-oriented content in the city's black press all demonstrated how efforts to promote and teach black history in Chicago fed the continued development of a "vibrant and ideologically diffuse African American public sphere."[134]

The Hall of Fame would be a recurrent feature in *Ebony* until the end of the decade, with reader ballots appearing in each November issue and new additions being announced in February to coincide with Negro History Week. In 1957, readers chose sociologist and civil rights activist Charles Spurgeon Johnson, who had served as the first black president of Fisk University.[135] The following year they voted for Carter G. Woodson, the man who had "helped put the

Negro back into the history books."[136] Although *Ebony* provided a glowing tribute to Woodson's historical importance, in keeping with its earlier emphasis on his role in the formation of Negro History Week, its description of the historian's personal life was less flattering and drew criticism from the *Journal of Negro History*.[137] While the journal's response to *Ebony*'s article was primarily a defense of Woodson's character, it also reflected underlying tensions over the ability of popular black periodicals to produce reliable or representative accounts of black history, an issue that would rear its head again during the early 1960s.

From a different perspective, Woodson's entry into the Hall of Fame, alongside the subsequent entry of blues musician William C. Handy, demonstrated another concern regarding *Ebony*'s historical coverage—its privileging of black male pioneers. By 1959, the *Ebony* Hall of Fame included fourteen inductees, of which only four were women.[138] Quantitative disparities were compounded by the frequent framing of black male pioneers as the "fathers" of their respective disciplines, such as Woodson's status as the "father of Negro history" or Handy's reputation as the "father of the Blues." Such language contributed to what Anna Pochmara has described as a "masculinization" of black history. In their efforts to "dig up" the black past, *Ebony* and other black periodicals helped to establish a patrilineal historical lineage that validated black male authorship and achievements by framing black history through the lens of heroic masculinity.[139]

The limits of *Ebony*'s historical content must be placed within the gender hierarchies of its own editorial team. With the notable exception of vocal female contributors such as Era Bell Thompson, *Ebony*'s editorial hierarchy was dominated by men, a fact replicated in periodicals across the country. The preponderance of black men in *Ebony*'s Hall of Fame and within its coverage of black history reflected the deeply gendered process of black historical knowledge creation at an editorial level—something that overlapped with the magazine's broader engagement with gender politics. *Ebony*'s penchant for scantily-clad cover models and Johnson's acceptance of advertisements for skin bleaches and hair relaxants drew regular accusations of colorism from its audience, while the contributions of black female celebrities were often defined through their role as wives or mothers.[140] As Christopher Tinson has noted, the magazine's retrogressive gender politics prompted fierce backlash from black feminists such as Evelyn Rodgers during the second half of the 1960s, while its coverage of black female activists often reflected the broader silencing of black women's contributions to the civil rights and Black Power movements.[141]

Similarly, in addressing the gendered limitations of *Ebony*'s historical content, I do not intend to isolate or decontextualize such imbalances from comparable disparities in the production and dissemination of African American history.

Male historians dominated the black history movement of the nineteenth and early twentieth centuries, and despite an increasing number of black women doing history work, only a handful of female historians joined the academy prior to the civil rights era.[142] It was not until the 1980s that a new wave of scholarship led by pioneering black female historians such as Darlene Clark Hine and Deborah Gray White forcefully demonstrated the "centrality of Black women to the history of America."[143] Given these broader concerns, while the limitations of *Ebony*'s historical coverage can (and should) be critiqued, we should also acknowledge that its content often celebrated the historical achievements of black women in ways that traditional textbooks, academic scholarship, and mainstream periodicals did not.

Coverage of the Hall of Fame in *Ebony* appears to have been curtailed at the end of the 1950s, although later booklets about the project were created to coincide with the celebration of Negro History Week and distributed to local schools with the help of the Chicago Urban League.[144] However, the project offered an important insight into *Ebony*'s expanding coverage of black history, something Johnson argued had served to increase "the Negro's pride in himself and his heritage."[145] This shift was driven by editors such as Bennett and Thompson, with the latter particularly outspoken regarding Johnson's failures to develop *Ebony* into a more progressive voice. In the summer of 1959, Thompson went as far as to threaten resignation unless Johnson agreed to a set of demands that included more profiles of black pioneers and the publication of a black history quarterly.[146] Such demands, coupled with what appeared to be "a growing interest in Black history" among the magazine's readers, led to Johnson's signing off on a major new black history series by Bennett—a series that would radically transform the editor's own role with *Ebony* and the magazine's broader significance as a historical text.[147]

CHAPTER 2

Tell Us of Our Past

In the July 1960 issue of *Ebony*, the magazine's "Backstage" feature called upon its readers to congratulate Bennett, who had just been unveiled as the periodical's first senior editor. Leading with an image of Bennett hunched studiously over his typewriter, the feature painted a lively portrait of an impromptu gathering held at the magazine's editorial offices in Chicago to mark the achievement.[1] Always the man for an occasion, Johnson provided bottles of champagne, and company staff banded together to toast Bennett's success. The editor's promotion may in fact have come sooner; in personal correspondence and on his curriculum vitae, Bennett listed the year of his transition to senior editor as 1958.[2] However, at least within the pages of *Ebony* itself, news of his promotion was postponed until summer 1960. As champagne glasses clinked at 1820 South Michigan Avenue, a fellow staffer leaned across to lightheartedly remind Bennett that he'd "come a long way from Mississippi." The senior editor surveyed the room before offering an introspective response: "We've all come a long way."[3]

Bennett's remarks could have been applied specifically to figures such as Era Bell Thompson, Allan Morrison, or Simeon Booker, who had all emerged as leading African American journalists during their time at the company. They could also have been used to describe the fortunes of *Ebony*, which in the space of fifteen short years had cemented its position as the most popular black periodical in the country. By the summer of 1960 the magazine's circulation had topped six hundred thousand, while advertising revenues were at an all-time high.[4] For its fifteenth-anniversary issue in November 1960, more than eight hundred thousand copies of *Ebony* had been printed, and its editors estimated that within a month the issue would have been read by "some four million people in all parts of the world." Its staff had grown from a handful to more than two hundred, and its offices had expanded to include branch offices in New York, Los Angeles, and Washington, D.C.[5]

However, "Backstage" declared that Bennett's remarks could be more broadly applied to the socioeconomic, cultural, and geographical transformations in African American life during the years following World War II. On the eve of the Japanese attack on Pearl Harbor, fewer than half of all African Americans lived in urban areas. By the dawn of the 1960s, nearly three-quarters had moved to towns and cities. In 1960, African American men earned an average of two-and-a-half times what their annual income had been on the eve of World War II, and the efforts of Johnson and other black corporate executives to celebrate middle-class tastes and celebrity culture had awakened corporate America to the economic clout of an upwardly mobile "Negro market."[6] Athletes such as baseball star Jackie Robinson had helped to crack the color line in American professional sport, while black entertainers such as Dorothy Dandridge and Nat King Cole had become household names. Reflecting on its first fifteen years in print, *Ebony*'s editors declared that both the magazine and "the world of color it interprets have made remarkable progress."[7]

Despite such positivity, it was also clear that across the nation African American rights continued to be denied. Emboldened by the actions of activists such as Robert Williams and his advocacy of armed self-defense, black citizens looked to push the pace of civil rights reform.[8] As the sit-in movement spread across the South, new organizations such as the Student Nonviolent Coordinating Committee emerged, which offered space for interracial communities of activists eager to push beyond the narrow boundaries of state-sanctioned dissent that had characterized the early Cold War era.[9] In *Ebony*, this change was reflected through articles such as "The Ghost of Marcus Garvey," which emphasized the connection between Garveyism and the reemergence of black nationalism during the years following World War II.[10] From a similar perspective, features such as "The Revolt of Negro Youth" suggested that a shift toward a "younger, more aggressive leadership" platform within the black freedom struggle was starting to take hold.[11]

As black activists in the 1950s and 1960s began to adopt more diverse methods and strategies of protest, they also came to understand their struggle through an increasingly transnational lens. In reflecting on Bennett's unveiling as senior editor in its July 1960 issue, it is striking that *Ebony* sought to place his remarks within this same diasporic framework. The magazine declared that Bennett "was thinking of 'a long way' in more than just time and space" and that his use of the phrase served to connect the Global South with the American South, linking "the coming violence in South Africa" and the "coming independence for the Belgian Congo and Nigeria" with the "revolt of Negro students" below the Mason-Dixon Line.[12] In the same issue, Bennett authored his most militant article to date—a searing exposé on the Sharpeville Massacre and the apartheid system in South Africa. The feature warned of a coming reckoning— the "Day of Blood"—where racial antagonisms would lead to a cataclysmic racial confrontation.[13] The editor's copy was accompanied by graphic images of black bodies strewn across Sharpeville's streets, marking the first time explicit images of mass racial violence had been printed on its pages since the Columbia race riot during the mid-1940s.[14]

The framing of Bennett's remarks in "Backstage," alongside the publication of his Sharpeville exposé in the May 1960 issue of *Ebony*, also reflected a growing interest in the African independence movement among black journalists and writers in the United States. As scholars such as Nicholas Grant have argued, black American periodicals became frequent commentators on the apartheid regime in South Africa during the 1950s, while Ghana's declaration of independence drew widespread coverage in the black press at home.[15] Johnson was part of a United States delegation to Ghana in 1957 headed by vice president Richard Nixon, and he returned to America with "a new spirit and new energy" to secure freedom at home.[16] Within the pages of *Ebony*, Thompson continued her role as a foreign correspondent, while Morrison and other contributors examined the political and diplomatic ties between the United States and Africa.[17] By the early 1960s, frustrations at home were compounded by a growing identification with the decolonization movement in Africa.[18] Writing for the *New York Times* in March 1961, James Baldwin declared that "at the rate things are going here, all of Africa will be free before we can get a lousy cup of coffee."[19]

An important part of this connection was a shared historical relationship, and *Ebony* began to devote more content to exploring the diasporic connections between Africa and the United States. In February 1961 Marc Crawford, who had previously worked as a reporter for *Jet* and who would go on become an award-winning journalist for *Life*, introduced *Ebony* readers to the work of prominent Africanist William Leo Hansberry.[20] Crawford's article echoed the tone established in much of *Ebony*'s earlier historical coverage, applauding Hansberry's intellectual contributions while denouncing the continued neglect of his achievements. Crawford also connected the professor's work to that of earlier black historians such as Du Bois, with Du Bois's 1915 work *The*

Negro named as a key factor in Hansberry's career as an Africanist.[21] Perhaps most interesting was its demand for an ethnocentric view of black history that looked to celebrate African heritage among black Americans. Hansberry complained that "to many Americans of African descent the feeling of being a Negro is often embarrassing . . . there is nothing in the prevailing literature that gives the Negro a sense of pride in African origin."[22]

The article was warmly received by *Ebony*'s audience, with Michigan resident Julius Brown celebrating the profile for presenting a "truer picture of African history." Brown linked the work of Hansberry to the appeal of black nationalism and pan-Africanism, arguing that "there is a growing proudness among Negro Americans in their ties with Africa. Your article serves to make this proudness greater."[23] Philadelphian Carolyn Walton agreed: "I know we are a great people despite what Uncle Charlie would like us to believe."[24] Three years later, the magazine would renew its connection to Hansberry by serializing parts of his co-edited book *Ageless Africa: A Pictorial History of the Golden Past*, a study that promised to unveil the "true story of the African past" as well as the continent's central role in the "development of world civilization."[25]

Tell Us of Our Past

Just a few months after Crawford's profile of William Hansberry, *Ebony* unveiled Bennett as the author of an expansive new "Negro History" series. The series was a major development in the magazine's black-history-themed content: while historical survey articles and profiles of black "pioneers" had appeared on a relatively consistent basis throughout the 1950s, Bennett's series marked the first sustained collection of articles that used black history as a unifying theme. The public rationale for the series' introduction was clear, with an issue of "Backstage" contending that it had been introduced because of "an overwhelming public demand" from *Ebony*'s readers to "tell us of our past."[26] Presenting this call for black history as a desire that stretched across class, occupational, and generational lines, its editors emphasized the role of black history as a unifying editorial device, something that would appeal to all sections of the black community and would help to counterbalance criticisms of *Ebony* as a bourgeoisie, middle-class periodical.

Explanations for the series' introduction also pointed to the growing presence of Africa in the minds of black Americans. "Backstage" noted that many of *Ebony*'s readers were "anxious to learn not only of their contributions to American history but also of the life of their ancestors in Africa. They ask for roots that go beyond the slave plantation of the South and the first slave ship that touched these shores."[27] Within Johnson Publishing, *Ebony*'s increasing Afrocentrism was mirrored by the revival of *Negro Digest*, which had been discontinued in 1951. Under the leadership of Hoyt Fuller, the periodical would evolve from a news-oriented digest into a diasporic literary journal—a shift most clearly seen through its rebranding as *Black World* during the early 1970s. The introduction of new black magazines such as *Freedomways* provided further evidence of desires to place diasporic concerns at the center of African American intellectual and cultural criticism.[28] The *Liberator* was among the most vocal exponents of this trend, positioning itself as "the voice of the Afro-American protest movement in the United States and the liberation movement of Africa" following its introduction in 1961.[29]

This sentiment was at the heart of Bennett's first article, "The African Past." The opening sentence set the tone, with Bennett pointing to a series of "revolutionary discoveries by archaeologists and historical anthropologists" prompting a fundamental shift in academic debates about African history. In rhetoric that echoed the lyrical prose of earlier black popular historians such as Joel Rogers, Bennett confirmed the indelible connection between black America and the motherland but also reiterated the citizenship rights and national identity of African Americans in the United States. The editor linked new research by East African archaeologists and anthropologists to prominent Africanists and African American historians such as Carter G. Woodson, Melville Herskovits, and John Hope Franklin. While *Ebony*'s earlier content had focused on "recovering" lost histories of black life and culture, Bennett sought to provide readers with a more historiographical and critically incisive perspective—showing a clear desire for his work to be taken seriously as an ambitious and well-researched historical project.

Efforts to develop a more "scholarly" perspective were also evidenced through the layout and formatting of *Ebony*'s "Negro History" series. Bennett's in-text citation of scholars and researchers was complemented by the somewhat unusual decision to include a bibliography at the end of the article, while the article's aesthetics looked to more clearly set out its educational function. As Maren Stange has eloquently argued, *Ebony*'s content was consciously modeled on the photo-essay format of *Life*, which was primarily directed by visual rather than literary content. In the majority of *Ebony*'s features, the text remained secondary to the power of the visual image as a way to "uphold familiar codes of journalistic objectivity." By relying on the presumed "transparency" of photography as a medium, the magazine leaned on visual content to separate black citizens from "the familiar markers of degradation, spectacle, and victimization" that proliferated in twentieth-century American visual culture.[30]

Yet in Bennett's series this relationship was altered in small but significant ways. Rather than functioning as the editorial centerpiece, images were used to complement and fortify the historical "objectivity" of the text itself. Where images were used, they were not the informal snapshot-style portraits or still-life images around which much of *Ebony*'s content was focused. Instead, Bennett's first article featured a series of maps, hieroglyphics, and ancient tomb paintings, as well as close-up images of West African masks and sculptures.[31] This trend was continued in the second installment of the "Negro History" series, which focused on the introduction and expansion of the transatlantic slave trade. Bennett's text was accompanied by impressionistic drawings of slave life composed by Norman Hunter, who alongside Herbert Temple was one of *Ebony*'s resident staff artists. Black-and-white vignettes accompanied Ghana Information Services images of West African slave forts and depots.[32]

Bennett's writing also continued an arc away from the more upbeat interpretation of black history that had characterized much of *Ebony*'s earlier content. The magazine's previous discussion of slavery had frequently carried an uplifting message of racial reconciliation, with one 1955 feature documenting a yearly "slave reunion" at a North Carolina plantation, where the children of slaves and the offspring of former slave owner Theophilus Hauser congregated to "share fried chicken, fables, and friendship."[33] By contrast, as Bennett's series delved into the history of American slavery, the editor rejected depictions of slavery as a paternalistic institution popularized by earlier white historians such as Ulrich B. Phillips. Instead, his visceral discussion of the transatlantic and domestic slave trade lingered on its extreme violence and racist underpinnings. As had been the case for the first article in his series, Bennett sought to develop a strong historiographical base for his writing, leaning on the controversial work of Stanley Elkins to emphasize the brutality of slavery as an institution comparable to Nazi concentration camps.[34]

However, while Elkins argued that the physical and psychological trauma inflicted by slavery had rendered many blacks submissive and docile "Sambos," Bennett chose instead to focus on the resilience of enslaved people and their willingness to fight against the people and system that oppressed them. Borrowing from the work of Kenneth Stampp, Herbert Aptheker, and other revisionist historians, the editor emphasized the diversity and ingenuity of slave resistance—ranging from sit-down strikes, slow-downs, and temporary absconding to outright rebellion.[35] In the fifth installment of his series, "Slave Revolts and Insurrections," Bennett explored the legacy of the Haitian Revolution and its impact across the black Atlantic, linking the actions of figures such as Toussaint L'Ouverture to Gabriel Prosser, Denmark Vesey, and other enslaved

Africans who fought for their freedom in North America. He concluded the piece with a detailed assessment of the Nat Turner Rebellion, which he credited for bringing a "generation of crisis" to its head.[36]

A Vital Contribution to the Dissemination of Historical Truths

If *Ebony* endeavored for the series to be taken seriously, then its editors would have been largely comforted by the response from its audience. Throughout the series' publication, the magazine printed more than fifty full or partial letters from readers that were overwhelmingly supportive of the project and its educational impact.[37] Indeed, many of the key trends that emerged through reader correspondence are encapsulated in the very first printed response to Bennett's series, which was published in September 1961. New York reader Ronnie Boone expressed satisfaction that *Ebony* had decided to begin the series, noting that when he was a student, "all I ever learned was that Negroes sprang up out of the cotton fields as slaves, picking cotton." He declared that Bennett's series was providing him with "a chance to learn all that I knew was true" and likened the magazine's content to biblical scripture: "Like Moses, who came to lead his people to the Promised Land, you have come and you are leading."[38]

While Boone's hyperbolic rhetoric offered an exaggerated portrayal of *Ebony*'s educational and intellectual interventions, his letter expressed a clear desire for greater access to black history material that reflected the continued inadequacies of the public-school system. One 1937 study of Southern school textbooks found that, out of a sample of fifty history textbooks, none contained significant examples of African American contributions to American society. Another study from the same period found that textbooks persistently identified African Americans as "unquestionably racially inferior."[39] Well into the 1950s and 1960s, textbooks across the country reinforced stereotypes of African American inferiority and uncritically accepted historiographical schools of thought that presented slavery as paternalistic and Emancipation as a "tragic mistake."[40] Although new historical surveys such as Franklin's *From Slavery to Freedom* had been enthusiastically greeted, many blacks continued to lack even basic access to historical texts that were not willfully misrepresentative. As a result, *Ebony*'s readers embraced its "Negro History" series as a valuable counterpoint to the "bad things that have been circulated against the Negro" by white scholars such as Carleton Putnam, whose 1961 study *Race and Reason* contended that miscegenation would bring about the demise of American civilization—a position that lead to the book becoming required high school reading in multiple Southern states.[41]

At the same time, not all readers were convinced of *Ebony*'s validity as a black history text. The result was a fascinating back-and-forth dialogue within the magazine's "Letters to the Editor" section. Readers adopted different strategies to situate *Ebony* as a reliable historical source, including contrasting its content to the inaccurate information they had received as students, repeatedly describing the magazine as a "book" or "historical text," and comparing Bennett's series with book-length studies such as E. Franklin Frazier's *The Negro Family in the United States* and Franklin's *From Slavery to Freedom*. For others, the magazine's status as a periodical marked it as less rigorous from a scholarly perspective and therefore less reliable than a book source. An unnamed Michigan reader declared that the first article in Bennett's series contained "many abuses of historical fact and has all the earmarks of a propaganda leaflet."[42] Rather than rely on research conducted by a lay historian such as Bennett, the letter's writer recommended that readers turn to peer-reviewed academic texts for a "closer approximation of the truth." To accentuate this point, the reader signed off with the anonymous yet pointed insignia, "A Historian."[43]

The response to *Ebony*'s "Negro History" series from "official" historical outlets such as the ASNLH was also revealing. In the March 1962 issue of the *Negro History Bulletin*, the organization expressed its approval at *Ebony*'s "pioneering stride . . . to bring Negro History to the masses."[44] The *Bulletin* opened its feature with two letters from William Boone, a member of *Ebony*'s promotions department who would go on to become its assistant circulation manager.[45] Boone's letters demonstrated *Ebony*'s desire to garner praise from important black history institutions and organizations such as the ASNLH, noting that "we will appreciate whatever comments or quotes you wish to make" in the organization's own publications. In response, the *Bulletin* expressed its support for *Ebony*'s attempt to "recover black history for a popular audience" and noted that the magazine was "making a vital contribution to the dissemination of historical truth."[46]

However, the *Bulletin*'s coverage of Bennett's series also looked to subtly distinguish itself and the work of the ASNLH from the kind of "popular" history presented in *Ebony*'s coverage. Praise for the magazine's content was couched with statements such as "the materials presented *seem* to be valid, interesting and worthwhile."[47] Similarly, the *Bulletin* centered *Ebony*'s importance on its ability to "span the gap between scholarly research and public education." From this perspective, *Ebony*'s coverage of black history was seen to be most valuable as a way of drawing members back to the ASNLH through "stimulating greater popular interest in the general area of Negro History" rather than supplementing or even supplanting its duty to "sponsor authentic research and publications."[48]

Through such rhetoric, the *Bulletin* sought to highlight the limitations of *Ebony*'s scholarly importance, even as it celebrated its broader impact as an outlet for popular black history.

Irrespective of such concerns, Bennett's "Negro History" series continued to attract acclaim from the vast majority of *Ebony*'s audience during the spring and summer of 1962, with a profile in the *Negro Digest* contending that the feature had elicited "a greater response than any other single project ever undertaken" in the magazine's history.[49] Chicagoan Charles Craig echoed this sentiment, declaring that Bennett was "doing a remarkable job in presenting facts of Negro history that I would imagine few people have read." Fellow reader Matthew Bonds was also impressed, describing the series as "an artistic and factual masterpiece" that had surpassed "many of the best histories on the subject."[50] As the series neared its denouement, reader disappointment was tempered by the magazine's reiteration of its intention to publish the series in book form, while rumors swirled of an ambitious special issue to mark the centenary of the Emancipation Proclamation.

Before the Mayflower

After months of anticipation, the book-length adaption of Bennett's "Negro History" series was released in fall 1962, titled *Before the Mayflower: A History of the Negro in America*.[51] Timed to coincide with the final installment of "Negro History," *Before the Mayflower* marked the logical continuation and extension of Bennett's writing in *Ebony*, with the text being heavily marketed across Johnson's magazines and through promotional pamphlets distributed to readers.[52] One such pamphlet featured a mosaic of newspaper reviews and press clippings, with quotes declaring that the text was "destined to become a valuable addition to the libraries of discerning Americans."[53] At times, the marketing campaign for *Before the Mayflower* bordered on the absurd, with the 1963 *Jet* pin-up calendar basing its pictures on the "landmarks and milestones" celebrated in Bennett's text. The result was a bizarre collection of images featuring scantily clad female models using props to "commemorate" important moments in black history, such as the 1954 *Brown vs. Board of Education* decision.[54] From a different perspective, the publication of *Before the Mayflower* played a major role in launching the Johnson Publishing Book Division, which would emerge as one of the largest black-owned publishers in the country during the 1960s and 1970s.[55]

It is clear that critiques of Bennett's "legitimacy" as a historian weighed heavily on his own mind as well as the minds of *Ebony*'s editorial team. In an October 1962 issue of "Backstage," which previewed the release of his book, *Ebony* informed readers that *Before the Mayflower* was "written in a popular style but is based on sound scholarship and documentation."[56] This marked a continuation of efforts to situate the series on the intersections of black academic and popular culture and as a publication that combined the scholarly approach of the *Negro History Bulletin* with the mass circulation of newspapers such as the *Courier*. Bennett reiterated this ambition in the preface to the first edition, where he explained that *Before the Mayflower* was "not, strictly speaking, a book for scholars; but it is as scholarly as fourteen months of research could make it."[57]

Just as the question of Bennett's credibility as an emerging historical voice had underpinned many of the initial responses to his "Negro History" series, so too was this concern addressed by reviewers of *Before the Mayflower*. Archie Jones of the *Chicago Sun-Times* reviewed Bennett's text alongside John Hope Franklin's 1963 study *The Emancipation Proclamation*, arguing that both works were an attempt to commemorate the impending centenary of the historic executive order. However, he appeared keen to distinguish their respective roles and writing styles. Franklin, as a "ranking historian," was commended for providing a dispassionate and objective account. By contrast, Jones contended that Bennett, as a "very successful Negro journalist, is trying to create a heroic tradition for the American Negro."[58] For Jones, Bennett's account was rooted in his training as a journalist rather than as a historian and therefore favored an emphasis on narrative and emotion over factual objectivity. He described Bennett's retelling of slavery as an "exaggeration by implication" that was "typical of heroic history." Jones advised readers that Franklin's study, as the more reasonable and historically reliable text, could "serve as an antidote for Bennett's emotion-laden work."[59]

One week later in the *Chicago Tribune*, Henrietta Buckmaster offered a rebuttal to many of the criticisms put forward in Jones's review. Buckmaster rejected the image of Bennett as an emotional and potentially unreliable narrator, applauding *Before the Mayflower* as a "moving record of human passion, put down coolly" and described the text as an impartial "balance sheet—a long balance sheet begun 1,000 years ago." Furthermore, whereas Jones had focused on the unsuitability of a journalist writing an historical account, Buckmaster emphasized the value of Bennett's contribution by highlighting the deficiencies of white-authored American history textbooks. Buckmaster asked her readers to consider how many of them had "read thru [sic] the chinks in their history books and discovered the slave revolts that, year after year, kept the South in turmoil."[60] The author's support of Bennett was further qualified by her own literary credentials, with Buckmaster being recognized as the author of *Let My People Go: The Story of the Underground Railroad and the Growth of the Abolition Movement*.[61]

This debate stretched to the book's broader educational value and significance, with multiple outlets critiquing its legitimacy as a "credible" black history text. Many responded positively, with the *Chicago Daily News* calling for Bennett's work to be "enshrined in the libraries of schools throughout the world," and Marion Jackson of the *Atlanta Daily World* describing the text as an "authoritative work which will win a special niche in the historical archives for its excellence."[62] Not to be outdone, Robert Johnson's review in his "Book of the Week" column for *Jet* declared it to be "THE book with THE most revealing insights into the Negro's persecuted past" and described *Before the Mayflower* as the singular text "Negroes MUST read and White America dare not ignore."[63] By contrast, a reviewer for the *Boston Globe* linked reservations over the work to Bennett's professional occupation as a "journalist [who] writes history," although they offered condescending praise for *Before the Mayflower*'s scope, which "might daunt a more academic historian." The review left readers with no doubts as to the book's limitations, declaring that "a balanced judgement, such as John Hope Franklin's *The Emancipation Proclamation*, it is not."[64]

Scholarly responses were also critical. Writing in the *Florida Historical Quarterly*, Michael Gannon contended that *Before the Mayflower* was a "popularization of American Negro history" that offered little new interpretation and "does not pretend to be an original piece of work."[65] Like other critics, Gannon was quick to identify Bennett's primary role as the senior editor of *Ebony*, noting that "his profession shows clearly in his book." The reviewer also took aim at Bennett's "dramatic" writing style, complaining that "the author reads at times like the narrator of 'Death Valley Days,'" a popular radio and television show that provided theatrical stories of the American West.[66] More immediately, Gannon's comparison of Bennett's work to melodrama, alongside his repeated emphasis on Bennett's experience as a journalist, formed the basis of his rationale for dismissing *Before the Mayflower*'s value as an original scholarly intervention.[67]

Such disputes over the book's scholarship and rigor underscored an enduring tension between, on the one hand, an appreciation of Bennett's writing on black history and, on the other, ambivalence over his standing as an historian. Even as critics of Bennett's work recognized its value, they sniffed at his lack of academic qualifications, as well as the tone and language used in *Before the Mayflower*. It was no surprise that critiques of Bennett's work frequently paired him with Franklin, whose work was regularly held up as an example of informed African American historical writing and who fulfilled the notion that black historians should "reflect a judiciousness in keeping with the temperament of one disciplined in objectivity and preciseness."[68] This desire for objectivity was coupled to the more "precise" language used by black professional historians, meaning that Bennett's rhetorical flourishes became equated with historical leaps of faith and ideological inconsistencies. It is worth noting that initial reviews of Franklin's text had criticized the historian on exactly these grounds, with Roi Ottley describing *From Slavery to Freedom* as an "unwieldy" history that lacked the "crisp, incisive observations expected of a first-rate journalist."[69]

The comparison to *From Slavery to Freedom* also betrayed the ways in which Franklin's text—as evidenced by its title—offered a more comforting vision of racial uplift in America that reinforced liberal faith in the fundamental soundness of American institutions. It is telling that critics of Bennett's work generally chose to compare his writing to Franklin's, rather than to texts such as W. E. B. Du Bois's *Black Reconstruction* or Rayford Logan's *The Betrayal of the Negro*. Yet this stance simplified the complexity of Franklin's own relationship to notions of historical objectivity, with the historian declaring during World War II that "as a social discipline the historical process should be forged into a mighty weapon for the preservation of peace."[70] It also held Bennett's work to a much higher standard than the historical profession writ large. In many ways Bennett's "Negro History" series and the content of *Before the Mayflower* provided a more balanced representation of black history than could be found in state-sanctioned history textbooks.[71] This fact was not lost on many of *Ebony*'s readers, who applauded Bennett for providing an "unslanted and documentary account" that sought to rectify enduring biases within the academy and American popular and political culture.[72]

The marketing of and reception to *Before the Mayflower*, at least within the pages of *Ebony*, helped to formalize Bennett's transition from the magazine's rank and file to a position as the Johnson Publishing in-house historian and one of the company's most prominent public faces. Perhaps the clearest evidence of this shift can be seen through a "Backstage" feature published shortly after the release of *Before the Mayflower*, which sought to substantiate Bennett's role as a "serious writer"—whether he was tackling "a light entertaining story about a gorgeous girl or a piece on the ultra-heavy side like his recently completed series on Negro history." Bennett's profile provided a level of insight into his personal life and daily routine that was rarely afforded to other editors, forming part of the magazine's efforts to craft what we might define as a "scholarly aesthetic." *Ebony* described its senior editor as "a real nice, chess-playing, pipe-smoking guy" who lived a quiet family life and could be regularly seen around the office with a "briefcase of soon-to-be-completed work." This quiet, scholarly demeanor apparently did little to dampen his growing celebrity, with *Ebony* reporting that as the first-day copies of *Before the Mayflower* arrived in the office, employees "stood in line before Bennett's office, books in hand, to get his autograph."[73]

The Emancipation Proclamation Special

If any readers had lingering doubts over *Ebony*'s newfound commitment to documenting black history, then they might well have been dispelled by the announcement of a major special issue to mark the one hundredth anniversary of the Emancipation Proclamation. Upon its publication in September 1963, the "Emancipation Proclamation" special marked the first time an entire issue of *Ebony* had been dedicated to assessing a historically significant theme or event. In the months leading up to its publication, the magazine's editors stoked reader anticipation, promising a blockbuster issue, which would be "the biggest *Ebony* ever printed."[74] True to their word, the "Emancipation Proclamation" special weighed in at an extraordinary 236 pages, more than 50 percent larger than the average length of the three preceding and succeeding issues. It was arguably the largest black periodical ever printed and would remain the largest issue of *Ebony* published until its fortieth-anniversary special in the mid-1980s. Drawing together a rich array of contributors, the special aimed to "assess the position of the Negro in America today, peer back into his past to see how he reached this position, and look forward somewhat into his future."[75]

Johnson took considerable pains to frame the special as a "blue-ribbon event"—a project that had been more than a year in the making and featured contributions from leading black writers, activists, and intellectuals such as poet Gwendolyn Brooks, psychologist Kenneth Clark, and NAACP field sec-retary Medgar Evers, whose contribution was published posthumously after the activist's murder by a white supremacist in June 1963.[76] Tellingly, the pub-lisher measured the Proclamation's shortcomings against the ongoing struggle for racial equality, noting that "in this summer of the Negro's discontent, the unfinished business of the Emancipation Proclamation is glaringly apparent."[77] Such rhetoric offered valuable insight into the evolution of Johnson's own posi-tion on civil rights and foreshadowed the more militant rhetoric adopted in later special issues, such as "The WHITE Problem in America." More broadly, it provided a measuring stick for *Ebony*'s changing relationship to, discussion of, and engagement with the African American past. The scope and tone of the "Emancipation Proclamation" issue would have been inconceivable less than a decade earlier, when *Ebony*'s discussion of the "black man's trek up from slavery" closely echoed both the language and the sentiment of Franklin's seminal 1947 study.[78]

For a comparison, we might look to the February 1950 feature on "The 15 Outstanding Events in Negro History" and contrast this piece with Bennett's thematically similar but ideologically distinct "Ten Most Dramatic Events in

Negro History" that was published in the September 1963 special. There was clear overlap between the two pieces, with events such as the first landing at Jamestown, the Boston Massacre, the Civil War, and the Emancipation Proclamation featured in both. However, whereas the first article provided a succinct and dispassionate overview of each event, Bennett's writing provided an altogether more militant retelling of such seminal moments—presenting them not as backward steps or triumphant leaps forward in a history of racial uplift but as sites of fracture, rupture, and retribution. In the first instance, the Nat Turner insurrection was presented as a valiant but ultimately failed attempt to secure freedom. In Bennett's retelling, Turner became a messianic figure, "a mystic with blood on his mind, a preacher with vengeance on his lips, a dreamer, a fanatic, a terrorist . . . an implacable foe of slaveholders and slave-breeders."[79]

Such language undoubtedly provided ammunition for critics of Bennett's prose but also reflected broader shifts in black print culture, civil rights activism, and the academy during the 1950s and early 1960s. The overriding tone of *Ebony*'s coverage in its "Emancipation Proclamation" special echoed that of black magazines such as *Freedomways*, which in its own retrospective on the centennial of the Emancipation Proclamation several months earlier had declared 1963 as the year of the "still un-free."[80] Similarly, new periodicals such as *Liberator* used the anniversary of the Emancipation Proclamation to remind readers of their position as more radical voices for black liberation compared to more venerable black periodicals such as *The Crisis*. In a personal reflection in *Liberator*'s centennial issue, James Baldwin argued, "I myself do not feel like the nation has anything to celebrate this year—certainly not one hundred years of Negro Freedom."[81]

Similarly, scholarly interpretations of black history were "certainly influenced by the escalation of the modern civil rights movement" during the 1950s and early 1960s, with the more measured, "conventional" histories such as *From Slavery to Freedom* being challenged by a new wave of scholarship that was less optimistic and increasingly activist oriented.[82] For figures such as Benjamin Quarles, the anniversary provided a moment to reconsider both the Emancipation Proclamation's significance and the broader role of African Americans within the Civil War.[83] The resurgence of black nationalism provided added bite to longstanding efforts by black intellectuals to push back against a white revisionist historiography of the war by highlighting, as Robert Cook has detailed, the "overriding importance of slavery as a factor in Civil War causation" as well as the "active role played by blacks in their liberation."[84]

These trends were indicative of how competing approaches to the commemoration of the Emancipation Proclamation fed into broader tensions surrounding the memorialization of the Civil War in American culture. Prompted by popular interest, the federal government had established the Civil War Centennial Commission in 1957, which sought to encourage citizen participation and a celebration of national unity. As John Bodnar has noted, federally sponsored commemorative events rarely engaged directly with the ongoing struggle for civil rights and instead attempted to promote language and activities "that were ceremonious and ritualistic."[85] Given the ongoing divisions engendered by Cold War geopolitics and the coalescing civil rights movement, it seemed a logical strategy for the federal government to depict the Civil War as "a defining moment when northerners and southerners finally became Americans."[86]

On a state level, appeals to racial and geographical unity were altogether more difficult to achieve. This was particularly true in the South, where state centennial commissions plotted a dangerous path between "expressing loyalty to the symbol of national unity and pride in the Southern cause."[87] Across the states of the former Confederacy, African Americans were routinely left out of the planning and employment of commemorative events. They fared somewhat better in the North, where state commissions looked to temper criticisms of their focus by appointing prominent black advisors such as John H. Johnson and John Hope Franklin.[88] In Illinois, Johnson was part of an American Negro Emancipation Centennial Commission that pushed back against the federal Centennial Commission's efforts to project a harmonious vision of the conflict by "recalling a different past and present."[89] However, as a group, black Americans "lacked the resources to compete effectively in the race to commemorate the Civil War" and were conspicuously absent at high-profile public events and services.[90]

From this perspective, the tone of *Ebony*'s "Emancipation Proclamation" special can be understood as both reliant on and responsive to specific shifts in the pattern of black activism and intellectual thought, and as part of long-standing efforts to create a distinct black "counter-memory" that controverted romanticized images of the conflict and its aftermath. Certainly, it is significant that the magazine chose the figure of Frederick Douglass to grace its Emancipation Proclamation cover, given that no contemporary Northerner had contributed "more to the war's ideological meaning and memory."[91] The abolitionist had fought tirelessly to turn American citizens against the Confederacy and had rallied against the "Lost Cause" narrative and other postwar attempts to downplay the significance of race in the conflict's origins and outcome. Up until his death, Douglass had repeatedly emphasized that "there was a right side and a wrong side in the late war which no sentiment ought to cause us to forget."[92]

The use of Douglass on the cover of the 1963 special was also rooted in his role as a unifying symbol of black history, a role that continued to hold water across the ideological and philosophical spectrum. As Eric Sundquist has noted, moderate critics could point to Douglass's inspirational transition from slavery to freedom as a symbol of "self-making and integrationist uplift," while radical activists could take heart from his more militant speeches and public addresses. Indeed, later Black Power icons such as Stokely Carmichael would venerate Douglass as an activist whose rhetoric offered a rejection of nonviolent protest and a call to arms.[93] In his profile of Douglass for the "Emancipation Proclamation" special, Bennett attempted to unify these competing narratives, arguing that Douglass "favored ballots, if possible, and bullets, if necessary."[94] At the same time, he called upon readers to recognize the activist blueprint provided by black pioneers, asking, "What does Douglass say to us today? What can we find in his life to nerve us for the trials of this hour?"[95]

While this emphasis on Douglass's emancipatory potential as a unifying symbol helped to generate wider engagement with the centennial, it came at the expense of a more substantive engagement with class or gender politics. Just as *Ebony*'s earlier engagement with black "pioneers" had been characterized by a preoccupation with the achievements of black men, so too was Douglass's impact as a historical figure tied to his embodiment of gendered norms and expectations. As a result, Bennett's article on Douglass appeared to internalize a gendered reading of black history that connected the achievements of exceptional "race men" to their relationship to black masculinity as a unifying historical principle.[96]

> First of all—and this is very important—Douglass was a man, in the deepest and truest sense of that much-abused word. Today—when there are so few men— black or white—we need the nobility of his example. Douglass knew—and we need that knowledge today—that to be a man is to be, precisely, responsible. He knew, too, that manhood is founded on self-respect and self-esteem.

This extract illuminates multiple assumptions that came to characterize much of *Ebony*'s historical content. First, the contributions of black male pioneers were seen to be rooted in their gendered identity as "race men." Second, this gendered identity was predicated on a clear sense of racial solidarity, respect, and self-determination. Third, and perhaps most important, these gendered characteristics provided a blueprint for black masculinity in the present against a backdrop of anxiety where few "good black men" remained. As previously noted, this did not negate Bennett's willingness to recognize and celebrate the historical contributions of black women. In many ways, *Ebony*'s discussion, past and present, of black women was more progressive than American society as a whole. However, the importance of normative gender relations would remain a prominent feature of the magazine's negotiation of black history into the 1970s and beyond.

Despite such flaws, the "Emancipation Proclamation" special was greeted with enthusiastic praise by the magazine's audience.[97] Like the reaction to Bennett's "Negro History" series, many of the letters that were published in response to the special issue reiterated the significance of *Ebony*'s role as an outlet for black history education. Readers described the special as "among the greatest books ever written on or about Negro history" and declared that "this issue is a history book in itself." Starnes Lewis noted that upon reading the special he immediately decided to have the issue bound like a book to preserve it and that he had advised all his friends "to bind their copies also and save [them] for future reference." Other members of the magazine's audience promised to keep the special as an "invaluable reference source" for future generations. James Dumpson, the New York Commissioner of Welfare, recommended to *Ebony*'s leadership that a pocket edition of the special could be produced to be "put in the hands of every child in every school of the country." Perhaps the greatest praise came from A. S. "Doc" Young, one of the special's many guest contributors, who trumpeted its impact as "one of the most titanic, most important 'books' ever published in America." Emboldened by this response, *Ebony* and Bennett would respond with a variety of new articles and series that attempted to more intimately connect black history to the ongoing battle for racial equality.[98]

CHAPTER 3

White Problems and
the Roots of Black Power

While black-history-oriented content had featured in *Ebony* since its introduction in 1945, the magazine's coverage of and engagement with the African American past significantly expanded during the late 1950s and early 1960s. Ambitious projects such as the *Ebony* Hall of Fame, while ultimately short lived, helped to lay the groundwork for the introduction of more substantial features, such as Lerone Bennett Jr.'s first "Negro History" series. *Ebony*'s special retrospective on the centennial of the Emancipation Proclamation in 1963 served as further evidence of its role in "boldly reconstructing" the black past.[1] The response of *Ebony*'s audience to such content, alongside the largely positive public reaction to Bennett's *Before the Mayflower*, consolidated *Ebony*'s role as a popular outlet for black historical education and the centrality of its senior editor to this mission. By the magazine's nineteenth anniversary in November 1964, its "Backstage" feature had become a popular place to showcase its role as a tool for "teaching the masses of the Negro the story of their own heritage."[2]

For much of its first two decades in print, *Ebony*'s historical features had been focused on celebrating the exceptionalism and self-made accomplishments of a predominantly male band of intrepid black pioneers, something that complemented the periodical's broader prerogative to "mirror the happier side of Negro life." This approach was in some ways maintained through subsequent black history series, such as Bennett's "Pioneers in Protest." However, even as *Ebony*'s coverage of black history attracted praise, its enduring emphasis on celebrity culture and conspicuous consumption drew the ire of purchasers and protes-tors alike.[3] For Bennett, this tension provided an opportunity to push for more politically oriented interpretations of the past, while for Johnson the publication of such content became a means of countering public criticism of his magazine as a mouthpiece for the "talented tenth."[4]

Following the publication of *Ebony*'s 1963 special, black frustrations at the pace of social change fed into a spate of urban uprisings in cities such as New York and Philadelphia—events that served as a precursor to an explosion of violence in the predominantly black neighborhood of Watts in Los Angeles in 1965.[5] While *Ebony*'s editors could not have predicted Watts, the uprising ran alongside the publication of "The WHITE Problem in America," a 1965 special that served to root the riots historically and to reiterate black history's practical application. Similarly, as black activists turned toward more radical strategies for liberation, black history would become a vital lens through which *Ebony*'s publisher and editors negotiated the ongoing struggle for equality in the pres-ent. This would become increasingly obvious following the emergence of Black Power on the national stage, which intersected with an ongoing black history series published in *Ebony* that focused on the impact of "Black Power" during Reconstruction.

Pioneers in Protest

Buoyed by the overwhelming response to *Ebony*'s "Emancipation Proclamation" special, Johnson continued to sign off on historically themed articles throughout late 1963 and early 1964. Now firmly established in his role as the magazine's in-house historian, Bennett provided a steady stream of black-history-oriented content, including a lengthy feature on Jean Baptiste Point Du Sable, a free black trader widely recognized as Chicago's first permanent settler.[6] True to form, Bennett spun a colorful portrayal of Du Sable's adventures on the shores of Lake Michigan, positioning his tale as a revelatory insight into the origins of modern Chicago that fired playful jabs at the magazine's earlier penchant for scandalous content. Bennett declared that only a handful of the city's residents were hip to "Chicago's deepest and best-kept secret: its father is a Negro."[7] Other *Ebony* staffers contributed further historical pieces, with Allan Morrison building on his earlier work through features such as a cover story on the role of black sol-diers during the Revolutionary War.[8]

In addition to in-house articles, *Ebony* showcased new historical research by historians and writers working outside of Johnson Publishing Company. G. Allen Foster, perhaps best known for his 1963 study *The Eyes and Ears of the*

Civil War, published two extracts from his longer work in *Ebony* in the immediate aftermath of its "Emancipation Proclamation" special.[9] The first article focused on African American spy John Scobell, who worked behind Confederate lines gathering information for Union troops.[10] The second feature told the story of Mary Louvestre, an enslaved Virginia woman who provided vital information on Confederate shipbuilding to the North. Foster's work was greeted just as enthusiastically as the historical writing of in-house contributors, with reader Fred Hemmerly contending that the Scobell profile was "surely one of the more delightful and heartfelt stories [he'd] ever read."[11] *Ebony* followed up its collaboration with Foster with a five-part preview of *Ageless Africa*, an illustrated history of the African continent, co-written by E. Harper Johnson and William Hansberry, which purported to capture "the grandeur of ancient and medieval Africa" for the first time. *Ebony* informed readers that the book's origins lay in the widespread attention Hansberry received after a profile of the historian was published in the magazine's February 1961 issue.[12]

Looking to capitalize on the success of his "Negro History" series, Bennett's second black history series, titled "Pioneers in Protest," debuted in March 1964 and promised to provide a range of "in-depth profiles of Negro and white pioneers of the freedom movement," beginning with a feature on African American scientist and abolitionist Benjamin Banneker. Bennett's article was far from the first effort by a black periodical to detail Banneker's accomplishments. More than a decade earlier, Jesse Zimmerman had written an in-depth profile of Banneker for *The Crisis* that provided a comprehensive retelling of his life and accomplishments.[13] However, while Zimmerman's account had focused on Banneker's professional attributes and scholarly acumen, Bennett offered a more activist-oriented summary of the scientist's life. The editor envisioned Banneker as a strident abolitionist who denounced slavery and "the hypocrisy of US patriots" such as Thomas Jefferson. Whereas Zimmerman emphasized Banneker's role as a "secretary of peace," Bennett championed him as "the first Negro of national stature to give vent to the Negro protest."[14]

This tone was extended to the series' coverage of black women—while "Pioneers in Protest" was dominated by the contributions of black (and white) men such as Banneker and John Brown, it also highlighted the impact of black women such as Sojourner Truth and Harriet Tubman, who were celebrated as militant leaders and black feminists long before such ideas were seriously considered within mainstream American media. Both Truth and Tubman were envisioned as "the archetypal image of a long line of fabulously heroic Negro women."[15] This message was particularly resolute in *Ebony*'s profile of Tubman, which pictured the abolitionist as a "great slave rebel, whose name struck terror in the hearts of Eastern Shore planters." Through a series of evocative vignettes, Bennett constructed an image of Tubman as a daring guerrilla leader, "black as the night, and as bold."[16]

Like his first "Negro History" series, the response to "Pioneers in Protest" from the magazine's readers appeared to be overwhelmingly positive. Missourian Emmett Hughes applauded Bennett for helping to recover "the history of the Negro and his contribution to American history as a whole," while other readers contended that Bennett's series was "a distinct service to the nation."[17] It was clear that the editor wished to draw stronger parallels between his exploration of African American history and the ongoing struggle for civil rights. Perhaps the best example of this can be seen through the fourth article in his series, which focused on the life of Frederick Douglass. Bennett forsook a conventional article layout in favor of a range of quotations taken from Douglass's speeches, books, and newspaper articles. Accompanying these words were a collection of photos referencing the modern civil rights movement, including images of the Birmingham church bombing, the Freedom Rides, and the site of Emmett Till's murder in Money, Mississippi.[18]

Efforts to connect black historical activism to the present were not limited to *Ebony*'s editorial content. The magazine's audience also highlighted the relationship between black past and present, as well as the direct ways in which *Ebony*'s historical content was contributing to racial progress. Indeed, some readers believed that features such as Bennett's "Pioneers in Protest" series or the magazine's serialization of *Ageless Africa* were "just as important as the sit-ins, the marches and rights bills because they assert the fact that we were as important to the progress of the world as any other race."[19] Shifts in *Ebony*'s coverage of black history intersected with a broader editorial move toward a more combative position on civil rights during the early 1960s, with Bennett's "Negro History" series complemented by exposés on school and residential segregation in the North and profiles of community activists and civil rights campaigners such as Earl Dickerson and Constance Baker Motley.[20]

The editor contended that a "new mood," characterized by open criticism of nonviolent direct action and the go-slow approach of established civil rights organizations, was pushing black America toward "a fateful eyeball-to-eyeball confrontation with Jim Crow."[21] Bennett expanded on such sentiments through public addresses, where he criticized the timidity of middle-class black leadership and detailed the "red-hot-rage in the Negro ghetto."[22] At a Capital Press Club event in June 1963, Bennett spoke of a "creeping contempt for moderates and liberals" among many younger black activists.[23] His words startled fellow panelists such as U.S Civil Rights Commission staff director Berl Bernhard and socialist historian Howard Zinn, who described Bennett in his diary as "much more militant in words than his magazine; you'd never suspect he edited something like that."[24] Bennett also followed *Before the Mayflower* with two more politically strident texts: *Confrontation: Black and White*, which contended that the "average white American is, and always has been, a gutless but ruthless bigot," and *The Negro Mood*, which expanded on his writing for *Ebony* to situate the black revolution of the 1960s "within the context of a long history of developing protest and social contention."[25]

While neither book would challenge the mass popularity of *Before the Mayflower*, they garnered praise from outlets such as the *Chicago Defender*, which applauded Bennett's "examination of the factors that have given rise to the present racial crisis."[26] Black literary critic and *Negro Digest* editor Hoyt Fuller described Bennett as a rare spokesman for the African American cause; one of the "few authentically *knowing* voices" among the hordes of "pseudo militants, tailgate sociologists, and superficial prognosticators."[27] John Henrik Clarke went further, suggesting that *The Negro Mood* in particular offered "an entirely new perspective for . . . the Negro rebellion."[28] For Josh McPhee, the title of *Confrontation*, alongside its striking cover design by Janet Helverson, appeared to signal an increasingly oppositional approach to race relations and a "codification of the visual binary of black and white."[29]

As the movement's focus began to shift northward following the March on Washington and passage of the 1964 Civil Rights Act, both *Ebony* and the nation were forced to adapt to a new racial climate and the "potentially explosive emotional upheaval in the ghettos of America" foretold by Bennett and other commentators.[30] Racial tensions in the supposed "melting pot" of the modern American city were hardly a postwar phenomenon. White mob attacks on black communities emerged as a recurrent feature of postbellum life in southern U.S. cities such as Wilmington (1898) and Atlanta (1906), as well as burgeoning black metropolises such as St. Louis (1917) and Chicago (1919).[31] Even as African American servicemen fought for democracy abroad, racial tensions and white violence contributed to race riots in Detroit, Harlem, and Los Angeles during 1943. The continued migration of African Americans out of the South following World War II further exacerbated existing patterns of workplace discrimination, residential discrimination, and anti-black prejudice.[32]

On July 16, 1964, just two weeks after Lyndon Johnson had signed the Civil Rights Act into law, a fifteen-year-old black boy named James Powell was shot and killed in an altercation with a white off-duty police officer in New York City. Over the following six days, widespread rioting led to at least one further death, hundreds of arrests, and intense altercations between predominantly black protestors and a predominantly white New York police force in Harlem.[33] Several hundred miles northwest on New York's north coast, rioting in Rochester led Governor Nelson Rockefeller to call in the National Guard. The following month, rioting occurred in a number of cities, including Philadelphia and Chicago, where Cook County sheriff and future Illinois governor Richard Ogilvie advised state and county police to broadcast through their squad-car loudspeakers that "if you shoot, we're going to fire back."[34]

The unrest of 1964 marked the beginning of a series of "long hot summers" that would arguably reach a peak during the nationwide uprisings in the aftermath of Dr. Martin Luther King's assassination in 1968, exposing the cracks in American race relations and urban policy that the Civil Rights Act of 1964 had attempted to shore up. Across the nation, law enforcement and government officials blamed "outside agitators" for disturbances, while news outlets focused on the damage caused by rioters, who were disparaged as "looters" and "hoodlums."[35] However, for protestors on the ground, the unrest was an expression of deep-rooted frustrations at the failure of local and federal government to address systemic urban inequalities. It was a tension that would come to characterize a new phase of the freedom struggle, which threatened to "drive a wedge between the civil rights movement and many white liberals."[36] In *The Negro Mood*, Bennett had asserted that, in order to succeed, new black strategies must be situated within "a long history of developing protest and social contention."[37] By the first quarter of 1965 his position had hardened; he advised Syracuse students in March that the country was in a "lull before the storm" and contended that "we are headed for a disaster . . . we need to make revolutionary changes now."[38]

Watts and *The WHITE Problem in America*

For many Americans, the storm Bennett and other commentators had forecast appeared to break in August 1965. Less than a week after the Voting Rights Act had been signed into law by President Johnson, the predominantly black neighborhood of Watts in Los Angeles erupted in flames. The inciting incident was a routine traffic stop by California Highway Patrolman Lee Minkus, who pulled over twenty-one-year-old Marquette Frye and his brother Ronald for reckless driving. As Minkus administered a sobriety test and placed Marquette under arrest, Ronald walked to the family home nearby, returning to the scene with his mother, Rena Price. A crowd quickly gathered, swelling to around a thousand people by the time the Fryes had been hustled into a patrol car. Rumors spread of police brutality, leading to an outburst of rage that quickly spiraled into a full-fledged riot.[39]

While the outbreak of rioting in the summer of 1964 had drawn alarm from many corners, it paled in comparison to events in Watts. Over the six days following the Fryes' arrest, South Los Angeles was transformed into a war zone, with rioting, arson, and looting extending over a forty-six-square-mile curfew zone. At least thirty-four people were killed, more than one thousand injured, and thousands more arrested; property damage was estimated in the hundreds of millions.[40] Just as news outlets had placed blame for unrest during 1964 on violent black agitators, the response to Watts provides an image of the city's black population as an incensed and insatiable mob. The *Los Angeles Times* reported that police officers were fighting "a virtual guerrilla war . . . with mobs of frenzied Negroes" and warned of roving packs of African Americans who "sacked stores and stoned passing autos virtually unrestrained."[41] *Life* magazine declared that on the flaming streets of Los Angeles, "swarms of Negroes grew into roaming mobs, looting, burning, beating, to the war cry of 'Get Whitey.'"[42] Mainstream news coverage focused on the "wild plundering" of rioters and framed the unrest as an outbreak of militant agitation and as a crisis of "law and order."[43] By contrast, African American news outlets such as the *Los Angeles Sentinel* and the *Chicago Defender* highlighted police brutality and general white indifference to endemic social problems as catalysts for the insurrection.[44]

Against the backdrop of the Watts riots in August 1965, *Ebony* published its second major special issue, "The WHITE Problem in America." Perhaps the most significant issue of the magazine yet published, the special painted a deeply critical portrait of urban segregation, white flight, and the continuing failures of economic and political elites to address the nation's systemic racial problems. The tone was set by an unusually strident statement from Johnson, which declared that the real obstacle to black progress was "Mr. Charlie, Whitey, The Man—the unthinking white man who is the symbol to Negroes of all those whites who have 'stood in the doorways' to keep the Negro back."[45] The publisher argued that since the onset of the Montgomery bus boycott in 1955, white commentators had attempted to "solve the race problem" through focusing on how best to integrate black citizens fully into American society. By contrast, Johnson suggested that "the answer lies in a more thorough study of the man who created the problem. In this issue we, as Negroes, look at the white man today with the hope that our effort will tempt him to look at himself more thoroughly."[46]

Johnson's statement marked a significant departure from his conservative approach to racial politics, which had helped to shape much of *Ebony*'s early content. For years the publisher had avoided questions about his commitment to the movement or had argued that any lack of militancy within his publications was compensated for by the number of jobs they provided for black editors, models, and salesmen.[47] More broadly, the special offered an incisive and expansive critique of white supremacy that sought to invert discussions of "the Negro problem" that had dominated postwar American social science. As Daryl Michael Scott has noted, both conservative and liberal white social scientists routinely sought to generate contempt toward or sympathy for blacks by emphasizing pathology and the "damaged black psyche."[48] Perhaps best characterized by the tone of Gunnar Myrdal's 1944 study *An American Dilemma*, this approach presented the plight of black citizens as a puzzle that could be slotted into its rightful place within the nation's democratic project through inclusion and rehabilitation.[49] By contrast, *Ebony* looked to inscribe the problem of racial discrimination as specifically "a problem of white prejudicial attitudes."[50]

This theme was taken up by figures such as African American writer John Oliver Killens, who contributed an extract from his essay collection *Black Man's Burden* to the special. Just as Johnson had attempted to invert discussions of the "Negro problem," so too did Killens reject the paternalistic trope of the "white man's burden" to assert that the true burden of American imperialism and white supremacy was levied on black communities at home and abroad.[51] Similarly, Bennett reiterated that "there is no Negro problem in America" and emphasized that in order to solve the race problem, the country must turn an interrogative lens on white America. "It was a stroke of genius," Bennett declared, "for white Americans to give Negro Americans the name of their problem, thereby focusing attention on symptoms (the Negro and the Negro community) instead of causes (the white man and the white community)."[52] In addressing uprisings such as the 1964 Harlem riots, Bennett pointed the finger of blame at the racist response of city police and the ghettoization of black urban communities, which had been created and sustained by white power structures.

Given its lengthy gestation, the overlap between the Los Angeles uprisings and the release of "The WHITE Problem in America" was largely accidental. As recently as March 1965, *Ebony* had named Los Angeles as one of the country's ten best cities for jobs, contending that it "practically assures" work for African Americans with Equal Opportunity Employers.[53] This was largely a consensus opinion, with the Urban League naming Los Angeles as "far and away the best city for blacks" based on housing, employment, and quality of life.[54] For many onlookers and media outlets, the Watts riots were so disturbing because they occurred in a city that was, at least in theory, both geographically and historically removed from the darker aspects of American racial politics. When Los Angeles police chief William Parker was interviewed in summer 1964, he soundly rejected suggestions of racial tension in the City of Angels, arguing that "any condition which contributed to chaos in other parts of the country" did not exist in his hometown. Just weeks before the uprisings in Watts, Parker reiterated that "there can be no race riots in Los Angeles."[55]

Although the timing of its release may have been coincidental, "The WHITE Problem in America" provided a powerful reader for the riots. Keith Gilyard has noted that Killens's comments about the limitations of nonviolent resistance "never seemed more persuasive" than when set against the unfolding chaos in Los Angeles.[56] From a different perspective, *Ebony* editor Ponchitta Pierce unveiled pervasive media biases in coverage of the Watts riots by discussing civil unrest in white-dominated suburban communities. As part of an exploration into crime in the suburbs, Pierce documented the aftermath of rioting in Hampton Beach and Laconia, picturing white suburban teenagers confronting National Guardsmen, looting businesses, and burning automobiles.[57] When placed alongside highly racialized coverage of "frenzied" mobs in Los Angeles, her article helped to underscore the hypocrisy of media outlets that denounced "race riots" but underplayed or failed to report on white-dominated riots in other areas of the country. More broadly, the special emphasized the historical antecedents for the new wave of urban riots sweeping the nation.[58]

For Johnson, the Watts riots helped to amplify the special issue and to emphasize the strategic value of its publication. The eye-catching cover and incisive editorial content of "The WHITE Problem in America" offered a timely rebuttal to continued criticisms of *Ebony* by more militant activists and journalists. In the aftermath of Watts, Eddie Ellis had published a two-part article in radical black magazine *Liberator* that questioned whether *Ebony* was truly a "black" magazine. Citing factors such as its failure to effectively document militant black activism and its continued reliance on white corporate advertising, Ellis declared that "if *Ebony* can't even be loyal to the 750,000 Negroes who read the magazine, we know *Ebony* has NO identification with, or loyalties to, the other 30 million BLACK captives in America."[59] Yet the issues of *Ebony* that paralleled Ellis's critique featured scores of letters applauding "The WHITE Problem" as a new high in black journalism and as a vital "ideological weapon" in the fight for full democracy and racial justice.[60]

Perhaps more important, "The WHITE Problem in America" helped to reframe public discussions of the magazine's own history. Published just a few months before *Ebony*'s twentieth anniversary, it offered persuasive evidence of the periodical's growing diversity and maturity. In its anniversary special, Johnson argued that *Ebony* had become "a spokesman for the full and equal treatment of Negroes in this day and age."[61] This sentiment was reinforced by press releases and taken up by external sources such as the *Philadelphia Tribune*, which identified "The WHITE Problem in America" as an example of Ebony's transition "from materialism to militancy."[62] Although Johnson was quick to spotlight such developments as a daring editorial move, this was not entirely true. As *The Crisis* noted in its own reflections on *Ebony*'s twentieth anniversary, the adoption of a more activist stance was "not only sound editorial policy, but also good business."[63] Far from alienating readers with their content, *Ebony*'s two special issues of 1963 and 1965 had been the bestselling issues in the magazine's history.[64] The attraction of a more militant historical perspective and the connections between black radical protest in past and present would become even clearer as calls for Black Power burst onto the national stage.

What We're Saying Now Is Black Power!

Among the editorial strategies *Ebony* endorsed in the aftermath of the 1964 riots was an effort to better document the influence of militant activists such as Malcolm X and the Deacons for Self-Defense, as well as a new wave of civil rights organizations rising to the forefront of the movement.[65] Groups such as the Congress of Racial Equality (CORE) were championed as the "wild child of civil rights," with protestors praised for combining the "toughness of a soldier with the restraint of a clergyman."[66] The Student Nonviolent Coordinating Committee was described in altogether more militant terms as "the most radical, the most controversial and perhaps the most creative of all civil rights organizations." In a detailed profile of the group published in the July 1965 issue of *Ebony*, SNCC was defined as a "revolutionary action agency dedicated to the proposition that racism is only one symptom of a deeper sickness at the heart of our society."[67]

One figure who was conspicuously absent from *Ebony*'s SNCC profile was Stokely Carmichael. Less than a year later, the activist's appearance at the Meredith march in Mississippi and his electrifying "Black Power" speech on June 16, 1966, would thrust him into the national spotlight.[68] Carmichael's call for Black Power would reverberate throughout the movement, creating a new language and new philosophy for racial protest and black identity and threatening the church-based middle-class black activist and white liberal coalition that had characterized the early phase of the postwar civil rights struggle. However, at the time of *Ebony*'s SNCC profile Carmichael was still a minor figure in SNCC's organizational hierarchy, with his influence confined to grassroots political organizing in Alabama.[69] The article focused instead on the leadership triumvirate of then-SNCC chairman John Lewis, Program Secretary Cleveland Sellers, and Executive Secretary James Forman.

In 1965 the sole voice championing the concept of "Black Power" in *Ebony* was Lerone Bennett Jr. The editor had used the phrase in earlier work, most notably an article published as part of his original "Negro History" series in *Ebony*, titled "Black Power in Dixie," which had focused on black political representation in the South during Reconstruction. In November 1965 Bennett began a new historical series titled "Black Power," which fleshed out the ideas put forward in this earlier article. It was presented as the first "detailed human portrait" of black politicians during Reconstruction, with Bennett emphasizing that the era was "remarkably similar to our own" and that a fuller understanding of the first Reconstruction "is indispensable for an understanding of the Second Reconstruction" of the 1960s.[70] "Look close at this scene as it stands now in 1867," Bennett advised his readers, "and mark well the revolutionary mood of the Negro masses."[71] *Ebony*'s audience was reminded of these similarities through direct legislative comparisons, such as pioneering public accommodations acts in South Carolina where "militant Negro legislators had to meet substantially the same arguments advanced 100 years later" for the passage of the 1964 Civil Rights Act.[72] Similarly, Bennett's slippage between the use of "black" and "Negro" throughout his series looked to create a rhetorical bridge between the revolutionary fervor of the 1870s and 1960s.

Ebony's depiction of a "Black Reconstruction" clearly took its cue from Du Bois's landmark 1935 study of the same name, which had sought to turn Reconstruction historiography on its head.[73] For much of the early twentieth century, representations of Reconstruction had been dominated by the Dunning School, whose sympathies lay with white Southerners who resisted federal efforts to maintain Reconstruction. As Eric Foner has argued, historians of the Dunning School insisted that black suffrage was a serious error of judgment that imposed the responsibilities of government on "childlike blacks . . . unprepared for freedom and incapable of properly exercising the political rights Northerners had thrust upon them."[74] Bennett's rehabilitation of Lieutenant Governor Oscar James Dunn of Louisiana and other Southern black legislators fed into a broader "reconstruction of Reconstruction" by revisionist historians who during the postwar years built upon Du Bois's portrayal of Reconstruction as an "idealistic effort to construct a democratic, interracial political order from the ashes of slavery."[75] The editor's words were complemented by impressionistic artwork created by Herbert Temple and illustrations taken from sympathetic period magazines such as *Harper's Weekly*.[76]

From a different perspective, Bennett's "Black Power" series reflected the ways in which growing support for nationalism within the movement had influenced the trajectory of African American historiography. Figures such as

Malcolm X, who would come to be recognized as a "spiritual adviser in absentia" for Black Power advocates, were deeply informed by their understanding of African American history's importance as an educational and political tool.[77] Through speeches such as "Black Man's History," X contended that "the thing that has made the so-called Negro in America fail, more than any other thing, is your, my, lack of knowledge concerning history."[78] X's emphasis on black history as a central component to African American collective identity, alongside the media's growing fascination with his image, made him arguably "black history's major popularizer" during the final years of his life.[79] Following his assassination in 1965, the vacuum created by his death would be filled by black historians and intellectuals such as Bennett, individuals who remained committed to utilizing African American history as "a weapon in the fight for racial equality."[80]

For Bennett, the application of Black Power during Reconstruction was rooted in the total realization of black people as political agents: "Did one want a birth certificate? It was necessary to see a black man. Was there trouble in the schools? It was necessary to see the predominantly black school commission. Perhaps the problem was a death certificate. The man to see was black."[81] Black policemen, black magistrates and black-dominated juries, black mayors, black railroad and oil company presidents—these were the things that justified "the power of blackness." Such rhetoric sought to present complex legal and structural issues in "terms the men in the streets could understand: a naked power struggle between two men, one white, one Negro."[82] While Bennett's writing style had always allowed for voluble prose, the fiery vignettes of death-or-glory black politicians littered throughout his "Black Power" series reflected a broader shift within black historiography during the 1960s toward a more activist-oriented style that characterized the work of Nathan Hare and other black academics who would play a key role in the development of the Black Studies movement.[83]

Following the April 1966 issue of *Ebony*, Bennett's "Black Power" series was placed on temporary hiatus due to the editor's ill health.[84] In its absence, popular conceptions of the slogan were realigned by events at the Meredith march. James Meredith, who had become the first black student to integrate the University of Mississippi in 1962, began a solo "March against Fear" from Memphis, Tennessee, to Jackson, Mississippi, on June 6, 1966, to protest continuing racial discrimination in the South and to promote African American voter registration. On the second day of his campaign, Meredith was gunned down by a white assailant near Hernando, Mississippi. Following the attack, a number of civil rights organizations vowed to continue the march. This included King and the SCLC, and Carmichael, who had recently replaced John Lewis as the chair of SNCC.[85] As the number of activists grew, so too did tensions between marchers and state troopers. Carmichael was arrested for trespassing on public property as the march reached Greenwood, Mississippi, on June 16. Following his release, the SNCC leader made a beeline for a rally at a local park, fuming that "this is the twenty-seventh time I have been arrested, and I ain't going to jail no more! The only way we gonna stop them white men from whuppin' us is to take over. . . . What we gonna start saying now is Black Power!"[86]

Carmichael's call for Black Power radically transformed the terms on which the black freedom struggle would be framed and debated. Aram Goudsouzian has argued that the slogan gained immediate traction because in just two words it powerfully captured "a generation of frustrations and aspirations: the slow pace of federal reform, the limits of nonviolence, the failings of white liberals, the need for political and economic control over black communities, [and] the yearning for pride."[87] More tellingly, it laid bare the tactical and ideological fault lines that had come to divide the SCLC and NAACP from the "take-no-prisoners approach" of younger organizations.[88] King initially sought to soften and mediate Carmichael's cry by defining Black Power as "the ability to wrest concessions from white authority on the road to interracial brotherhood."[89] However, the weeks that followed demonstrated that Carmichael's and King's understandings of the "Black Power phenomenon" were, at least in public, fundamentally different—King envisioned Black Power as a nihilistic and reactionary force, whereas Carmichael was directed by his belief that Black Power was "the proper articulation of the needs of the people."[90]

When CORE voted unanimously to endorse Black Power at the organization's National Convention in Baltimore on July 4, the national press reacted with horror.[91] The *New York Times* declared that the unity of civil rights organizations had been "shattered by the rising cry of 'black power'" and drew direct links between the slogan and outbreaks of ghetto violence.[92] Other newspapers such as the *Chicago Sun-Times* doubted whether Black Power meant anything more than "bricks and stones and Molotov cocktails."[93] If Carmichael's call had come eighteen months earlier, it may well have found a more sympathetic audience among veteran civil rights beat journalists such as Claude Sitton of the *New York Times*.[94] As it was, by the summer of 1966 many beat journalists had been reassigned to cover the emerging war in Vietnam.[95] Reporters less familiar with Carmichael and the SNCC were quicker to reiterate the stance of vice president Hubert Humphrey, who rejected Black Power as "apartheid," and NAACP executive director Roy Wilkins, who argued that supporters of the slogan had "formally chosen the racist route" and that separatism was equivalent to "black group suicide."[96]

A General and Timeless Goal

To many commentators, Black Power was a dangerous "new" slogan that marked a juncture between nonviolent civil rights activism and an increasingly revolutionary age.[97] Yet for Carmichael it was hardly a new phenomenon; he would later declare that "we'd been talking about nothing else in the Delta for years."[98] As scholars such as Rhonda Williams and William Van Deburg have demonstrated, while calls for Black Power during the second half of the 1960s, as well as mainstream condemnations of it, may have been temporally unique, they were an extension of the "general and timeless goal" of black nationhood, self-determination, race consciousness and pride.[99] This same lens can be applied to *Ebony* itself, given the magazine's multiple references to "Black Power" in different guises prior to the introduction of Bennett's series. Indeed, Williams has argued that a 1957 interview with Paul Robeson in *Ebony* marked the "print debut" of Black Power, alongside a 1954 travelogue by Richard Wright.[100] In this fascinating exchange with contributor Carl Rowan, Robeson articulated his understanding of Black Power as a call for radical proletariat action within the black diaspora, connecting the growing power of black Americans to the "black power that now is flexing its muscles in Asia and Africa."[101]

When *Ebony*'s "Black Power" series returned in July 1966, the magazine made no reference to how the slogan's popular image had been fundamentally altered by Carmichael's speech at the Meredith march. However, Bennett's writing continued to draw explicit parallels between "radical Reconstruction" and contemporary events such as the Selma-to-Montgomery march. He contrasted the shutdown on the Edmund Pettus bridge with events a century earlier, when "the real Edmund Pettus was fuming in his Selma law office while black *and* white men tramped through the Selma streets, singing a harshly militant We *Have* Overcome."[102] In doing so, Bennett looked to establish Black Power not as a departure from but a continuation of the movement's political and social goals. This position was reinforced by activists such as CORE chairman Floyd McKissick, who argued that Black Power was "a concept as old as the first American immigrant who sought to share in the government of this land."[103]

A little over two months after Carmichael's call for Black Power, Bennett penned an explosive profile of the activist in the September 1966 issue of *Ebony*, titled "Stokely Carmichael: Architect of Black Power."[104] On first glance, Bennett's article appeared to tap into the sensationalistic media coverage of Carmichael that had proliferated following the Meredith march; most notably through his opening description of a tense highway car chase and showdown between Carmichael and a car of racist white men.[105] Indeed, journalists such as A. S.

"Doc" Young believed that "such childishness as racing down a Southern high-way" demonstrated Carmichael's unsuitability for leadership, while some of the magazine's readers pointed to Bennett's image of a freewheeling, bare-chested Carmichael as evidence of his true status as an "irresponsible, jive-talking juve-nile."[106] However, on closer reading, Bennett's work appears to challenge this negative portrait of Carmichael with a description of controlled aggression and self-confidence—an empowering embodiment of his controversial slogan. Similarly, in contrast to suggestions that Carmichael was personally hostile to elder movement statesmen, the article pictured him walking arm in arm with King at the Meredith march and cavorting with "friendly critic" Bayard Rustin.[107]

Critically, Bennett's profile offered Carmichael space to present an in-depth account of his own understanding and definition of Black Power; an opportu-nity other media outlets often denied. When magazine's such as *Life* engaged with Black Power, they were more concerned with fretting over how the slogan should be defined than allowing Carmichael an opportunity to outline his own understanding of the concept.[108] In much of his early media exposure following the Meredith march, Peniel Joseph contends that Carmichael's complex persona and political philosophy was "boiled down to a simple duality: the intelligent, well-spoken and handsome college graduate and former sit-in activist vs. the fire-breathing and violence-prone militant."[109] However, as Goudsouzian has noted, on the rare occasions he was given time and space by sympathetic jour-nalists, Carmichael sought to frame Black Power "in universal and democratic terms, as a logical outgrowth of the civil rights movement."[110] Perhaps nowhere was this clearer than in his *Ebony* profile.

In keeping with Bennett's depiction of Black Power during Reconstruction, Carmichael emphasized that political power was at the heart of the Black Power concept. He described Black Power as "the massed political, economic, emo-tional and physical strength of the black community exercised in the interest of the total black community."[111] In bullet-pointed prose, Carmichael argued that Black Power was a declaration of independence, a demand for black control in black majority cities and counties, an effort to expose the limits of white power when confronted with a unified black group, a demand for independent political groups and cooperatives, and a call for black class solidarity. In turn, Bennett linked this doctrine to the deeply rooted notions of Black Power imagined dur-ing the nineteenth century. "Black Power does not mean more of the kind of power black people have in Northern urban ghettos," Bennett explained. "What it means, Carmichael says, is a kind and degree of power black people have not had in this country since Reconstruction."[112]

Accordingly, while Joseph has suggested that Bennett's article helped to cast Carmichael's as "the soul of a new movement," it also appeared to solidify

Carmichael's role within an existing one.[113] It was no coincidence that Bennett opened the feature with an encounter that echoed the type of "naked power struggle" that had characterized so many of his previous "Black Power" articles.[114] His depiction of Carmichael's highway standoff located the encounter within a timeless (and gendered) struggle for respect, where "a man had challenged a man—and a man had answered."[115] Similarly, the feature positioned Carmichael as the living embodiment of previous black radical leaders—seen through interactions between Carmichael and figures such as Harlem bookstore owner Lewis Michaux. As Carmichael viewed an image of Malcolm X, Michaux informed him that "Malcolm X is still living. When you walked in, Malcolm smiled."[116]

Black Power Is 100 Years Old

In the issues that followed Bennett's profile of Carmichael, *Ebony* offered two quite different visions of Black Power. The first came through articles by figures such as King and Carl Rowan, who warned that Black Power was a "phony cry" and that a recommitment to nonviolence offered "the only road to freedom."[117] Gesturing toward his own leftward shift following the March on Washington and the Watts riots, King noted the deep-rooted inequalities that underpinned the outbreaks of urban rioting during the mid-1960s, suggesting that the unrest was "brought on by long-neglected poverty, humiliation, oppression, and exploitation."[118] However, like other commentators, he criticized the emergence of Black Power as a series of "unplanned, uncontrollable temper tantrums" and warned that "wholesale slaughter" might be the result if black militants attempted to wage open war on American society.[119] To reinforce this message, *Ebony* reprinted images from its earlier coverage of the Sharpeville massacre alongside King's words. Syndicated columnist and "voice of reason" Rowan was less generous in a November 1966 article, offering a deeply critical depiction of Black Power as "a plain old-fashioned hoax."[120] In the author's opinion, Carmichael's "outpouring of Negro anger and emotion" had dealt a critical blow to the movement's leadership and direction.

The second came through the continuation of Bennett's series, which reiterated the liberatory potential of Black Power and the connection between its nineteenth- and twentieth-century iterations. Just as King's reservations had been used to equate black militancy with black violence, Bennett cataloged the fears of postbellum journalists such as James Shepherd Pike, who "recoiled in horror" at the potential transformation of Southern society under black leadership.[121] However, whereas King saw only a violent resolution to an exertion of Black Power, Bennett's series articulated its scope for political and economic liberation: "the black man was in power, and, despite that fact or perhaps because of it, South Carolina was thriving."[122] Similarly, it was with no small sense of irony that Bennett followed reports of a "white backlash" to the modern emergence of Black Power by detailing "the first white backlash" to Black Power during Reconstruction.[123] From this perspective, the true "horror" of Black Power lay not in its radical potential but in the "counter-revolutionary campaign of terror" waged against it by racist white terrorists.[124]

In retrospect, it is clear that Bennett's series and his profile of Carmichael played a major role in familiarizing millions of Ebony's readers with the concept of Black Power, and his work offered an alternative perspective on Black Power to the one that dominated American mainstream media. The timing of the magazine's "Black Power" series was certainly significant, given it predated Carmichael's speech at the Meredith march by six months and continued throughout the following months, helping to shape reader responses to the slogan in real time. That is not to say that the magazine's audience was united in its support for Black Power. Many readers expressed reservations over Carmichael's rhetoric and "all that 'Black Power' nonsense."[125] However, Bennett's empathetic and considerate discussion of Black Power formed an important counterbalance to the criticisms of commentators who believed it to be an "ill-defined, juvenile posture at best or an incendiary, fear-inducing catchphrase at worst."[126]

The extent to which Carmichael's own call for Black Power was inspired by Bennett's writing is considerably more difficult to decipher. Following the Meredith march, Bennett would claim in speeches that he had "first coined the phrase 'Black Power'"—a sentiment that was supported by figures such as Howard Meyer.[127] Certainly the rhetoric of Bennett's articles, books, and public speeches in the years preceding the Meredith march would come to play a familiar role in Carmichael's desire for black people to "move into a position where they can define what freedom is, what a white liberal is, what black nationalism is, [and] what power is."[128] Although little record of any personal correspondence between the pair exists, anecdotal evidence points to a considerable professional and intellectual respect that was formalized through collaboration on Carmichael's profile in Ebony. Bennett would continue to speak highly of Carmichael in the aftermath of the feature, while Before the Mayflower was cited as a key text in Carmichael and Charles Hamilton's 1967 work Black Power: The Politics of Liberation.[129]

Perhaps the clearest evidence of Carmichael's awareness of Bennett's work can be seen through Carmichael's speeches, wherein he cited Bennett by name on multiple occasions. In an address made in Chicago following the West Side riots in July 1966, Carmichael declared that "we have to tell them we are going to use the term 'Black Power' and we are going to define it because Black Power speaks to us."[130] He argued that this definition was rooted within a broader black radical tradition and that this would only be appreciated through reading and learning from black activists and historians themselves. "We have to study black history. . . . You should know who John Hullett is, who Fannie Lou Hamer is, [and] who Lerone Bennett is." The following year during a speech in Seattle, Carmichael reiterated Bennett's standing in the context of some of the great black political and intellectual figureheads: "We need to know who our heroes are. Our books must have Frederick Douglass. They must have Denmark Vesey. They must have Nat Turner. They must have Dr. W. E. B. Du Bois. They must have Richard Wright. They must have J. A. Rogers. They must have Lerone Bennett."[131]

Given *Ebony*'s audience and reputation as a leading black periodical, one might have expected journalists and political commentators to have examined the magazine's "Black Power" series in helping to frame their own critiques of the slogan following the Meredith march. However, the series was almost completely ignored in the national media following Carmichael's call for Black Power in June. This seems puzzling, given that *Ebony*'s "Black Power" series offered perhaps the most detailed and comprehensive literary use of the slogan in the buildup to the Meredith march, that it had been widely read and circulated, and that it had explicitly looked to connect Black Power during the first Reconstruction to the "Second Reconstruction" of the 1960s. One reason for this neglect might have stemmed from *Ebony*'s continuing reputation as an upbeat and whimsical magazine with little serious political or intellectual weight. Without close reading, it was easy for critics to dismiss its radical potential out of hand, particularly when the magazine continued to be attacked for "playing down negro militancy, muffling its pleas for negro equality with the muted tones of Uncle Tom eloquence, and denying the beauty of blackness."[132]

However, this explanation does not account for the broader disparity of influence generated by *Ebony*'s Black Power coverage. For example, both Rowan and King's criticisms of Black Power in *Ebony* were picked up by multiple press outlets, including major newspapers such as the *Boston Globe* and the *Washington Post*. Rowan in particular was praised for putting the "ranting about 'Black Power'" into proper perspective.[133] More conservative black newspapers such as the *Philadelphia Tribune* also supported Rowan's position, echoing his contention that activists who embraced the "false ideas" of Black Power were "inviting disaster."[134] By contrast, mainstream outlets avoided discussion of the magazine's "Black Power" series, while Bennett's profile of Carmichael was similarly dismissed. When viewed in this light, such neglect would appear less of an oversight than a rejection of a particular representation of Black Power that sought to establish its deep historical roots.

In the absence of significant exposure in the mainstream press, *Ebony*'s readers were left to offer their own interpretation of Bennett's "Black Power" series. Like the response to his earlier series, many in the magazine's audience pointed to its role in addressing the inadequacies of formal education. Dale Harlan, a white lawyer and politician, contended that "our school books never taught us that the black man had anywhere near the status, respect and power that I have learned he had through your articles."[135] One unnamed reader, writing from Soledad State Prison in California, informed *Ebony*'s editors that "Africa's Golden Past" and "Black Power" had become vital research materials for a black culture and history class developed by some of the inmates. The author declared that "through your magazine and this class, many of us have attained new values and an unprecedented pride of self and race."[136] In turn, Bennett's profile of Carmichael drew praise for relieving skepticism over Black Power and helping to counteract to the "nefarious" twisting of Black Power by the mainstream press.[137]

Perhaps most interesting was the increasing willingness of *Ebony*'s readers to take up Bennett's challenge for them to connect his historical vignettes of "Black Power" during Reconstruction to the slogan's reemergence during the 1960s. Harlan argued that the historical context provided by *Ebony*'s "Black Power" series made the case for black liberation clear and, by extension, the "current problems in the South and the rest of the nation even more difficult for me to understand."[138] Illinois native David Blackwell was altogether more forceful, declaring that "if we don't want a repeat performance of what happened to black people 100 years ago, we better think about either abandoning this country or adopting some new ideas on how we are going to live here with Whitey."[139]

Other readers drew a direct line between Bennett's series and Carmichael's rhetoric, with Brooklyn resident John Edwards noting that his reading of *Ebony*'s "Black Power" series had led him to truly understand "what Mr. Carmichael meant by the term and where he got his now popular war cry." Suggesting Bennett's direct influence over Carmichael's adoption of the slogan, and linking the rise of Black Power following the Meredith march to the struggles of black politicians during Reconstruction, Edwards argued that "Mr. Carmichael is evidently trying to retain for the Southern black man the birth right that was snatched from him almost 100 years ago."[140] Bennett reiterated this theme in the concluding article in his series, where he contrasted the struggle for Reconstruction that overshadowed the centennial of the Declaration of Independence in the 1870s with "the Black Revolution [that] overshadowed the centennial of the Emancipation Proclamation" in the 1960s.[141] This message would be maintained as the series transitioned into book form, mimicking the trajectory of previous series "Negro History" and "Pioneers in Protest." Published the Johnson Book Division at the end of 1967, Bennett's *Black Power, U.S.A.* was marketed under the declaration that "BLACK POWER is 100 years old."[142]

CHAPTER 4

Learning Is an All-Black Thing

By the denouement of Bennett's "Black Power" series in early 1967, Todd Steven Burroughs suggests that *Ebony* had solidified its importance as a "vital forum for black history."[1] The magazine's history-themed articles and series had become a major part of its content—not just as popular features in their own right, but also, as the intersections between Bennett's "Black Power" series and coalescing Black Power movement demonstrated, a critical lens through which *Ebony*'s audience could navigate the shifting currents of African American protest, politics, and popular culture.[2] While Johnson may not have fully supported efforts to expand *Ebony*'s role as an outlet for black history education during its early years, he had come to revel in this function by the second half of the 1960s. In August 1968 the publisher declared to readers that "from the yellowed pages of forgotten newspapers and from the writings of black historians who have themselves compiled volumes of black history, we have become one of the most authoritative sources of black history in the world today."[3]

Through such effusive claims, Johnson demonstrated his understanding of the magazine's value as a "history book" against the backdrop of continuing textbook omission and misrepresentation, systemic racial disparities within the public-school system, and growing concerns over a "crisis" of identity among African American youth. At the same time, such announcements revealed a keen awareness of how to translate the popularity of *Ebony*'s black history content into financial gain. Using features such as "Backstage" and "Letters to the Editor," as well as a raft of internal advertising features, Johnson looked to champion *Ebony*'s value as a pedagogical tool and its status as "the most cut-up magazine in America."[4] These efforts would be extended through the Johnson Publishing Book Division, which released a series of textbooks designed to inform young African Americans "that theirs is a proud heritage [that] grows stronger every year."[5]

Johnson's August 1968 statement also reflected a desire to situate *Ebony* within a broader push for black-authored historical perspectives and a demand for educational empowerment, which had become an integral part of the modern black freedom movement. As William Van Deburg has argued, African American history became a "wellspring of group strength and staying power" that was a powerful weapon in and an important part of the struggle for black-centered education and, ultimately, black liberation.[6] This belief underpinned widespread demands for curricular reform and helped to catalyze the creation of black independent schools and the black revolution on campus.[7] *Ebony*'s coverage of these battles, alongside the decision to profile and publish some of their most influential voices, can be linked to the efforts of a small band of left-leaning journalists and editors who pushed to expand discussions of Black Power, black education, and the politics of African American history in *Ebony* and other Johnson Publishing periodicals during this period.[8]

Perhaps most important, Johnson's portrayal of *Ebony* as an "authoritative" source of black history gestured toward the continued importance of Lerone Bennett Jr. in both guiding and legitimating the magazine's engagement with the African American past.[9] Bennett's reputation as a prominent black public intellectual and "profound scholar in social history" afforded him significant leeway to pursue a more militant editorial and philosophical position on *Ebony*'s pages, where he championed black history as a "pragmatic tool for African American liberation and consciousness building."[10] This position was bolstered by Bennett's deepening relationship with institutions such as Northwestern University, where the editor took up a teaching role, and the Institute of the Black World in Atlanta, where Bennett helped to shape the "search for a new understanding of black America's past and present."[11]

For more radically oriented readers, Bennett's contributions to *Ebony* became the magazine's "saving grace," allowing them to overlook its continued emphasis on black celebrity and consumer culture.[12] The editor rewarded his audience with a series of provocative articles that, as Cleve Washington noted in a 1972 profile, pushed toward "defining and interpreting history consistently from a black perspective."[13] However, even as Bennett's reputation as a "Black Power historian" helped to offset criticisms of the magazine's content, the gap between his own ideology and the magazine's position as a consumer periodical became more apparent.[14] Such tensions would be played out within institutions across the country as black educators and activists sought to advance a "black curriculum" and continued to redefine the boundaries of the movement and the terms of their struggle.

Ebony in the Classroom

Bennett's repeated attacks on the Dunning School throughout his "Black Power" series were just the latest example of *Ebony*'s attempts to correct the "abundance of outright untruths" about black history, as well as a reflection of growing public dissatisfaction with the failures of the American educational system.[15] Jonathan Zimmerman has argued that black activists took a three-pronged approach to agitating for curricular reform. First, they argued that less pernicious representations of African Americans within school textbooks could help "persuade stubborn whites to revise their views on present-day quests for racial justice."[16] Second, they contended that new books would help to put into practice the aims of landmark civil rights legislation, such as the 1964 Civil Rights Act and 1965 Voting Rights Act, by disrupting racial stereotypes and increasing white racial literacy of black historical accomplishments. Third, they warned that the continued invisibility or misrepresentation of African Americans within school textbooks promoted "feelings of separateness and inferiority" among black schoolchildren.[17]

In the aftermath of the Watts riots and the emergence of Black Power on the national stage, such demands became a pressing political issue. The NAACP and other civil rights organizations launched national drives to replace "distorted" textbooks with studies that would "treat the Negro fairly."[18] At a House Sub-Committee hearing on black representation in textbooks, U.S. Commissioner of Education Harold Howe admitted that "the role of the American Negro . . . has been blurred, confused and simply ignored by textbook writers."[19] In a February 1967 op-ed for the *Negro Digest*, Vice President Hubert Humphrey denounced the pervasive "Negro history gap" in American schools and declared that "the shared pride in Negro history and achievement is a solid foundation upon which to build a new and healthy climate of mutual respect and understanding among all elements of society."[20] However, such rhetoric was not always reinforced through public policy. While the 1965 Elementary and Secondary Education Act set aside around $400 million for the purchase of "multi-ethnic" and "multi-racial" books, the federal government was reluctant to enforce curricular reform on a local level, meaning that many school districts continued to utilize "lily-white" publications.[21]

One month after Humphrey's remarks were published in the *Digest*, Bennett penned a forceful critique of the "built-in biases of the American educational system." The editor supplemented the traditional "Rs" of reading, writing and arithmetic with a fourth—Racism—contending that this R permeated "the whole curriculum and provides the framework within which the learning process occurs."[22] Echoing the three-pronged attack of other educational activists, Bennett argued that the widespread use of "textbooks filled with evasions, half-truths and distortions" had left a disastrous impact on race relations, providing white Americans with a false sense of racial exclusivity over a land "created by the blood and sweat of men and women of all races and creeds" and depriving black students of a true picture of their own history. These sentiments would be reiterated by other contributors, such as Charles Harrison, who provided readers with a list of suggested textbook revisions and advocated for specialized teacher training to help students "gain both facts and perspectives about the Negro in the story of our national past."[23]

Anger over textbook biases complemented anxieties over the continuing impact of Jim Crow schooling in the South and municipal neglect of African American students in black urban communities across the country.[24] The plight of the "ghetto school" was a subject that drew regular coverage in *Ebony*, with Alex Poinsett entrusted with penning many of the magazine's educational features. A Chicago native, Poinsett had attended Englewood High School on the South Side, and his familiarity with the city's school system had been reinforced by his role in the magazine's coverage of the Chicago school boycotts during the first half of the 1960s.[25] In *Ebony*'s 1967 special issue on "Negro Youth in America," Poinsett denounced ghetto schools as "an educational wasteland" and suggested that public education for inner-city black students, at least in its current iteration, was "an exercise in futility."[26] This tone was maintained by his publisher, with Johnson warning that the failures of the nation's educational system were producing a generation of younger African Americans who were divorced from their past and facing "a massive crisis of identity."[27]

These concerns were reinforced by readers, who regularly complained to *Ebony*'s editors about the inadequacies of their own education and the lack of a black history curriculum. Responding to Bennett's article on textbook bias, Michigan reader Betty Peters contended that when her high school history teacher arranged for a debate on slavery in the United States, "our class couldn't discuss the subject factually or intelligently because we had no textbook or information in our school library about slavery." Estelle Lowery mirrored such concerns, admitting, "I feel a little silly when Negro history is brought up because I don't know enough to really be proud of my race." Poinsett's efforts to highlight the plight of ghetto schooling was also applauded by readers like Stanley Ferdinand, who praised the editor for drawing attention to the "still existing dual but ineq-uitable public-school system."[28]

While such responses spoke to systemic concerns regarding the lack of black historical representation within the American educational system, they had the secondary benefit of reinforcing *Ebony*'s own importance as a "history book." Conscious of the desire for black-authored resources that offered a positive representation of African American history, Johnson began to more aggressively promote *Ebony*'s value as an educational tool for black children. Press releases documented its role as "supplementary reading for many high school and college classes."[29] The magazine's now yearly special issues became a major part of this drive, with tens of thousands of extra copies printed for distribution to schools and community organizations.[30] Correspondence from black students, school-teachers, and educators filled the magazine's "Letters to the Editor" section after each new special issue or historical feature, declaring that *Ebony* would be read "a thousand years from now, not only by scholars and specialized students, but also by the citizenry at large, as part of their general education in the history of this age."[31]

Another part of this campaign was the expansion of *Ebony*'s school sub-scription program, with its editors contending that many schoolteachers took out two subscriptions—"one to read and keep and the other as their principal source of positive pictures to fill their bulletin boards."[32] The school subscription program was promoted through a series of internal advertising features that championed *Ebony*'s role as "a unique teaching and learning source" and argued that "no other publication in the world affords the potential that *Ebony* does for aiding the Black student in his quest for identity, self-esteem and education for living."[33] Featuring pictures of smiling black children armed with scissors, such adverts positioned *Ebony* as "the most cut-up magazine in America"—a title that alluded to the longer history of African American scrapbook making as a tool for historical education and paralleled the similar educational reuse of publications such as the *Black Panther* community newspaper.[34]

The magazine also produced a series of activity booklets titled "*Ebony* in the Classroom," which became a prominent feature of its efforts to solicit more school and classroom subscriptions. Multiple versions of the booklet were produced in collaboration with different authors. One contributor was Ber-nadette Harris, a Chicago Public Schools teacher and the sister of John Mou-toussamy, a prominent African American architect and designer of the iconic Johnson Publishing headquarters at 820 South Michigan Avenue in Chicago, which the company moved into during the early 1970s.[35] Another version of the booklet was produced in collaboration with Darwin Walton, a public-school educator and an accomplished children's book author whose acclaimed *What Color Are You?* was released through the Johnson Book Division.[36] Other materials aimed toward black children included a series of "*Ebony* Photopaks" that could be ordered directly through the company and featured themes such as "Famous Negroes of the Past."[37] This emphasis on child education would feed into the launch of youth-oriented magazine *Ebony, Jr!* in 1973, which targeted black elementary students with black-history-oriented stories, cartoons, and games.[38]

In addition to its emphasis on children's education, *Ebony* featured regular mailing and advertising content that highlighted its educational value for a broader audience. Projects such as the "*Ebony* in the Classroom" booklet were complemented by adult-oriented brochures such as "Buried Afro-American History," which informed potential subscribers why the publication "digs up the black past."[39] *Ebony*'s editors also contributed to a range of different compendiums and reference works published by the Johnson Book Division, including *The Negro Handbook*, a 535-page reference work that was advertised as "a concise and accurate reference work" and "a book that the whole family will use." Like *Ebony*'s own content, the perception of factual accuracy became a key selling point for the work, with readers advised, "Don't Argue . . . Look It Up! In *The Negro Handbook*."[40]

Perhaps the most significant textbook produced by the Book Division came in 1971 with the release of the first edition of the multivolume *Ebony Pictorial History of Black America*. Guided by Bennett and produced by a team of *Ebony* editors, the initial three volumes of the project ran close to one thousand pages and would be further expanded by additional volumes throughout the 1970s.[41] In his introduction to the first volume, Bennett located the project within a larger effort by *Ebony* and the Book Division to "meet the demand for facts and interpretation of the black experience." Advertisements for the project did not hold back, declaring it to be "the most complete and authentic popular history of African-Americans ever produced" and one of the "crowning achievements in the 25-year mission of *Ebony* magazine to build and project the image of the black man in America."[42]

"Abe" Lincoln, Nat Turner, and Black Power Historiography

While advertisements for the *Ebony Pictorial History of Black America* emphasized that it was a collaborative editorial project, they also noted Bennett's role in guiding the project to fruition. This focus on Bennett's influence was a recurrent feature in much of the Book Division's promotional material that appeared in the magazine. Pictures of books such as *Before the Mayflower* and *Black Power, U.S.A.* were foregrounded in advertisements for "The *Ebony* Bookshop," which purported to offer readers access to "today's most vital books by, about and related to BLACK PEOPLE."[43] Bennett also featured in stand-alone advertisements that focused solely on his individual publishing endeavors. Full-length images of Bennett looking intently into the camera and sporting his trademark pipe were accompanied with text that asked the magazine's readers, "Are you reading him?"[44]

Such features reflected Bennett's burgeoning reputation as a public intellectual but also served to remind readers of his centrality to the magazine's historical production. Johnson relied heavily on Bennett's contributions to support of his claim that the magazine had become "one of the most authoritative sources of black history in the world today."[45] Because of this, the publisher afforded Bennett "carte blanche" to challenge the institutional and intellectual norms that had contributed to a neglect of African American history and an uncritical celebration of prominent white Americans.[46] If much of the magazine's earlier content had been unwilling to attack white historians or historical figures directly, a series of provocative articles published following the completion of his "Black Power" series illustrated Bennett's increasing editorial and ideological control, beginning with "Was Abe Lincoln a White Supremacist?" in February 1968.

During its early years, *Ebony* had remained a staunch defender of Lincoln's contributions to uplifting the black race. For example, a February 1948 editorial had addressed growing criticism of Lincoln's reputation, including his "increasing slander and vituperation" within some sections of the African American community. While noting that Lincoln's racial attitudes were far from perfect, the editorial swiftly rebuffed "those myopic Negroes who libel the memory of Lincoln," choosing instead to present an image of the sixteenth president as a "swift, zealous, radical and determined" advocate for civil rights.[47] Although Bennett had looked to reassess Lincoln's significance during his writing during the early 1960s by shifting focus from Lincoln's role as the "Great Emancipator" to the efforts of African Americans to win their own freedom during slavery and the Civil War, his representation of Lincoln remained largely in step with the perspectives of mainstream biographers such as Carl Sandburg.[48]

This would change dramatically in his February 1968 article, with Bennett declaring that, on every issue relating to black Americans, Lincoln was "the very essence of the white supremacist with good intentions."[49] While the editor acknowledged his former admiration of the sixteenth president, he sharply criticized Lincoln as a racist who "believed until his death that black people and white people would be much better off separated—preferably with the Atlantic Ocean or some other large and deep body of water between them." The editor also rejected scholarly claims that Lincoln's survival may have averted the failures of Reconstruction, contending that the president's racial prejudices would have ensured "a Reconstruction of the white people, by the white people, and for the white people." Perhaps most damning, Bennett saw Lincoln's failures as a threat to his personal mythology as the "Great Emancipator" but not his place within the American historical canon. He argued that "in the final analysis, Lincoln must be seen as the embodiment, not the transcendence, of the American tradition, which is, as we all know, a racist tradition."[50]

The acerbic tone of Bennett's Lincoln exposé was striking, given that the editor had expressed concerns over the president's shortcomings in much milder terms through earlier works like *Before the Mayflower* and *What Manner of Man*, his 1964 biography of Dr. Martin Luther King Jr.[51] Numerous scholars have questioned the claims Bennett made in his 1968 article and later book-length contribution *Forced into Glory*, criticizing his "Lincoln-bashing" as ideologically driven and intellectually suspect.[52] Yet as historian John Barr has noted, much of this work has considered Bennett's 1968 article in isolation, without an understanding of how his ideas about Lincoln had changed or where they sat within a longer history of Lincoln critiques from African American scholars such as W. E. B. Du Bois. Bennett was hardly the first black historian to critique Lincoln's racial attitudes.[53] However, *Ebony*'s vast circulation ensured that these criticisms "did not remain cloistered within the African American community but migrated into venues that reached even larger audiences."[54]

To substantiate the article's creditability, *Ebony* reminded its readers of Bennett's credentials as a "sensitive writer and meticulous researcher," and numerous black press outlets praised the editor's work and supported his conclusions.[55] By contrast, a host of prominent white critics rejected Bennett's article out of hand as an inflammatory and irresponsible piece. This response was led by *New York Times* editor Herbert Mitgang, who published a bristling riposte in the *New York Times Magazine* titled "Was Lincoln Just a Honkie?"[56] Through the use of racially loaded phrases such as "Honkie," Mitgang clearly sought to align Bennett with more outspoken Black Power activists such as H. Rap Brown, who had incited public outrage with his description of Lyndon Johnson as a "white honky cracker" and an "outlaw from Texas."[57] In a similar vein, the journalist attempted to draw parallels between reinterpretations of Lincoln's legacy by black nationalist historians and the rise of Black Power, which threatened to "inflame American cities in a new Civil War."[58]

Mitgang's review led to a contentious back-and-forth debate between the *New York Times* and *Ebony* editors during the weeks following the article's publication.[59] Bennett declared Mitgang's assessment of his writing to be "a parody of the traditional Lincoln hagiography."[60] The historian contended that in keeping with most Lincoln apologists, "Mr. Mitgang finds himself arguing desperately and rather pathetically with Lincoln."[61] Mitgang was unwilling to let the matter die, firing back in a letter that reiterated his earlier criticism of *Ebony*'s content and warned that Lincoln should "not be put in the meat grinder of black nationalist revisionism. To do so is slanted, up-dated history that ignores the time, the place and the man."[62] Other white writers such as Mark Krug supported Mitgang's warning that Bennett would be at least partially to blame if racial tension spilled over into violence.[63]

Yet by dismissing Bennett's article as the kneejerk response of an anti-white polemicist, critics failed to grasp the cultural and political implications of Bennett's argument. As Allen Guelzo rightly notes, while the editor's critique was interpreted by some as an ad hominem attack, it reflected a deep-rooted suspicion on the part of Black Power advocates of "Lincoln, the Proclamation, or anything else white liberals had to offer."[64] It was a position that resonated with figures such as black writer Julius Lester, who contended that African Americans "have no reason to feel grateful to Abraham Lincoln . . . he was in office to preserve the Union, not free the slaves.[65] As African American activists and intellectuals sought to inject Black Power sensibilities into their discussion of the nation's past, the rejection of white-authored and white-centered historical narratives became an important part of the "process of cutting loose from white America."[66] If looking to reappraise the racial attitudes and philosophies of supposedly unimpeachable white "allies" such as Lincoln was one feature of this trend, another was an attempt to rebuff perceived attacks on radical black heroes, particularly by white historians.

One scholar who learned this the hard way was William Styron, a prominent white novelist and essayist who published *The Confessions of Nat Turner* in late 1967.[67] Written in the first person, Styron's book recounted Turner's legendary 1831 slave revolt in Virginia as told through the "confession" of Turner to white lawyer Thomas Gray. Styron sold the work as "less an 'historical novel' in conventional terms than a meditation on history," arguing that 1831 was simultaneously "a long time ago and only yesterday."[68] While the book received adulation from the white literary establishment, a bevy of prominent black intellectuals railed against Styron's portrayal of Turner.[69] Some of the most strident critiques were published in a collection edited by John Henrik Clarke, *William Styron's Nat Turner: Ten Black Writers Respond*, which accused Styron of misappropriating black history for his own racist motivations.[70] Clarke and his co-authors argued that by tarnishing Turner's reputation, Styron was by implication attacking "the stature of the black freedom fighters of the 1960s."[71]

Bennett was among the select group of black writers invited to contribute to Clarke's collection, and sections of his chapter were reprinted in *Ebony* in October 1968, introducing many of the magazine's readers to the Styron controversy for the first time.[72] Bennett's main point of attack was the source upon which it was based, with the editor describing lawyer Thomas Gray as "a treacherous and unctuously condescending white man who is trying to worm his way into the black psyche for purposes of white aggrandizement."[73] Like his fellow contributors, Bennett understood Styron's text to be an unsubstantiated attack on black masculinity and, by extension, on the black freedom struggle itself. He rejected Styron's depiction of Turner as an "impotent, cowardly, irresolute creature," and instead asserted that the "real" Nat Turner was a "virile, commanding, courageous figure." For Bennett, the representation of Turner in *Confessions* was not only the antithesis of his historical character but "the antithesis of blackness . . . a neurasthenic, Hamlet-like white intellectual in blackface."[74]

Whereas Bennett's Lincoln profile in *Ebony* had been met with a fierce backlash, the black backlash to Styron's work prompted its own response from white scholars such as Eugene Genovese, who chided *William Styron's Nat Turner* as an example of the misplaced chattering of the "black intelligentsia" and argued that the book demanded attention "not so much because of the questions it raises about Styron's novel as for what it reveals about the thinking of intellectuals in the Black Power movement."[75] Certainly, Clarke's collection reinforced some of the more unsavory undercurrents of black nationalist thinking, most notably a preoccupation with heroic black heterosexual masculinity. Styron's depiction of Turner's sexuality was a central concern for many contributors, with suggestions that Turner had lusted after a white woman and had experienced a homosexual encounter being roundly condemned.[76] Tellingly, none of the ten contributors whose work featured in Clarke's collection were women.

However, as was the case with his Lincoln article, Bennett's contribution to *William Styron's Nat Turner* offers an example of his efforts to move toward "defining and interpreting history consistently from a black perspective."[77] In the same way that "Was Abe Lincoln a White Supremacist?" can be read less as a specific attack on the sixteenth president and more as a critique of white male myth making, so too can *William Styron's Nat Turner* be understood as not merely the rejection of a single work but as "a polemic and corrective that introduced a spectrum of opinion mostly ignored in the mainstream press."[78] These features also provide important examples of *Ebony*'s growing role in disseminating radical historical ideas to a mainstream audience, a move that prompted a lively debate between readers in its "Letters to the Editor" section. For some, the editor's Lincoln article was part of a conspiracy to "degrade the honor of men we have revered through the ages." For others, it was a "lucid presentation of facts that have for too long been glossed over in our educational institutions."[79]

The Black Revolution on Campus

Bennett's efforts to move toward interpreting history from a "black perspective" was part of growing demands for black-centered educational initiatives and the promotion of a "black curriculum." Whereas civil rights activists had pushed for better educational opportunities through school integration, more radical activists rejected assimilation into the established educational and cultural hierarchy and began to agitate for greater educational control and self-determination.[80] In some cities, this demand manifested itself through the creation of Pan-African nationalist schools, a trend Russell Rickford has argued represented a shift from "the pursuit of reform within a liberal democracy to the attempt to build the infrastructure of an independent black nation."[81] *Ebony* documented the push for black independent schooling through profiles of activists such as Albert Vann, head of the Afro-American Teachers Association in New York City, and institutions such as the Nairobi Day School in East Palo Alto, California, where classroom study was directed by the philosophy that "learning is an all-black thing."[82]

Demands for educational reform and educational autonomy quickly spread from grade school to college campuses. During the years following World War II, black historians had begun to enter the white academy, with John Hope Franklin becoming the first African American to head a history department at a predominantly white institution when he joined Brooklyn College in 1956.[83] However, black students were not satisfied with piecemeal appointments and pushed for greater institutional representation. In 1967 students at San Francisco State University vocalized concerns about the lack of black perspectives within the college's curriculum and proposed the development of an Institute for Black Studies. At Howard University, one of the nation's premier black colleges, sociologist Nathan Hare was dismissed after producing a Black University Manifesto and leading a series of campus protests.[84] Following his departure, Hare published a withering attack on the college's leadership in *Ebony*, accusing Howard's administrators of installing a "plantation regime" and pointing to a growing divide between "black students and Negro professors."[85]

Hare's rhetorical distinction between "black" students and "Negro" faculty reflected the weaponization of language as a form of identity politics by Black Power activists, who claimed a "new vocabulary in which the word 'black' is reserved for "black brothers and sisters who are emancipating themselves," and the word "Negro" is used contemptuously for negroes "who are still in Whitey's bag."[86] In doing so, he articulated the willingness of young black men and women to push for revolutionary change in American higher education. Black campus activism did not abruptly emerge during the 1960s, with earlier struggles such as the New Negro Campus Movement of the 1920s and 1930s providing important antecedents to the educational activism of black college students during the Black Power era.[87] However, as Martha Biondi has eloquently argued in *The Black Revolution on Campus*, a collective feeling of power and purpose among African American college students underpinned a dramatic period of "conflict, crackdown, negotiation and reform that profoundly transformed college life" during the late 1960s and early 1970s. Across the country, student activists staged sit-ins, disrupted faculty meetings and college football games, and even threatened to shut down institutions altogether.[88]

Bennett profiled the black campus movement in more depth in the May 1968 issue of *Ebony*, where he spoke of a black cultural revolution that was "convulsing the campuses of America."[89] Echoing both the tone and rhetoric of Hare's earlier article and extending it to contestations affecting higher education institutions across the country, Bennett described this revolution as a "new and portentous front in the black liberation movement" that pitted "students against administrators, the young against the old, 'Negroes' against 'Blacks,' and 'Negroes' and 'Blacks' against whites." The editor noted that student demands focused on the implementation of "a relevant black education with in-depth studies of Afro-American history and culture and the political and economic problems of the Afro-American community." In a more abstract sense, Bennett suggested that student activists were "engaged in a painful and necessary labor of self-discovery, self-legitimization and self-definition."[90]

On a local level, the "black college revolt" in Chicago came to center on Northwestern University, an elite private research institution located in the northern suburb of Evanston. The college had featured prominently in statewide battles to end Jim Crow practices in Illinois during the 1930s, and attempts to diversify the student body continued to be thwarted during the years following World War II.[91] In 1963 students affiliated with the Human Relations Committee began an investigation into the use of racial quotas by the undergraduate admissions office, a move that incurred the wrath of the university's administrators.[92] As late as fall 1965, the number of African American freshmen enrolled at the institution could be counted on the fingers of one hand.[93] To make matters worse, the tiny percentage of black students who were part of the college's student body faced major challenges, such as segregation in dormitories and residential housing. Northwestern's refusal to impose sanctions against local landlords who actively discriminated against black students was one of a range of factors that fed the development of black student activism on campus.[94]

Ongoing discrimination sparked the growth of a new militancy among Northwestern's black student body, with the creation of a black undergraduate group "For Members Only" (FMO) in 1967 quickly followed by an Afro-American Student Union (AASU). FMO was led by Kathryn Ogletree, a freshman from the West Side of Chicago, while the AASU was headed by James Turner, a graduate student based in the Sociology Department who would later become the founding director of the Africana Studies and Research Center at Cornell University. In April 1968 Ogletree and Turner put forward a list of demands to Northwestern's faculty and administrative staff, including, but not limited to, clear steps to address racism on campus and the establishment of a Black Studies Department.[95] When the college's administration responded with a series of rebuffs and inadequate concessions, students decided to take matters into their own hands. In the first week of May, more than one hundred students affiliated with FMO and the AASU staged the first major sit-in in Northwestern's history by occupying the Bursar's Office, hanging a sign on the door that read "Closed for Business 'till Racism at NU Is Ended."[96]

Although Northwestern president J. Roscoe Miller initially attempted to get the protestors arrested, many faculty members appeared sympathetic to their cause. The administration would eventually acquiesce to some student demands, most significantly through instigating plans for the development of a Department of Afro-American Studies.[97] Students were also invited to suggest potential visiting lecturers as a way of developing courses relating to black history and culture. Bennett's positive portrayal of Turner and other Northwestern activists in his *Ebony* profile of the black campus movement had been well received by the university's black student body, and the editor emerged as a clear favorite to fulfil a role as visiting lecturer. According to Biondi, demands for Bennett to be appointed as a visiting lecturer reflected a desire to "inject a movement sensibility and critical edge to the forging of a Black studies curriculum in Evanston," with Bennett's strong connections to Chicago and burgeoning reputation as an activist-intellectual resonating with the new militancy of Northwestern's black student body.[98]

Bennett formally began his year as a visiting professor of history in Northwestern's College of Arts and Sciences at the beginning of September 1968.[99]

While his role would divert attention from his position as *Ebony*'s senior editor, a professorship at a highly ranked research institution served to bolster his standing as a "noted black historian" and, by extension, provided further ballast to Johnson's claims that *Ebony* was an "authoritative" black history text.[100] During the decades following World War II, Northwestern had endeavored to build one of the country's leading cohort of American history scholars, and Bennett's colleagues included Richard Leopold, a leading historian of the military and diplomacy, and George Fredrickson, who was in the process of completing his seminal 1971 study, *The Black Image in the White Mind*.[101] Bennett would also work alongside a number of talented teaching assistants, including Ibrahim Sundiata, who would go onto become the chairman of Howard University's History Department and a noted black history scholar.[102]

The editor certainly committed himself to his role as a visiting faculty member, requesting a one-year leave of absence from *Ebony* and Johnson Publishing to focus on his new teaching responsibilities. Bennett would ultimately continue to publish pieces in the magazine throughout his tenure at Northwestern, although many of his contributions were composed of recycled material from earlier work or extracts from publications such as *The Negro Mood* and the revised edition of *Before the Mayflower*.[103] Bennett also made good use of his published work in his classes, with a survey module on post–Civil War African American history leaning heavily on *Before the Mayflower*, *Pioneers in Protest*, and *Black Power, U.S.A.*, as well as revisionist work by scholars such as Du Bois and Aptheker.[104] His lectures, alongside those of fellow visiting professor and Trinidadian Marxist C. L. R. James, proved to be wildly popular, and Bennett's time at Northwestern cemented his standing with the university's students and their desire to see him installed in a more permanent role.[105]

The intellectual cachet provided by his position at Northwestern also furnished Bennett with opportunities to develop other intellectual and political connections. In December 1968 the editor participated in a special working group on Black Power at the University of Chicago that included renowned black political and social scientists such as St. Clair Drake and Charles Hamilton.[106] A few months later, Bennett was invited to become one of the founding members of a Black Academy of Arts and Letters headed by C. Eric Lincoln, which would be "dedicated to the definition, study and fostering of arts, letters and culture of black people."[107] Among the academy's board of directors was Vincent Harding, a figure well known to Bennett from his time as a graduate student at the University of Chicago during the mid-1960s. Following the completion of his doctorate, Harding had taken up a position at Spelman College in Atlanta. Alongside figures such as Stephen Henderson—a good friend and former classmate of Bennett's at Morehouse—Harding began to piece together plans for a think tank that would become a national center for black studies and black intellectual thought. By summer 1969, the Institute of the Black World had come into being, headed by Harding, Henderson, and William Strickland, and featuring Bennett as a senior research associate.[108]

Of Time, Space, and Revolution

Bennett's experiences outside of Johnson Publishing during this period filtered into his contributions to *Ebony*, which increasingly showcased his desire to move away from white-oriented histories and historical methodologies to advocate for an interpretation of the past that spoke directly to the African American experience. Like many Black Power historians, Bennett came to argue that "history has charged black people with responsibility for completing the American Revolution" and that only black history was qualified to "answer to challenges of [our] times."[109] This philosophy prompted a flattening of the intervals between time and space and the embrace of a "developmental" rather than a chronological interpretation of the past. This concept was clearly at play in the first article of a new history series, "The Making of Black America," which began serialization in the June 1969 issue of *Ebony*. Bennett looked to draw a direct line between major moments in African American history through the month of August.[110]

> It was in August . . . that 300,000 men and women marched on Washington D.C. It was in August that Watts exploded. It was in August, on a hot and heavy day in the 19th century, that Nat Turner rode. And it was in another August . . . that a Dutch man of war sailed up the river James and landed the first generation of Afro-Americans at Jamestown, Virginia.

It appeared more than coincidence that August was also the month favored for the publication of *Ebony*'s annual special issue. Two months after the beginning of Bennett's latest history series, *Ebony* released "The Black Revolution." In an opening article that set the tone for the special, titled "Of Time, Space, and Revolution," Bennett situated the black revolt of the 1960s as both a historical mandate and a synthesis of black radical activism across generational and geographical lines. He contended that "a *real* revolution introduces a new time and a new space and a new relation to both time and space."[111] Through this notion, Bennett applied his understanding of black history as a "living" history to the black revolution as a social and political movement, arguing that the act of revolution enabled radical black pioneers to speak directly to each other across both space and time. This articulation of black history's form and function was the latest example of Bennett's evolving editorial and political philosophy, some-thing we can trace through his previous historical interventions in *Ebony* and that was influenced by his deepening collaborations with Black Power activists and intellectuals on a local, national, and international scale.

Bennett's article also documented his developing belief that an understand-ing of and engagement with black history provided more than just a tool for educational and cultural uplift; it was a moral and intellectual requirement. Bennett contended that "we have a mandate from history, a mandate from the living, the dead, and the unborn, to make this moment count by using the time and resources history has given."[112] The notion of black history as a form of per-sonal responsibility would become an increasingly prominent part of Bennett's writing from the late 1960s onward and can be read as a response to perceived fractures in African American communities across fault lines of generation, class, gender, and geography. However, as chapters 5 and 6 will demonstrate, this notion of black history as personal responsibility—that the "God of History helps those who help themselves"—came to sit uneasily alongside the coded language of "personal responsibility" and racialized social pathology used by the New Right and the Reagan administration.[113]

Perhaps most important, "Of Time, Space, and Revolution" demonstrated the extent to which Bennett was able parlay his editorial influence at *Ebony* into a serious intellectual and philosophical discussion of black history and Black Power on the magazine's pages. By injecting an explicitly class-conscious critique of black history into a publication that unashamedly celebrated the achievements of the "talented tenth," Bennett threatened to disrupt *Ebony*'s well-established celebration of black entrepreneurship, celebrity culture, and conspicuous consumption.[114] Of course, we should not overstate the impact of such work—the bulk of *Ebony*'s content remained wedded to "mirror[ing] the happier side of Negro life," and its emphasis on celebrity culture continued to draw criticism from black radical activists as well as members of its own staff.[115] When *Ebony* assistant editor John Woodford quit the magazine during the late 1960s to take up a position at *Muhammad Speaks*, he assailed Johnson for his failure to publicly support prominent Black Power activists, his kowtowing to corporate advertisers, and for a bevy of other reasons he perceived "as insults to the Afro American community and myself."[116]

Nevertheless, Korey Bowers Brown suggests that "The Black Revolution" provided a powerful example of the ways in which more militant editorial voices within Johnson Publishing Company had placed pressure on Johnson "to alter *Ebony*'s traditional mission."[117] As Jonathan Fenderson has noted, a small but influential band of leftist journalists and editors had coalesced within

Johnson Publishing by the mid-1960s, people who sought to expand its discussion of "civil rights, nationalism, the politics of African American history, anticolonialism, Black Power and Black Arts (and aesthetics)."[118] Perhaps the most incisive voice for this cohort was Hoyt Fuller, who transformed the revived *Negro Digest* into a critical mouthpiece for the Black Power and Black Arts movements. By the time it was rebranded as *Black World* in 1970 to better reflect its diasporic focus, the *Digest* had cemented a position as the most influential black cultural journal in the country.[119] James Smethurst has argued that, absent its influence and impact as an outlet for black poets, literary critics, and intellectuals, "the articulation of the Black Arts movement as a national phenomenon would have been far different and more limited."[120]

Within *Ebony*, Hans Massaquoi, Alex Poinsett, and Allan Morrison (prior to his premature death in 1968) were among the more senior staffers who devoted considerable attention to Black Power, urban inequality, and educational bias during the second half of the 1960s, while international editor Era Bell Thompson continued to promote a diasporic perspective on black political activism.[121] The addition of new editors such as A. Peter Bailey, who had previously worked alongside Malcolm X at the Organization of Afro-American Unity, and David Llorens, who had been an active participant of the Student Nonviolent Coordinating Committee and would go on to head up the Black Studies Department at Washington University in 1970, also reflected a clear effort "to recruit young writers with militant sensibilities."[122] Indeed, against the backdrop of perceived fractures in African American political culture between civil rights integrationists and black nationalists, the production of "The Black Revolution" can be read as a productive collaboration between an older generation of leftist writers and a new cohort of Black Power journalists.[123]

The result was unquestionably a high point of *Ebony*'s engagement with Black Power and black political, cultural, and historical militancy. The special featured a wide array of contributions from black activists, politicians, historians, and philosophers that aimed to "discuss the Black Revolution in terms that black people can understand."[124] A confrontational tone was established from the onset, with Johnson declaring that "we stand today, a nation more divided black against white than at any time in history. The promise of the March on Washington is dead. Dr. Martin Luther King is dead. Very much alive is a virulent white racism that threatens to destroy not only black people but American democracy."[125] Other notable features included a manifesto from imprisoned Black Panther leader Huey Newton, a profile of cultural nationalist Amiri Baraka, who was seen to be "hard at work building the Black Nation," and a discussion of the relationship between black arts and black liberation by Larry Neal, a prominent cultural critic and major figure in the Black Arts movement.[126]

If "The Black Revolution" can be read as evidence of *Ebony*'s apparent "embrace of Black Power principles," then it is telling how central debates about black history and black-centered education were to this approach.[127] In addition to Bennett's analysis of the relationship between black history and black liberation, the special featured multiple contributions from participants in the black campus movement. Black doctoral student James Turner used his own impact as a student activist at Northwestern as a window into the "political socialization of black students."[128] Turner's article was complemented by a feature by Vincent Harding, who praised the ongoing black campus movement as the "vanguard" of the revolutionary struggle.[129] As Jeffrey Ogbar has argued, such articles helped to position "The Black Revolution" as one of the most important literary attempts to take a "broad look at black resistance to racial subjugation from as early as the colonial era through to the urban unrest of the 1960s."[130] From a different perspective, these contributions underlined the efforts of black educational activists to utilize *Ebony*'s popularity as a means of advancing their own political projects.

The Challenge of Blackness

Vincent Harding was identified to *Ebony*'s audience by his nascent role as the director of the Institute of the Black World, and he took advantage of this platform to promote the Institute as a "base of operations" that could connect the campus movement to American society. Harding was preoccupied with developing a "Black University perspective" that underscored the importance of establishing close connections between Black Studies programs and black communities, intellectual opposition to traditional analytical approaches to race, and structural autonomy. Translating these aims into a clear organizational philosophy for the institute initially proved difficult, although Derrick White has suggested that its activities were most readily informed by the combination of "a black nationalist perspective with an American pragmatism." Critically, the similarities between Bennett and Harding's approach to black history, alongside Bennett's strategic value as an *Ebony* insider, helped to position the editor as a major influence as the institute began to establish a reputation as a home for many of the nation's most prominent black theorists and radical intellectuals.[131]

Three months after the publication of "The Black Revolution" the IBW convened its first Black Studies Conference in Atlanta, an event that Turner would later be describe as "the founding convention for the field."[132] Bennett was entrusted with delivering the conference's keynote address, which he used to set out his own vision for the institute as a space for "defining, defending, and illustrating blackness." Harding would describe the speech as a "personal distillation and clarification . . . of the collective experiences of the staff of the Institute," and White has argued that Bennett's address "justified the IBW's purpose, provided a broad framework for Black Studies, and shaped the organization's trajectory" into the 1970s.[133] It would later be adapted for publication as the institute's first "Black Paper," with African American philosopher John McClendon positioning it as "one of the seminal essays on the philosophy of Blackness" to emerge out of the Black Power era.[134]

Harding and other Institute affiliates clearly held Bennett's scholarship in high esteem, with Sterling Stuckey positioning Bennett alongside Harding as one of the institute's "twin threats" following his address at its 1969 Black Studies Conference.[135] Yet it is also true that Bennett's influence within the organization was predicated, at least in part, on his role within Johnson Publishing Company. Harding made little secret of his desire to exploit *Ebony* as an outlet to promote the development of Black Studies and the institute's own projects. Harding's two-part series on "Black Students and the 'Impossible' Revolution" would be followed by an in-depth profile of the institute, authored by Alex Poinsett and further outlining the revolutionary shift away from "Negro History"—an interpretation of the past that "recorded the groans, chains and prayers of black America without challenging white America's basic values"—and toward "Black History" as a discipline that "exposes, discloses and reinterprets America."[136]

In summer 1970, Harding and Henderson endeavored to push this notion further through another two-part series in *Ebony* that outlined their understanding of the "Black University perspective" in more detail. Harding rejected the parameters of "integration" or "separation" in defining the format and function of the Black University, declaring that such terms were definitions "we have allowed a still arrogant white world to impose upon us."[137] This sentiment reflected the attitudes of Bennett, who rejected the squabble between integration or separation among black activists as a "false choice" and called for "liberation by any means necessary."[138] Harding put forward the concept of the Black University as an educational and intellectual space that attempted to break with the "familiar patterns of white domination and control over black higher education." For both men, the realization of the Black University was rooted an understanding that history formed the foundation for the development of Black Studies as a scholarly discipline.[139]

Harding also looked to develop the institute's relationship with Johnson Publishing through the company's Book Division. Harding informed Bennett,

Hoyt Fuller, and other Johnson Publishing staffers of the institute's desire to establish a relationship with "a serious black publisher," and Johnson indicated his interest in pursuing a potential collaboration.[140] In August 1970 Fuller outlined these plans in an extensive memo to institute staff, describing a "cooperative book publishing venture" that would lead to an institute imprint under the Johnson Book Division banner. Harding also hoped to instigate a regular book review feature in *Ebony*, edited by the institute's staff, who would contribute an "orientation designed to enhance the IBW-JPC publishing venture and to validate certain books and viewpoints."[141] However, the project was never realized—most likely torpedoed by escalating costs attached to the construction of the company's new corporate headquarters in Chicago.[142]

The Black University

Despite its failure to launch, the prospective publishing venture with the Institute of the Black World provides an illustrative example of Johnson Publishing's deepening engagement with the philosophy of black history and the question of Afrocentric education during the late 1960s and early 1970s. This position was pushed most forcefully through Harding's notion of the Black University, with his contributions to *Ebony* complemented by a series of three separate special issues of the *Negro Digest* between 1968 and 1970. Other contributors such as Gerald McWorter and Nathan Hare reiterated the need for "leveling the existing university structure" and instituting new pedagogical approaches that centered the black community "in its reach toward unity, self-determination, the acquisition and use of political and economic power, and the protection of the freedom of the human spirit."[143] In addition to the institute's proposed publishing venture, other potential projects connected to Johnson Publishing included sponsoring a black-oriented institution of higher learning located in the Chicago area, based on a "university without walls" model that fed into the Black University idea.[144]

On a national level the black campus movement prompted an anxious response from university administrators and led to a flurry of new opportunities for black activists and educators. However, it also stoked tensions between black militancy, liberal anxiety, and the persistence of white racism on campus. At Cornell University, an occupation of the university's student union by African American students led to the creation of a Black Studies program in 1969 and, coupled with the arrival of firebrand black activists and writers such as Don Lee, revealed deep fissures between the student body and faculty. Student activists aimed to recruit movement veterans such as Cleveland Sellers, a former program director for SNCC who arrived at Cornell in spring 1969 to lead a course on black ideology.[145] As Donald Downs has noted, black activists appealed to students who wanted instructors versed "making history, not just studying it." By contrast, more conservative faculty members were horrified by Sellers's appointment, viewing him as "an ideologue rather than a scholar."[146]

It is important to note that the influx of black activists and intellectuals onto the campuses of predominantly white colleges was not universally welcomed by those within the black community. At Cornell, Lee taught freshman courses on black literature and remained largely free to pursue his interests as a "revolutionary poet."[147] Yet his position stood in opposition to the concept of the Black University envisioned by Harding, who had warned that the proliferation of Black Studies courses at major white colleges and universities threatened to coopt the Black University concept and to defuse its radical political potential.[148] It was a bitter blow when, less than eighteen months after the publication of his "Black University" series in *Ebony*, Harding discovered that Bennett had accepted a position as the first chair of the Department of African American Studies at Northwestern. In a passionate letter to his colleague, Harding expressed dismay that Bennett had chosen to align himself with a white institution and hoped that "the decision [was] not an irreversible one."[149]

During the interlude following Bennett's term as a visiting lecturer, the college had labored uncertainly toward the establishment of a formal Black Studies program. A Committee on Afro-American Studies set up by Dean Robert Strotz in spring 1969 had met with dogged resistance from students, who campaigned for more control over course design and charged the committee with a "profound lack of direction and purpose." In October 1971 Northwestern's board of trustees finally ratified the creation of a Department of African American Studies and, following consultation with black students, quickly settled upon Bennett as their choice for the position of chair.[150] Raymond Mack was entrusted with reaching out to the editor, declaring that Northwestern was eager to finalize circumstances "which will make it possible for you to help us build the best academic Department of Afro-American Studies in the country. Our black students want it; our white students need it; our entire university community will benefit from it."[151]

In her excellent account of the black campus movement at Northwestern, Martha Biondi has suggested that Bennett was not "particularly interested in a career in academia."[152] However, in personal correspondence with Northwestern administrators, Bennett outlined a series of demands that suggested a desire to develop a long-term relationship with the university. Key was a demand for assurances from senior administrators that funds would be available for the continued growth of the department, noting that "provisions should be made for adding two or three faculty members a year (after the 1972–73 term) for the next four or five years."[153] Bennett also highlighted the need to develop a comprehensive Black Studies collection within the university's library, arguing that if Northwestern desired to build one of the country's leading Black Studies departments, it would require "substantial funds for primary and secondary sources." Perhaps most important, Bennett demanded special provisions to ensure the "integrity and authority of the Department" within Northwestern's institutional apparatus through full ownership of course direction and definition and a "broad authority to establish the boundaries of the field and the qualifications of members of the Department."[154]

Ebony applauded the appointment, declaring that its senior editor had "earned the right to be listed among the most outstanding writers, scholars and thinkers in the United States today."[155] For the magazine, Bennett's new position provided further vindication for its self-anointed role as "one of the most authoritative sources of black history in the world."[156] His appointment also drew acclaim from Northwestern's faculty and student body. Laurence Nobles, acting dean for the College of Arts and Humanities, lauded Bennett as "one of the most distinguished scholars in his field."[157] The *Daily Northwestern* reported that black students had "reacted with overwhelming approval" to the appointment, with many expressing hopes that Bennett's reputation as a public intellectual could propel the fledgling department into a position as "the foremost center of black studies in the country."[158]

However, internal tensions and disagreements arose almost immediately over hiring policies for new staff. As detailed in the list of demands presented to Northwestern prior to his acceptance of the role, Bennett argued that his position as chair should provide him with sole authority over who would join the fledgling department. Other faculty members such as Sterling Stuckey, with whom Bennett had previously crossed swords at the Institute of the Black World, rejected the editor's approach as "authoritarian" and argued that his attitude "made cooperation impossible."[159] Just a few months after his initial appointment, Bennett penned a letter of resignation, declaring that "recent developments have made it necessary for me to withdraw from the Northwestern situation." Feeling betrayed by Stuckey and other colleagues, Bennett concluded that "it would be inadvisable of me to attempt to organize a Department without the full support of all elements on the campus."[160]

Bennett's resignation generated uproar among Northwestern's black student body, who felt his leadership and sense of judgement had been unfairly questioned and that his lack of a terminal degree had been used to undermine his position.[161] Students penned a series of letters to Bennett, describing his return as "vital" for the development of an effective and politically engaged Black Studies department.[162] Following a heated meeting between black students and members of the Afro-American Studies Committee, students contacted the editor again, arguing that "to allow your energy and commitment to be stifled by the irresponsible acts of members of the CAAS would be a mistake."[163] The conflict threatened to drag on into the new academic year, with FMO arranging a series of a press conferences to demand Bennett's reinstatement and presenting Strotz with a petition signed by four hundred students.[164]

While Bennett felt slighted by his treatment at Northwestern, his brief foray into academia helped to illuminate many of the benefits his role at *Ebony* afforded. The prospect of heading up the development of Northwestern's Black Studies program was, at least initially, impossible to resist. Yet attempts to secure administrative and intellectual autonomy for nascent Black Studies programs often proved to be less a project in black self-determination and more a complex process of negotiation—something that led to turmoil at institutions such as Cornell and Boston University, where thirteen members of its recently formed Afro-American Studies Center resigned in April 1971 following a dispute with university administration.[165] Compared to the institutional shackles of academia, Bennett's role at *Ebony* provided immense flexibility to explore the intersections of black history and black radical activism and a more substantial platform for his role as a public intellectual. As Molefi Kete Asante has noted, Bennett's role as *Ebony*'s in-house historian offered "an unusual independence and guarantee of wide readership that could not be claimed by any comparable author."[166]

For at least a few short years during the high point of *Ebony*'s engagement with Black Power, this editorial independence was expanded to allow other staffers and contributors to examine the "black revolution" in more detail. That specials such as "The Black Revolution" were produced in *Ebony*, a magazine described by Craig Werner as arguably "the *least* radical black publication" on the market, reflected the degree to which black periodicals, and American culture more broadly, appeared to become at least temporarily more receptive to black radical perspectives and structural critiques of American politics and society.[167] A "Black Power" approach to American history and black-centered education emerged as a vital element of such critiques within *Ebony*. However, as the movement began to fragment and factionalize, tensions would deepen between Bennett's continued advocacy of a radical historical perspective and *Ebony*'s broader, if uneven, retreat toward a less political and more commemorative vision of the African American past.

CHAPTER 5

We Can Seize the Opportunity

*E*bony's evolution into a prominent source for popular black history during the 1950s and 1960s was a complex and, at times, highly contested project. A diverse cast of editors and contributors attempted to present readers with a "true" interpretation of the African American past, contributing to larger struggles for black historical representation, black-centered education, and the development of a "black curriculum."[1] The magazine's role as a "history book" was supplemented by the educational projects of connected Johnson Publishing enterprises such as the Book Division, which sought to publish black history "in full perspective," and bolstered by Lerone Bennett Jr.'s public standing as a Black Power historian.[2] In turn, the magazine's readers looked to *Ebony*'s senior editor and other black historians as sources of "authentic" knowledge about the African American past. Writing in response to Bennett's February 1971 article on "The World of the Slave," Evanston resident William Henderson applauded the editor's contribution and dismissed a similar piece by white historian Eugene Genovese as simply "part of the white historical community's effort to 'cash in' on a neglected side of the American story."[3]

Anxieties over efforts on the part of whites to "cash in" on the African American past provided a reminder that by its twenty-fifth anniversary, *Ebony* was just one voice in an increasingly crowded black history marketplace. Indeed, Johnson's desire to substantiate *Ebony*'s role as "one of the most authoritative sources of black history in the world today" can be read as a direct reaction to the shifting role and increasing marketability of African American history within the nation's popular and political culture. The role of "white money" in the establishment of Black Studies programs, the proliferation of black-history-oriented television programs and specials, and the newfound willingness of white politicians to champion the historical contributions of black people all seemed to offer evidence of black history's relocation from the margins to the mainstream of American political and popular culture.[4] This shift was also promoted by American businesses: from the mid-1960s onward, *Ebony*'s pages became populated by advertising campaigns that embraced black history as a form of corporate social responsibility.[5]

While the various corporate and political black history projects that flourished during this period helped to stimulate greater interest in and engagement with the African American past, this "turn" toward black history also served a range of pragmatic and ideological purposes. As black radical activists and coalitions became increasingly marginalized, American politicians, mainstream media outlets, and corporate advertisers framed the commemoration and consumption of black history as a tool that could help to reconcile the nation as well as to separate it from the "riot and revolt" of the 1960s. For *Ebony*, the appeal of black history also began to change, as the magazine contended with market segmentation and the fracturing of African American communities along lines of class, gender, sexuality, and geography. While Bennett continued to advocate for an activist-oriented interpretation of the past, other sections of the magazine's content began to promote a more nostalgic perspective that emphasized black history's value as a racially unifying device through black heritage tourism and similar endeavors.

These competing "uses" of black history would coalesce around the American bicentennial during the mid-1970s. For prominent white politicians, the bicentennial provided, as president Gerald Ford detailed in his landmark address on the celebration of Black History Month, a moment to reflect on "the impressive contributions of black Americans to our national life and culture."[6] More significantly, federal recognition of Black History Month was used to reaffirm a belief that the civil rights years had led to a full reconciliation between African Americans and the nation. This stance was challenged by black activists and civil rights organizations, who denounced the bicentennial as a distraction from economic pressures, a deepening "urban crisis," and lingering racial inequities. In *Ebony*, Bennett's rejection of the bicentennial, and his reservations over the repackaging of "Black Heritage" more broadly, complicated the magazine's own attempts to commemorate the anniversary and its ongoing celebration of black celebrity and conspicuous consumption.

From the Margins to the Mainstream

During its first two decades in print, *Ebony*'s black history content had fed into the first phase of the postwar "black history revival" identified by scholars such as Vincent Harding. The initial impetus for this "revival" stemmed mainly from grassroots educational activists, with localized demands for curricular reform and greater historical representation catalyzing community activism across the country.[7] The black press documented these efforts, with many black periodicals attempting to address community concerns directly through the creation of new history-themed features and series that sought to disseminate black history content to a mass audience. From a similar perspective, black scholars pushed for what John Hope Franklin described as a "new Negro history," which demanded "the same justice in history that is sought in other spheres."[8]

In cities such as Detroit, protests against the continued use of racially biased textbooks by school boards and commissions prompted the creation of supplementary teaching materials that offered a more representative account of black history.[9] Efforts to democratize representations of black history within the public sphere were also rewarded with small victories. Pressure from black activists on both the local and federal levels meant that some efforts were made to include black perspectives in centennial commemorations of the Civil War and the Emancipation Proclamation. In Chicago, groups such as the National Conference of Negro Artists looked to reclaim public narratives of slavery and abolition.[10] In the South, African American leaders pushed back against white segregationists and their glorification of the Confederacy by promoting emancipationist readings of the conflict.[11]

Despite such gains, efforts to promote black history between the end of World War II and the early 1960s often faltered on the back of white intransigence. However, the growing appeal of black nationalism, the emergence of Black Power, and the impact of urban uprisings in cities such as Chicago, New York, and Los Angeles led to a spate of handwringing from white liberals and a renewed interest in black history as a societal safety valve. For Robert Harris, the result was a groundswell of interest in the African American past, which "permeated practically every sector of American society."[12] As detailed in chapter 4, efforts to establish black studies programs on college campuses across the country became one important part of this trend, with the "long hot summers" prompting an outpouring of new scholarship on race relations and the black experience. In a later study of black historians and the historical profession, August Meier and Elliott Rudwick argued that by the end of the

1960s, Afro-American history had become fashionable, "a 'hot' subject finally legitimated as a scholarly specialty."[13]

In the realm of national politics, the House of Representatives' Committee on Education and Labor sponsored hearings to establish a National Commission on Negro History and Culture, which would promote efforts to collect and preserve "historical materials dealing with Negro history and culture" and investigate the possibility of a national museum of black history and culture.[14] A bevy of black intellectual and historical experts lent their support to the initiative, including Charles Wesley, executive director of the Association for the Study of Negro Life and History, and Charles Wright, president of the International Afro-American Museum in Detroit.[15] While the Commission would not move beyond the planning stages, such efforts reflected growing federal awareness of what Vice President Hubert Humphrey had described as the "Negro history gap" in his February 1967 op-ed for *Negro Digest* and preceded more substantive federal efforts to recognize black historical contributions during the 1970s.[16]

Other sympathetic politicians such as Democratic representative Jim Scheuer framed public ignorance of the African American past as a moral crime and took aim at the country's media industries for failing "to portray the distinguished past contributions of the Negro in America."[17] Scheuer's criticisms reiterated the findings of the National Advisory Commission on Civil Disorders, which had been set up to investigate the causes of the 1967 riots. In its final report, the commission underscored the idea that American media had contributed to the unrest by providing little insight into "the difficulties and frustrations of being a Negro in the United States" and by failing to effectively communicate "a sense of Negro culture, thought or history."[18] This verdict had been influenced by scores of testimonies from black educators and activists, including Lerone Bennett Jr., who had informed the commission that American textbooks were "woefully deficient in teaching white children anything about black people and in teaching black people anything about themselves."[19]

Such criticisms had an immediate effect. In summer 1968, an estimated audience of twenty-two million people tuned into CBS to watch the first installment of an ambitious new series titled *Black History: Lost, Stolen or Strayed*. Narrated by popular black entertainer Bill Cosby, the show would go on to win an Emmy for Outstanding News Documentary.[20] Echoing the sentiments Johnson expressed in his introduction to *Ebony*'s 1967 special issue on "Negro Youth in America," *Lost, Stolen or Strayed* underscored the connection between a lack of black history education and "a fundamentally flawed and lost sense of self" among many black youths. At the program's conclusion, Cosby appeared onscreen to address viewers directly, linking a "crisis" of self-identity among African American children to "the way black history got lost, stolen or strayed" and accentuating the need for greater historical representation as a route to further racial healing and reconciliation.

An even more impressive televisual project would begin the following year with the introduction of *Black Heritage: A History of Afro-Americans*, which ran for more than four months.[21] A collaborative project between Columbia University and WCBS-TV, *Black Heritage* featured 108 thirty-minute lectures that aimed to give the American public a taste of the kind of black history courses being introduced on colleges campuses across the country. The series was coordinated by Vincent Harding, William Strickland, and John Henrik Clarke and featured an eclectic roster of contributors, including Benjamin Quarles, Sterling Stuckey, and Lerone Bennett Jr.[22] These projects would lay the groundwork for more commercially oriented black-history-themed television shows, most notably the ABC miniseries adaptation of Alex Haley's *Roots* saga, which, following its release in 1977, became one of the highest-rated American television series of all time.[23]

What *Jet* contributor Valerie Bradley described as the "new surge in black history and culture" also affected mainstream print media outlets.[24] Several months after the launch of *Black History*, readers of *Life* magazine were greeted with a close-up cover image of Frederick Douglass that mimicked the cover of *Ebony*'s seminal 1963 special issue marking the centennial of the Emancipation Proclamation. *Ebony*'s 1963 special, coming on the back of its first "Negro History" series and the launch of the Johnson Book Division, had played a pivotal role in cementing its importance as an outlet for popular black history. In turn, *Life* informed its audience that Douglass's appearance on its cover marked the beginning of a new series, *The Search for a Black Past*, developed in collaboration with John Hope Franklin and other prominent black historians. Echoing the long-standing complaints of black periodicals, *Life*'s national affairs editor Roger Butterfield contended that "American historians, with few exceptions, have never dealt properly with the American Negro," and he outlined the publication's efforts to take "a fresh look at Negro history."[25]

Black History Inc.

Perhaps the most intriguing aspect of black history's transition from the margins to the mainstream can be seen through its embrace by corporate advertisers. The commercial potential of black history was hardly a new concept for Johnson. As this book has repeatedly noted, the publisher's willingness to expand *Ebony*'s historical coverage was undoubtedly linked to his awareness of how reader desires to "tell us of our past" could be translated into magazine sales.[26] An uptick in black-history-oriented material from the early 1960s onward corresponded with a significant rise in *Ebony*'s advertising revenues, which nearly tripled between 1962 and 1969, and its monthly circulation, which jumped from around 550,000 in 1960 to well over one million by the end of the decade. The success of the Johnson Book Division provided further evidence of black history's marketability and helped to draw the attention of American businesses. Indeed, Jason Chambers has suggested that *The Negro Handbook*, while ostensibly a general-interest reference book on black life and culture, was more influential as "a guide to black America for white corporations."[27]

As advertisers looked to secure a stake in the "Negro market," they turned to black history as a marketing strategy, drawing on the experience of a diverse cast of black historians and black advertising executives in the process.[28] Several years before his collaboration with *Life*, Franklin was tapped by Pepsi-Cola to act as a consultant on "Adventures in Negro History," a series of films and records.[29] Working alongside Harvey Russell, who had been hired by Pepsi as a vice president of the company's "special markets" division, Franklin helped to write material and introduced the project at its Chicago premiere in December 1964.[30] The historian lauded Pepsi for "its imagination, skill, sensitivity, and understanding" and placed the company in the vanguard of the movement to tell "the story of the Negro."[31]

Another prominent black expert guiding major corporations toward the African American past was black advertising executive Clarence Holte, known as the "Jackie Robinson" of the advertising industry.[32] The adman was an enthusiastic purveyor of black history, amassing arguably the "finest private collection" of black history texts in the country, which he proudly exhibited in a feature article for *Ebony* in April 1970.[33] Through his position at BBDO, one of the nation's largest advertising companies, Holte oversaw the development of black-history-themed advertising campaigns for an array of major companies. In contrast with some of the more heavy-handed advertising campaigns created to attract black consumers during the 1960s and early 1970s, corporate appeals to black history, Chambers suggests, were enthusiastically received by many African Americans, providing advertisers with an "almost effortless way to demonstrate their insight into blacks' role in America."[34]

As the nation's leading black consumer magazine, *Ebony* became a vital outlet for a wide range of black history advertising campaigns. One prominent example of this trend can be seen through the Old Taylor series "Ingenious Americans," produced in collaboration with Holte and BBDO. The series profiled black pioneers such as inventor Garrett A. Morgan, surgeon Daniel Hale Williams, and explorer Matthew Alexander Henson, providing readers with a succinct biography and an impressionistic sketch of the historical figure in question.[35] By the sixth installment of the series in March 1967, the sketches had been replaced by photographs of sculptured busts produced from a series on "Negro Giants in History" by African American sculptor Inge Hardison. *Ebony*'s readers were invited to purchase their own miniature copies of each bust for the "non-profit price" of five dollars.[36]

One of the most popular black history advertising campaigns to appear in *Ebony* during this period was a black history calendar produced by the Seagram Company. Presented as a "proud record of Negro achievement in American history," the calendar featured one illustration of a "distinguished black American" for each month.[37] In addition, each individual day on the calendar provided "an interesting and significant fact about the valuable contributions Negroes have made to American history."[38] The company's in-house magazine celebrated the arrival of the Negro Historical Calendar as "a sales tool that says (and sells) Seagram in a new and imaginative way," and by 1972 company representative Steven Lockett estimated that more than one hundred thousand copies of the calendar were being distributed annually.[39] By highlighting the calendar's significance as an important educational tool, Seagram was able to situate the calendar's production within broader appeals to educational diversity and the development of Black Studies. This point was made clear through advertising features that described the calendar to *Ebony* readers as "your own Black Studies program."[40]

However, while editors and contributors such as Bennett and Harding used *Ebony*'s pages to present the emergence of Black Studies as a radical challenge to historical orthodoxies, campaigns such as Old Taylor's "Ingenious Americans" and the Seagram black history calendar adopted a somewhat different position. Through their emphasis on individual (and overwhelmingly male) black pioneers, black-history-oriented advertising offered a return to the "contributionist" depiction of black history that had dominated much of *Ebony*'s earlier content.[41] In the process, such advertising campaigns undermined the radical potential of black history and the connections between black militancy in the past and present, even as they were presented as positive contributions to popular black history education and as evidence of corporate America's awareness of and sympathy for black consumers and the African American community.

Celebrating a Shared Past

Differences in the black history philosophies presented through *Ebony*'s editorial and advertising content were just one example of larger tensions affecting the magazine's depiction of the past. For much of its first twenty-five years in print, the simple act of printing black-history-oriented material had positioned *Ebony* as a voice opposed to the continued neglect of black heritage within American educational and political culture. Yet as black history began to permeate practically every area of society and as black-authored historical perspectives entered the cultural mainstream, this oppositional stance became less compelling.[42] Increasing efforts by American media outlets to engage with black history were compounded by the emergence of new black magazines such as *Black Enterprise* and *Essence*, which marked the first serious challenges to Johnson's domination of the black magazine market since the early 1950s.[43] *Essence* was particularly keen to distinguish itself as an exciting alternative to its more venerable market rival, with sales director Clarence Smith informing prospective advertisers that "the *Essence* woman is not reading *Ebony*. That's her parents' magazine . . . the *Essence* woman is ahead of the old pack and shaping a new curve."[44]

Perhaps Johnson's most pressing concern was maintaining *Ebony*'s reputation as a general-interest publication that catered to all African Americans in the face of increasingly visible fractures between and within black communities across the country. By the early 1970s, The "crisis" Johnson feared was occurring among African American youths had been expanded to address the black community writ large. "We are moving in a crisis of identity," the publisher declared in 1973; "everyone wants to identify with his own."[45] As ideological tensions between competing strategies for black liberation became more pronounced, Johnson fretted that "to a stranger, black people in this country could easily appear to be hopelessly divided."[46] For detractors, the fragmentation of the civil rights coalition was indicative of the nation's apparent balkanization into a "tangle of race-conscious minorities" and social groups who had decided to turn their backs on the American flag in the pursuit of identity politics.[47]

The impact of the women's rights movement and a surge in black feminist consciousness also revealed gendered hierarchies of power and deep-rooted frustrations regarding the place of African American women within black communities and American society. As more recent movement historians have detailed, black female activists played a pivotal role in grassroots organizing and helped to midwife the transition from civil rights to Black Power, even as their logistical and intellectual contributions to the movement were consistently sidelined or ignored.[48] For cultural nationalists such as Amiri Baraka and Ron Karenga, the role of black women in the revolution was predicated on "submitting to their natural roles" as wives and mothers.[49] Institutional sexism was also ingrained politically, with the relative lack of black elected female officials and the contentious black male response to Shirley Chisholm's 1972 presidential campaign revealing deeply entrenched patterns of black patriarchy within electoral politics.

Ebony's own gender politics had come under repeated fire during the 1960s from black feminist activists such as Evelyn Rodgers and Dona Humphrey, who criticized the magazine's aesthetic and political depiction of black women.[50] While *Ebony* did provide space for black radical activists such as Angela Davis to outline their ideas, its discussion of Black Power, and of black activism more generally, was heavily gendered and clearly privileged the influence of black men.[51] This is perhaps most obvious through its 1969 special issue on "The Black Revolution"—in both its visual depiction of radical activism and its overwhelming reliance on black male contributors and subjects.[52] The magazine also helped to exacerbate such tensions through a spate of articles criticizing "women's lib" and warning of a "battle brewing between Black men and women."[53] In response, readers such as Mary Kenyatta contended that "black women cannot afford to wait till 'after the revolution' to deal with our oppression."[54]

In turn, the struggle for gay liberation emboldened black activists to address heteronormativity and pervasive homophobia within the movement. As scholars such as Thaddeus Russell have noted, the postwar civil rights coalition made it clear that "the price of admission to American society for African Americans would be a surrender to heterosexual norms."[55] A revived interest in black nationalism exacerbated such tensions, with many Black Power activists, as well as some of the early proponents of Black Studies, theorizing homosexuality as a "disease" originating in white society.[56] Yet even as some black activists entrenched themselves within patriarchal and homophobic discourses of black advancement, others pushed back against the marginalization of queer black voices within the movement. Against this backdrop, *Ebony* found itself criticized by both black social conservatives and cultural nationalists such as Baraka, who understood black queerness as an acquired condition of "white degeneracy," and by progressive readers and queer activists who denounced its heterosexist brand of respectability politics.[57]

Perhaps the most significant divisions occurred along class lines, with the fortunes of working- and middle-class black Americans rapidly diverging in the years following the landmark civil rights legislation of the 1960s. Andrew Weise has positioned the flight of middle-class African Americans from historically black enclaves to suburban communities, something which accelerated significantly during the decades following World War II, as one of the century's most significant demographic shifts.[58] This transition was aided by an emerging black professional class that benefited from changes in public policy, stiffer legislative opposition to workplace discrimination, and greater educational opportunities.[59] However, the increasing mobility and affluence of middle-class African Americans contrasted with the fortunes of the black working class, leading the lived experience of each group to become "qualitatively different and dramatically more divergent."[60] *Ebony* editors such as Alex Poinsett warned readers that two roads were emerging within black America: a high road that led "from well-kept homes, through well-financed schools to colleges and universities, then on to a lucrative life in the suburbs" and a low road that meandered "out of racial ghettos, through dark and ageing classrooms and then back to the dismal slums."[61]

These intersecting factors led to another subtle but significant shift in *Ebony*'s coverage of black history. During its early years, the magazine's black history content had been used to bolster its underlying mission of racial uplift and the celebration of African American achievement. As movement activism gathered pace, its discussion of the African American past became more activist-oriented; black history became a way of rationalizing ideological or philosophical differences between movement activists and a means of establishing antecedents to the ongoing struggle for civil rights. This was a strategy that Bennett had eloquently employed through features such as his "Black Power" series, where he had defended the rhetoric of Black Power advocates by situating them within a longer tradition of black militant activism, and articles such as "Of Time, Space, and Revolution," which had looked to contract the chronological and philosophical distances between black radicalism in the past and present.

However, as anxieties over the "balkanization" of black America grew during the second half of the 1960s, this message would again shift. While Bennett remained wedded to an activist-oriented interpretation of black history and forcefully expressed this position through his articles and features, other sections of *Ebony*'s content began to focus more on black history's function as a force for intraracial reconciliation. This was particularly true across class lines, with the magazine reminding its readers that "whether born slum poor, middle class comfortable or truly rich, there is one thing every Negro American youth today must remember—he is a Negro."[62] For middle- and upper-class African Americans, black history provided an opportunity to reconnect with their roots and a reminder of their responsibility to less fortunate kin. For the black working class, a "pride in the past" offered a route to racial uplift and a way to "forge swiftly ahead."[63]

One manifestation of this trend can be seen through the magazine's promotion of black heritage tourism from the mid-1960s onward, something that can be connected to the growth of heritage tourism in the United States as a significant cultural and economic phenomenon.[64] This strategy offered a dual pay-off, allowing the magazine to celebrate the possibilities of a "post–civil rights" tourism industry for black consumers while also reiterating the continued importance of black history.[65] As early as 1966, *Ebony* was reassuring members of its audience who were considering a vacation to the South that they were now protected by federal and state antidiscrimination laws and that while provincial areas and back-road sojourns should still be avoided, the "nightmares of yesterday's travel" were over.[66] As Southern resorts learned that the African American tourism industry was a multi-billion-dollar business, discrimination was allegedly replaced with inviting smiles and outstretched palms eager for African American dollars.[67] For its part, *Ebony*'s promotion of black travel in the South was increasingly directed by a politics of nostalgia that presented readers with the opportunity to "go back home."[68]

This celebration of black heritage tourism quickly spread to other regions. By the early 1970s *Ebony* was imploring its readers to "discover black history" through domestic travel to some of the many "monuments to black heroes [that] dot the nation." The magazine provided a guide that listed dozens of black history sites, ranging from the Beckwourth Pass in California to the Crispus Attucks monument in Boston, Massachusetts. As a collective, these disparate sites were celebrated as "stubborn reminders of the full richness and diversity of black American history."[69] The magazine also began to offer in-depth reviews of popular black history attractions such as the Frederick Douglass National Historic Site in Washington, D.C., which had been taken over by the federal government in 1963 and subsequently added to the National Registry of Historic Houses.[70] *Ebony* informed its readers that simply by visiting the building, readers could "share in the life of famed statesman, abolitionist and civil rights pioneer Frederick Douglass." From this perspective, participation in black heritage tourism became a direct intervention in the continuing struggle for racial equality.[71]

Old Illusions, New Souths, and the Black Revolution

While many of *Ebony*'s readers responded positively to the magazine's focus on black heritage tourism, its senior editor was less enthusiastic about the apparent commercialization of black history through its editorial and advertising content. As journalist Cleve Washington recognized, Bennett was keenly aware that *Ebony*'s "basic commercial thrust [did] not create an ideal atmosphere for the presentation of serious work."[72] These frustrations had been evident to colleagues such as Vincent Harding, who encouraged Bennett to "phase out of JPC" and establish himself within more radical black institutions.[73] During the 1960s

Bennett had repeatedly defended *Ebony* against criticisms that its content ideal-ized white middle-class values.[74] For Bennett, the magazine's editorial limita-tions were offset by its value as a mouthpiece for popular black history, which allowed him to disseminate his material "to a wider audience than is normally available to a historian on a continuous basis."[75] However, the proliferation of black history advertising, as well as the magazine's celebration of black heritage tourism, appeared to vex the historian and illuminated his own shift toward a more explicitly class-conscious and, in some ways, anti-capitalist black his-tory philosophy.

This shift would perhaps be best expressed through a series titled "The Making of Black America," which was published in the magazine between June 1969 and February 1974. The longest running and arguably most ambitious of Bennett's black history series for *Ebony*, "The Making of Black America" would go on to be published by the Johnson Book Division in 1975 as *The Shaping of Black America*. In a review of the book, John Henrik Clarke described the text as Bennett's "most profound commentary to date on the nature of the black experience."[76] The panoramic focus of the book shared clear parallels with *Before the Mayflower*. However, Bennett emphasized that whereas his first black history series and book project offered a "chronological history," "The Mak-ing of Black America" and *The Shaping of Black America* were intended to be a "developmental history" that offered "a new conceptual envelope for black American history."[77]

Against the commercialization of black history in the present, Bennett pro-vided readers with a striking survey of the historical relationship between black labor and black capital, beginning with the arrival of the first slave ships carrying the "black gold that made capitalism possible in America." Rejecting contem-porary notions that the first white settlers saw black Africans and "immediately started planting Jim Crow signs," Bennett emphasized the market forces that brought the first generation of Africans to the New World as indentured laborers and highlighted the similarity of their condition to that of white laborers who were "packed like herring into foul and steaming ships, sometimes called slave ships . . . and sold, as the first blacks were sold, by the captains of the ships or the agents of captains of ships.[78] Bennett's preoccupation with white servitude as the "historic proving ground for the mechanisms of control and subordination used in Afro-American slavery" would persist through subsequent articles.[79]

In turn, Bennett situated the history of African Americans within a larger imperial project that led to the "world-wide colonization of peoples of color by Europeans" driven by "the exploitation of the labor power and the resources of the colonized." Descriptions of black America as an "internal colony" became a popular conceptual device for Black Power activists following the publication of Stokely Carmichael and Charles V. Hamilton's 1967 manifesto, *Black Power: The Politics of Liberation in America*. Rejecting the postwar social science approaches to racial politics by scholars such as Gunnar Myrdal, Carmichael and Hamilton contended that "there is no 'American Dilemma' because black people in this country form a colony, and it is not in the interest of the colonial power to liberate them."[80] This position was also taken up by Black Power historians, with Bennett's 1969 article "Of Time, Space, and Revolution" offering an illustrative example of how critiques of colonialism by intellectuals such as Frantz Fanon and Kwame Nkrumah became fused with the rhetoric of black activists in the United States to promote the development of "radical black ethnic nationalist thought."[81] Bennett's work was too radical for some readers, with William Taylor contending that the editor's work would be more at home "in the propaganda sheets of black revolutionaries."[82]

Perhaps more important, Bennett's emphasis on systems of power and his efforts to trace the arc of black labor "from legal slavery to economic slavery to para-colonialism" provided a much deeper engagement with class politics, Marxist historiography, and the marketplace than had been present in earlier series. Indeed, sections of "The Making of Black America" appeared better suited to the pages of black revolutionary periodicals on the left, such as *Liberator* and *Umbra*, which contended that black consumer magazines had "sacrificed their own heritage to business interests."[83] This critique of racialized capitalism, which black Marxist historians such as Cedric Robinson would later express more forcefully, had significant implications for Bennett's relationship with *Ebony*.[84] Even as the magazine embraced black entrepreneurship and participation in American consumer society as an avenue for racial progress, Bennett attacked sections of the black middle class who he said were "hooked on conspicuous consumption and the feverish race for status."[85]

The editor also railed against *Ebony*'s celebration of the "New South," which he suggested was an overly optimistic and ahistorical framing of the new black tourism and business opportunities readers could take advantage of below the Mason-Dixon Line. In the magazine's 1971 special on "The South Today," a series of upbeat articles celebrated black social and political gains following the *Brown v. Board of Education* decision and the passage of the Civil Rights and Voting Rights Acts. In southern cities such as Atlanta, the magazine reported that "racial peace reigns," while other features offered an idyllic picture of the scene awaiting black migrants returning "home," where "the stars twinkle brightly, and the moon still reflects a romantic glow. The air is fresh and good. And the water is clean."[86] Louisiana governor John McKeithen championed the South's role in "bringing our black citizens into the mainstream," as seen through his own decision to appoint Leonard Burns as chairman of the state's Tourist Development Commission.[87]

By contrast, Bennett pointed to a host of enduring concerns, most notably the South's deep-rooted racism and troubling embrace of discriminatory racial practices endemic in the North, including "white flight to the suburbs and the use of zoning regulations and urban renewal to create Dixie-style Harlems." From this perspective, the "New South" of the 1960s and 1970s was merely the latest in a long line of "New Souths" stretching back to the failed promises of Reconstruction. Accordingly, appeals to romanticized notions of the region's climate and hospitality, alongside the South's "infinite capacity for deluding itself with myths and lies," risked downplaying the continuing impact of white supremacy and ignoring the precedents established by the region's own history, factors that increased the chances of "a retreat into tokenism and disaster."[88]

The philosophical tensions between Bennett's continued attempts to promote an activist-oriented discussion of black history on *Ebony*'s pages and the magazine's editorial and advertising focus on black heritage tourism can be situated within a national retreat from black radical politics. By the early 1970s, federal programs such as COINTELPRO had successfully infiltrated and undermined major Black Power organizations, while leading black radical activists such as Stokely Carmichael had either fled the country or had seen their influence dramatically diminish.[89] On a local level, the Illinois branch of the Black Panther Party was rocked by the murder of chairman Fred Hampton by FBI operatives and the Chicago Police Department in December 1969.[90] References to "Black Power" in *Ebony* became less oriented around notions of black revolution, as expressed in its 1969 special issue, and primarily concerned with the impact of black public officials in local and state government.[91]

Political efforts to promote black history and the marginalization of black radicals were closely linked. For conservative politicians, "black heritage" offered an alternative to, and arguably a distraction from, more radical forms of black political activism. In 1971, Johnson Publishing representatives LeRoy Jeffries and Alex Poinsett joined Richard Nixon at the White House to help launch the thirty-fourth annual celebration of Negro History Week, presenting the president with a collection of black history texts by the Book Division for inclusion into the presidential library.[92] Even Alabama governor and ardent segregationist George Wallace, whose third-party presidential campaign in 1968 had drawn support from white extremist groups such as the Ku Klux Klan, appeared to get the message. By 1973, the man who stood as possibly the nation's "preeminent symbol of white racism and recalcitrance" was urging fellow Alabamians to respect "the many contributions that African-Americans have made to our state and nation" as part of commemorative events marking black history week.[93]

We Can Seize the Opportunity

For American media outlets, advertisers, and politicians, the American bicentennial provided a powerful moment around which disparate understandings of racial politics, black history, and African American activism coalesced. Hopes that the bicentennial could act as a moment of racial reconciliation can be situated within broader efforts to position the nation's two-hundredth birthday as a moment of calm amid the choppy waters of the 1970s. The impact of the Watergate scandal, the protracted end to the Vietnam conflict, anxieties over the breakdown of the American nuclear family, and the onset of economic malaise all contributed to a sense that the nation was entering a period of decline. At the end of the decade, president Jimmy Carter would describe the nation's struggles as a "crisis of confidence . . . that strikes at the very heart and soul and spirit of our national will."[94] Against this backdrop, Walter Hixson has suggested that a self-referential celebration of the nation's history carried significant bipartisan appeal that promised to offset anxieties about the future of the nation.[95]

Formal plans for the bicentennial had begun in earnest with the creation of the American Revolution Bicentennial Commission on July 4, 1966, less than a week after Stokely Carmichael's speech at the Meredith march had thrust Black Power into the national spotlight; anxieties over black radical activism formed an influential backdrop to the commission's early work. It is striking that federal efforts to undermine the black revolution of the 1960s were paralleled by the government's desire to champion the American Revolution as part of the "Bicentennial Era." In a televised address from the National Archives in 1971, Nixon declared that "the American Revolution is unfinished business with important roles still open for each of us to play." Through presenting American history as a tool of political and psychological empowerment, the president borrowed from the rhetoric of black nationalist activists and historians while continuing to frame Black Power as a reactionary and ahistorical force. Nixon's approach complemented his administration's efforts to coopt Black Power through other projects, such as an embrace of Black Capitalism.[96]

As Natasha Zaretsky has noted, this strategy also revealed how political elites looked to channel demands for cultural autonomy stemming from the various social movements of the 1960s and 1970s into creating "a sense of national unity precisely through a carefully coordinated showcasing of difference."[97]

Bicentennial planners sought to address activist concerns regarding the limitations of a singular historical narrative by adopting a pluralist approach that attempted to incorporate individual and group identity differences into a national mosaic. At the same time, government officials looked to channel this approach into public affirmations of citizen loyalty, a move that John Bodnar argues sought to downplay "a decade of dissent and divisiveness during which governmental authorities had actually inflicted violence upon some of its youngest and poorest citizens."[98]

This sentiment was reflected on a local as well as national level. For postindustrial cities with major African American populations, the bicentennial was heralded as both an economic opportunity and an occasion for racial reconciliation. Major new projects such as a "Bicentennial Black Museum" in Philadelphia sought to celebrate black history as part of the bicentennial's broader theme of national pride and unity.[99] In Washington, D.C., organizer Robert Lester justified $125 million in federal government spending on bicentennial projects by arguing that "we need to change the image of Washington from that of a crime capital with poverty and corruption, to that of a host city."[100] Coleman Young, the first African American mayor of Detroit, believed the bicentennial could provide a much-needed boost to the city's flagging infrastructure and economy.[101] A press release from the mayor's office declared that by capitalizing on the bicentennial to develop Detroit as a labor history center, black and white residents could help to "build bridges in a polarized city."[102]

However, many black public officials remained ambivalent about the relevance of the bicentennial for African Americans, or their role in its commemoration. Bob Nunn, the National Park Service's equal opportunities director, was vocal about the lack of minority input into planning and programming of the bicentennial.[103] In Philadelphia, black leaders argued that the cost of various bicentennial projects merely served to draw important funds away from those in need. The city's bicentennial plans were also derided for creating "a bonanza" for the city's developers and elite business interests yet failing to provide for "the third of Philadelphia's population that lives in black ghettos."[104] Similarly, in Washington, D.C., there appeared to be a split between the ambitions of the city's political elite, who framed the bicentennial's impact primarily in terms of tourism revenues, and the expectations of black residents, who "saw the celebration more as an opportunity to rebuild and improve the city's black neighborhoods."[105]

Criticisms of the bicentennial, alongside pressure from black history organizations such as the ASNLH, led Gerald Ford to issue an official message on the commemoration of black history week in 1975.[106] One year later, the president

formally recognized the expansion of black history week into a month-long celebration, and linked this decision to celebrations of the nation's two-hundredth
anniversary.[107] Ford declared that "in the Bicentennial year of our Independence,
we can review with admiration the impressive contributions of black Americans
to our national life and culture."[108] This proclamation was indicative of the ways
in which bicentennial planners emphasized the theme of "cultural pluralism"
and embraced black history as part of an open invitation for Americans of all
backgrounds to be integrated into a new multicultural and multiracial national
"mosaic."[109]

Yet at the same time, Ford's address framed both the celebration of black history month and the commemoration of the American bicentennial more broadly,
as a point of departure—a moment at which national attention could finally
shift from the ongoing struggle of the civil rights movement to a triumphant
retelling of its successes. The president declared that the 1970s bore evidence of
"the full integration of black people into every area of national life," a statement
that ignored the enduring effects of structural and institutional racism within
American society and the rise of the New Right.[110] Ford also used his address as
an opportunity to smooth over the nation's fraught racial history, asserting that
"in celebrating Black History Month, we can take satisfaction from this recent
progress in the realization of the ideals envisioned by our Founding Fathers." In
doing so, the president dislocated the commemoration of black history from a
critique of the Founding Fathers racial prejudices and presented the bicentennial as an opportunity for the "restoration of traditional values and a nostalgic
and exclusive reading of the American past."[111]

An Affront to Truth and Freedom

Against this contested backdrop, *Ebony*'s 1975 special was dedicated to com-
memorating the bicentennial as "200 Years of Black Trials and Triumphs."[112]
Assistant art director Cecil Ferguson produced a cover montage featuring a
diverse assortment of black pioneers and challenged the magazine's readers to
name them, suggesting that "a good student of black history will recognize every
person and event."[113] However, as Virginia Fowler has noted, the special's cover
reiterated a patrilineal black history narrative and reflected broader gender disparities in the bicentennial's commemoration, which Nikki Giovanni and other
black feminist writers criticized.[114] Such concerns were taken up by *Ebony* readers like Doris Dingle, who informed the magazine's editors that while she was
appreciative of their efforts to promote black historical achievements, she found
it disturbing "that 13 full faces of men and approximately 17 vignettes of men

appear on the cover—and only two women."[115] Editorially, the magazine's content also reflected tensions over the anniversary's commemoration, admitting that "for black Americans, the Bicentennial . . . will be somewhat of a dilemma."[116] In his publisher's statement Johnson attempted to bridge this divide, framing the special as "not a celebration of the Bicentennial but an assessment of 200 years of black American history . . . we cannot celebrate but we can commemorate two centuries of brave progress against tremendous odds."[117]

Ebony's assessment of the anniversary was framed around a major three-part response to the question of whether African Americans should celebrate the bicentennial, featuring contributions from Joseph Jackson, president of the National Baptist Convention; Vernon Jordan, director of the Urban League Vernon; and Lerone Bennett Jr. Jackson offered the most effusive support, arguing that by rejecting the bicentennial, African Americans would merely "deny their own history and their contributions to the life of this great nation."[118] Jordan was more ambivalent, recognizing the bicentennial as an opportunity to re-center African Americans in public history narratives but also worrying that the anniversary would result in a gaudy affair "full of noise and clamor but with little substance." Despite his reservations, Jordan concluded that black participation in the bicentennial festivities should be encouraged, so long as it was done "on our own terms and with the goal of adding substance and a black perspective to an event badly in need of both."[119]

By contrast, Bennett's response provided little scope for reconciliation, offering a deeply pessimistic interpretation of the bicentennial's commemoration as "astounding," "frightening," and "dangerous."[120] If Bennett's previous descriptions of the "New South" had demonstrated reservations over elements of *Ebony*'s coverage, then his strident rejection of the bicentennial confirmed this position. The historian denounced the bicentennial as an embodiment of the "essential schizophrenia of America life."[121] Bennett declared that the anniversary was "an affront to truth and freedom. It is a desecration of the ideal. It is a mirage, an illusion." He positioned the bicentennial as an explicitly negative force and as an event that threatened to undermine the activist potential of black history and the historical contributions of black activists: "No for Martin King and Malcolm X and Medgar Evers," Bennett declared. "No for Harriet Tubman. No for Nat Turner. . . . For the Living, for the Dead, for the Unborn: No. No. No."[122]

As Keith Mayes has noted, Bennett and other prominent black critics of the bicentennial envisioned the anniversary as "an example of a cultural revolution incomplete: as a denial of new knowledge about blacks that the movement ushered in; and as another year to prohibit blacks from the American historical narrative."[123] Bennett argued that anything less than a complete rejection of the bicentennial would be a betrayal of an enduring obligation to the ancestors. Many of his readers appeared to share the editor's reservations. The October 1975 edition of "Backstage" noted that the bicentennial issue had "really stirred up the letter writers" and that most of the responses received from *Ebony*'s readers supported Bennett's position.[124] John Thibeaux dismissed the bicentennial as "only another of the white man's coverups," while Gregory Williams rejected the anniversary as little more than a tribute to "400 years of blood, sweat and tears, unemployment, lynchings, hunger and benign neglect."[125]

The debate over the bicentennial brought into full view underlying fractures between Bennett's writing and *Ebony*'s overarching editorial philosophy. For perhaps the first time, Bennett can be seen to have vocalized his frustrations at *Ebony*'s content within the publication itself. In his attack on the bicentennial, Bennett alluded to *Ebony*'s apparent complicity in encouraging a shift away from collective black activism through its emphasis on consumption and personal fulfilment. He said that "the issue is not whether we have more Cadillacs than the cocoa farmers of Ghana. The issue is freedom."[126] These remarks can be read as a critique of Johnson's belief in conspicuous consumption as an "instrument of aggression" in the struggle for equal rights, which was perhaps most famously expressed through a 1949 article titled "Why Negroes Buy Cadillacs."[127] More broadly, by rejecting style and status as "false and extraneous issues," Bennett's article offered a rebuttal to *Ebony*'s position as a consumer magazine. By contrast, other elements of *Ebony*'s content offered a less critical image of the bicentennial, with the magazine's annual vacation guide imploring readers to "Discover Yourself—It's the Bicentennial Year."[128]

Bennett doubled down on this position outside of Johnson Publishing through a flurry of invited television and public-speaking engagements where he reiterated his opposition to the bicentennial.[129] The editor also rejected invitations to participate in "white-washed" bicentennial activities sponsored by institutions such as Chicago Public Library, asserting that it was hypocritical "to celebrate a freedom that does not exist."[130] More broadly, Bennett venomously attacked the apparent change of heart that had led to an increased focus on black history within the American academy and popular culture. Despite the proliferating "images and echoes of Black Heritage," Bennett warned that "slavery and the subordination of black people are still the dominant passions of the United States. He declared, "Black heritage sells soap, whiskey and detergent. It sells everything, in fact, except the meaning of black heritage and the humanity of black people."[131]

Despite such strident rhetoric, Bennett appeared more willing to engage with the question of black heritage if his own work was considered. For example, the *Chicago Defender* reported that Bennett was one notable figure present at the headquarters of the Illinois Bell Telephone Company during May 1975 for a week-long exhibition of books by black Americans designed to "explore the heritage of black culture in this country."[132] In the very same issue of *Ebony* that Bennett used to launch his attack on the bicentennial, a Bell advertisement celebrated the role of African American Lewis Latimer in the development of the telephone: "Today, as the nation begins to celebrate its bicentennial and the Bell System its centennial, it is fitting to note that Black men and women continue to be important members of the Bell team."[133] The delicate balance between critical commentary and celebration could also be seen through other outlets such as *Black Journal*, which coupled appearances by bicentennial skeptics such as Bennett with a "Blackcentennial" game-show segment hosted by comedian Nipsey Russell.[134]

Illinois Bell was just one in a wave of different advertisers to produce bicentennial-themed advertising campaigns that ran in *Ebony* and other black periodicals throughout 1975 and 1976. Among the most prominent advertisements to tap into this trend came from travel providers, who extended appeals to black heritage tourism, which *Ebony* had introduced at the end of the 1960s. American Airlines invited readers to "take an American Bicentennial vacation and watch your history books come to life" at sites such as the Frederick Douglass home in Washington, D.C.[135] United Airlines offered a special bicentennial fare to allow black passengers to "celebrate yesterday's heroes," including abolitionist Harriet Tubman and Chicago's black founder Jean Baptiste Du Sable.[136] Amtrak advertisements featured an illustrated map showing hundreds of black history landmarks and promised readers that "Amtrak can take you to more of them."[137]

As Tammy Gordon has noted, these advertisements demonstrated growing corporate awareness of the buying power of black consumers, with public relations experts such as D. Parke Gibson later contending that the "Negro market" more than doubled in value during the decade between 1968 and 1978.[138] By using black history as a marketing strategy, corporate advertisers were able to alleviate fears about anti-black hostility within the tourism industry and encourage black patronage as means to satiate a "renewed interest in their own history."[139] More significantly, when published alongside Bennett's historical treatises, such features often worked to blunt his militancy and to moderate the reception of his work on the part of *Ebony*'s readers. At the same time, such ads diverted reader attention away from Bennett's reservations regarding the bicentennial with laudatory profiles of black pioneers that promoted full participation in bicentennial activities and an embrace of conspicuous consumption as a route to black historical education.

The shift toward a more commemorative perspective on black history in many elements of *Ebony*'s editorial and advertising content was paralleled by a retreat from coverage of, and critical engagement with, Black Power and black radical activism. In February 1976—the same month in which Ford announced the ratification of Black History Month—an article by Alex Poinsett offered *Ebony*'s obituary for the black revolution.[140] Poinsett asserted that the revolution was "in prison these days, or exiled overseas, or in the hip pocket of an FBI agent," and that the few revolutionaries who remained were clutching to the strands of "a seemingly unrealizable dream."[141] While readers such as Sekou Kenyatta offered a more upbeat version of this narrative, arguing that many black radicals were "probably now studying for his or her master's in college classrooms across the nation," they acknowledged that the high tide of revolutionary consciousness that had swept across the nation during the late 1960s was over. Mallard Benton Jr., writing from Decatur, Georgia, suggested that while black revolutionaries remained, they had "assumed pseudo assimilated roles in this society as a matter of survival."[142]

Two months after the publication of Poinsett's article, Johnson discontinued *Black World* and fired editor Hoyt Fuller. Rumors of *Black World*'s cancellation had been swirling since the beginning of the decade—privately bolstered by allegations of Fuller's "shameless anti-Semitism" and a policy of benign neglect toward the magazine—but the end still came as a surprise to many of its supporters.[143] Jonathan Fenderson has argued that the magazine's sudden cancellation did more than pull the rug out from under the feet of Fuller, who had been a loyal employee for close to two decades; it eradicated a singularly important outlet for the Black Arts and Black Power movements and removed the most radical voice under the Johnson canon.[144] While philosophical differences with Fuller may well have factored into his firing, Johnson framed the publication's demise as a purely business decision, announcing that he was no longer willing to absorb the magazine's recurrent losses.[145] Irrespective of the underlying rationale for his decision, Fenderson suggests that Johnson's actions demonstrated his belief that the public appetite for black militancy had markedly waned and reconfirmed his desire to keep the company heading firmly "down the road of Black capitalism, corporate advertising, and conspicuous consumption."[146]

Similarly, the narrative of failure that came to characterize *Ebony*'s depiction of Black Power in the 1970s no longer seemed to deserve a place within a triumphant history of black America that functioned as a narrative of racial uplift. From this perspective, the path toward full inclusion within American society would come not through radical action but through "a shift to the middle." For *Ebony* contributor B. J. Mason, this transition was embodied by the

trajectory of Black Panther leader Bobby Seale, whose efforts to enter politics during the 1970s appeared to signal a metamorphosis "from militance to
middle-classism."[147] While journalists such as Ellis Cose expressed dismay at
the cancellation of *Black World* and the shifting tenor of Johnson's publications,
Ebony's core audience appeared largely unresponsive to or unconcerned over
such developments.[148] If writers such as Askia Muhammad warned that "the
time is gone for requiems and roses to dead heroes," the bicentennial provided
an opportune moment to celebrate black history and to separate it from the
ongoing struggle for racial equality.[149]

CHAPTER 6

A Hero to Be Remembered

The multivalent tone of *Ebony*'s bicentennial special reflected deeper tensions within its own coverage of black history. During the 1970s and into the early 1980s, many elements of the magazine's historical coverage can be seen to have moved toward a less critically incisive representation of the past, reflecting the efforts of mainstream media outlets and politicians to frame discussions of black history around commemoration rather than the militant pursuit of civil rights. At the same time, Bennett continued to use *Ebony* as a bully pulpit, asserting that "history is knowledge because it is a practical perspective and a practical orientation" and reiterating its centrality to the ongoing black freedom struggle.[1] Such content provides us with a powerful example of what Houston Baker has described as the "twin rhetorics of nostalgia and critical memory" — a tension between, on the one hand, a desire to construct a conciliatory and racially unifying image of the past "filled with golden virtues, golden men and sterling events" and, on the other hand, an ambition to utilize black history and historical memory as "the very faculty of revolution."[2]

In the aftermath of Dr. Martin Luther King Jr.'s assassination in April 1968, public efforts to commemorate his life and legacy provided a key battleground for these competing discourses. Almost immediately following King's death, civil rights stalwart and Democratic representative John Conyers introduced a bill in Congress to establish a national holiday in his honor, and as the 1970s progressed, a national movement coalesced in support of this effort.[3] When

Ronald Reagan finally signed a 1983 bill ratifying the King holiday, many black politicians and activists contended that victory for the holiday movement was a watershed moment in the battle for black historical representation and in "legalizing the legacy" of both King's individual significance and the broader impact of the civil rights movement.[4] However, by reframing King as a champion of colorblind individualism, Reagan and other conservatives attempted to justify attacks on civil rights and affirmative action programs, demonstrating how appeals to black history came to be caught up in the politics of the culture wars.[5]

Against this backdrop, Bennett used *Ebony* to frame King's influence through the lens of "critical memory." Both inside and outside the magazine's pages, Bennett looked to remind his audience of King's radical philosophy and democratic socialism. For him, the movement to establish a national holiday for King was one that forced America to face up to its original sin of racism and the continuing significance of race in the lives of all of its citizens.[6] This sentiment would come to a head in a January 1986 special issue titled "The Living King," wherein Bennett reiterated King's significance as a race-conscious activist for social justice. Yet at the same time, *Ebony*'s wider engagement with the King holiday reflected its shift toward a more nostalgic interpretation of the black past as a way of reaffirming the shared values and historical experiences of African Americans, something that privileged the cultural and moral values of previous black generations and underscored pervasive anxieties over the future of black history.

The Prince of Peace Is Dead

King's relationship with Johnson Publishing can be traced back to his emergence on the national stage during the 1950s. One of the magazine's first major profiles of the civil rights leader was published in July 1956, providing a detailed eight-point plan for racial progress. In highlighting King's desire to "mobilize for an all-out fight for first-class citizenship," the tone of *Ebony*'s coverage was more combative than that of white-oriented outlets such as *Time*, which tended to downplay more confrontational elements of King's nonviolent philosophy and emphasize his "Christian meekness."[7] Given Bennett's familiarity with King— the pair had been classmates at Morehouse during the late 1940s and were both proteges of Benjamin Mays—it is unsurprising that *Ebony*'s senior editor was entrusted with penning the profile.[8] Bennett sought to place King within a historical lineage of the "new Negro" that echoed the rhetorical flourishes of Garveyism but also gently critiqued King's class privilege and use of religious symbolism, describing how King's disciples "reached out to touch the threads of his faultlessly-tailored suit."[9]

Over the years following the Montgomery bus boycott, King emerged as a master of utilizing popular media to further the civil rights cause. A prominent example of his talents in this area can be seen in his relationship with *Ebony*, with preacher and periodical developing a mutually beneficial alliance during the late 1950s and early 1960s, facilitated by King's relationship with Bennett.[10] Mentions of *Ebony* in personal correspondence demonstrate that King kept a close eye on and was receptive to the tone of its coverage.[11] In turn, Tony Atwater has contended that Johnson's personal admiration for King led to his magazines supporting the minister "financially as well as ideologically."[12] King even contributed a column to *Ebony* for more than a year, titled "Advice for Living," before an assassination attempt by Izola Curry in September 1958 forced him to cut down on media commitments.[13] Echoing the magazine's own middle-class sensibilities, King's column warned teenage readers against the vagaries of rock music and premarital sex, and took every opportunity to reaffirm his commitment to nonviolent direct action.[14]

King also became an important part of *Ebony*'s expanding black history coverage, with Bennett keen to situate his emergence as a movement figurehead within a longer black activist tradition. King appeared on the cover of *Ebony* in November 1962 to promote "From Booker T. to Martin L.," the last article in Bennett's "Negro History" series. Throughout this series, and again in its book-length counterpart *Before the Mayflower*, Bennett claimed that King was "a cause and effect of revolutionary change in [the] mood of Negro America" and the increasing "militancy and effectiveness" of black protest.[15] This sentiment was expanded in 1964 with the publication of Bennett's *What Manner of Man*, which provided one of the first substantive biographies of King.[16] Echoing the tone of his writing in *Ebony*, Bennett sought to reaffirm King's position at the forefront of the "second Reconstruction" of the 1960s and as the "spiritual descendant of Frederick Douglass."[17] The biography was well received, with Illinois governor Otto Kerner contending that its publication secured Bennett's "place of distinction in the literary world."[18]

While King had enjoyed widespread support in the black press during the 1950s, the growing influence of black nationalism during the early 1960s fed into the emergence of a new wave of "little black magazines" that were less accommodating of the minister's commitment to nonviolent direct action.[19] The *Liberator* emerged as one notable critic, with Peniel Joseph arguing that its firebrand editor, Dan Watts, possessed both "the means and determination to harass the civil rights leader."[20] While some of its staffers may have harbored reservations over the effectiveness of King's gradualist approach, *Ebony* remained a staunch defender of the minister.[21] In the face of growing criticism from more militant aspects of the movement, the magazine penned an impassioned photo-editorial tribute to King in its December 1964 issue, declaring that his name had become a global symbol for "the peaceful fight for rights—passive resistance, boycotts, strikes, and a steadfast bravery that does not allow one backward step even at a daily risk to one's own life."[22] Elements of the magazine's audience were more willing to criticize King, with Chicago-based community activists Lawrence Landry and Odis Hyde among a number of readers to disparage his response to the rise of Black Power.[23]

If commentary from *Ebony*'s audience reflected growing dissatisfaction with King's approach among some sectors of the black community, the magazine also provided the minister with a mouthpiece to outline the evolution of his own activist philosophy. In a contribution to the magazine's 1965 special issue on "The WHITE Problem in America," King suggested that white Southerners were making a "Marxist analysis of history more accurate" than appeals to Christian morality, noting that "businessmen act much more quickly from economic considerations than do churchmen from moral considerations."[24] The following year, he penned an *Ebony* article that suggested the liberation of colonized peoples across the world was dependent on the ability of black Americans "to reform the structures of racist imperialism from within."[25] By March 1968, *Ebony* was reporting that King had joined black nationalist leader Ron Karenga and "scores of lesser-known militants" in supporting a potential boycott of the Summer Olympics.[26] Such coverage can be linked with more recent scholarly efforts to elevate King's political radicalism, with Cornel West championing King's impact as "a staunch anti-colonial and anti-imperial thinker and fighter . . . [with] closeted democratic socialist leanings."[27]

From the viewpoint of the twenty-first century, the image of King as a democratic socialist and anti-imperial freedom fighter is one that remains largely absent in popular memory and dislocated from his status as an American hero. Yet we would do well to remember that acts of commemoration have their own politics, and that the now ubiquitous efforts to lionize King by American politicians, businesses, and media companies were far from assured at the time of his death. As Jason Sokol has noted, many white Americans rejected King as "a communist, a rabble-rouser and an agitator," and his shift from racial to economic justice during the later years of his life did little to soften this position.[28] The minister's opposition to the war in Vietnam also led to him being attacked by establishment politicians and media outlets with "ferocious abandon."[29] At his funeral, college mentor Benjamin Mays declared that "the American people are in part responsible for Martin Luther King Jr.'s death. The assassin heard enough condemnation of King and Negroes to feel that he had public support. He knew that millions hated King."[30]

However, while white (and nonwhite) animosities toward King continued to fester, the minister's demise sparked a marked shift in public opinion that was both authentic and strategic.[31] Media eulogizing of King helped to soothe previous opposition to his activism, ensuring that a man regularly accused by white detractors such as FBI director J. Edgar Hoover of harboring dangerously anti-American tendencies could take up the "mantle of moderation."[32] Devorah Heitner has noted how the spasms of violence that accompanied King's assassination prompted some media executives to consider more seriously the recommendations of the Kerner Report.[33] King's death also stimulated a more sustained attempt to address the "Negro history gap" through projects such as the Bill Cosby–fronted *Black History: Lost, Stolen or Strayed* and the Vincent Harding vehicle *Black Heritage: A History of Afro-Americans*.[34] Similarly, King's death helped to accelerate the push for black-centered educational programs, with Harding noting in his contribution to *Ebony*'s 1969 special on "The Black Revolution" that the "surge toward Black Studies . . . was greatly heightened by [King's] assassination."[35]

The King Holiday Movement

As the fires that burned across the nation in the aftermath of King's death were extinguished, the focus of movement insiders turned to the question of how best to honor his life's work. Gary Daynes has argued that two overlapping but competing approaches emerged—a "tributary style" that pushed for a more activist-oriented account of his life and a "memorial style" that prioritized cementing King's individual legacy.[36] While black academics such as Syracuse professor Charles Willie warned that attempts to idolize King were a disservice to both the minister and the black community, Coretta Scott King and the King family appeared more concerned with elevating their patriarch—something that came to center on the development of the King Center in Atlanta.[37] As a trustee of the King Center, Bennett asserted that the institution should provide a "concrete manifestation of our *duty* to pick up Dr. King's torch and advance on the trenches of the four evils he identified in his last published article—the evils of racism, militarism, poverty, and materialism."[38] However, this approach risked being absorbed into the center's role of what *Ebony* and other black periodicals characterized as a "monument to a martyr."[39]

Broader discussions of how to commemorate King's life came to focus on whether his birthday should be made a national holiday. Almost immediately following King's assassination, Democratic representative John Conyers had introduced a bill to toward this end.[40] The bill quickly gained the support of the King estate, as well as influential black leaders such as Ralph Abernathy, who used his role as the president of the SCLC to declare King's birthday "a national people's holiday."[41] The issue also became a political crutch, with president Richard Nixon and Democratic challenger George McGovern courting black voters during the 1972 campaign by entertaining the possibility of a holiday in King's honor.[42] By the end of the decade, support for the King holiday had coalesced into a truly national movement. A 1979 petition set up by the King Center to coincide with the fiftieth anniversary of King's birth garnered more than three hundred thousand signatures, and Conyers's bill would reach the House floor for the first time in the same year.[43]

While support for the holiday continued to grow, tensions persisted over how best to frame its significance. An emphasis on national unity and commemoration was necessary to render King more palatable for the white majority but served to strip the minister of his racial and regional identity. Furthermore, descriptions of King as a transcendent American hero sat uneasily alongside the rhetoric of colorblindness advocated by the New Right, whose relentless focus on individual opportunity sought to downplay entrenched racial inequities.[44] The rightward shift in American politics that swept Ronald Reagan to victory in the 1980 presidential campaign also prompted a notable shift in the approach of conservatives to the holiday debate. Prior to Reagan's election many conservatives had either ignored the holiday movement or had opposed it on economic or ideological grounds. However, as Daynes notes, by the early 1980s conservatives had gotten wise to how the King holiday could provide a "useful forum for their civil rights policies."[45]

This shift was embodied by Reagan's highly public volte-face on the subject. The president had remained a consistent opponent to the holiday throughout the 1970s, providing support for figures such as North Carolinian senator and conservative firebrand Jesse Helms to lobby aggressively against its ratification. After his election Reagan continued to cast aspersions over King's character and reputed communist affiliations.[46] However, as it became clear that public and political support was pushing the holiday toward fruition, Reagan began to moderate his position, grudgingly conceding that "though Dr. King and I may not have exactly had identical political philosophies, we did share a deep belief in freedom."[47] On November 2, 1983, when Reagan signed into law the bill to establish a national holiday for King, there was little sign of resentment for the man whom Michael Eric Dyson has characterized as Reagan's "bitter ideological enemy," with the president praising King as "a man whose words and deeds . . . stirred our nation to the very depths of its soul."[48]

For many activists, the struggle to establish a holiday in King's memory marked a milestone in America's racial history. Their victory appeared to be a decisive act in a proxy war for federal recognition of black history and, by extension, the "centuries-old fight for equal rights."[49] Civil rights veteran Jesse Jackson declared that Reagan's actions had "institutionalized" the black freedom struggle and its place within American history. NAACP executive director Benjamin Hooks echoed this sentiment, describing the bill as recognition of "the historic accomplishments of all black Americans."[50] In *Ebony*, the triumph of the holiday movement, alongside successes such as Harold Washington's victory in the 1983 Chicago mayoral race, was held up as evidence that black America constituted "a viable, powerful segment of the nation—a force that will have to be recognized by the nation's political leaders and power brokers." In doing so, black leaders and publications reiterated the centrality of race to discussions of King's legacy and the continuing significance of race for African Americans of all backgrounds.[51]

Yet for Reagan, the holiday appeared to symbolize something quite different. Upon signing the bill, the president pointed to King's 1963 address at the March on Washington as the culmination of his life's work and the high point of America's efforts to face down its crisis of racial discrimination. Similarly, Reagan linked King's memory to legislative victories such as the 1964 Civil Rights Act and 1965 Voting Rights Act, which he argued led people "to treat each other not as blacks and whites, but as fellow Americans."[52] This narrative ignored widespread opposition to the implementation of legislative change across the country and ongoing efforts to limit black enfranchisement and to stymie desegregation.[53] In addition, it discounted the more radical critique of American capitalism and imperialism that developed during the later years of King's life, ensuring that the King who dreamed of "brotherhood and the integration of buses, schools and lunch counters" would be memorialized, while the minister who "attacked capitalism [and] talked about the redistribution of the nation's resources" would be ignored.[54]

In this way, Reagan's words sought to position the civil rights movement as a "single halcyon decade" frozen between the mid-1950s and the 1960s, an approach that largely limited its impact to the South and to the pursuit of specific, noneconomic goals. As Jacquelyn Dowd Hall notes in her seminal 2005 article on the long civil rights movement, this framing positions the pursuit of civil rights as an accomplishment rather than a goal and prevents "one of the most remarkable mass movements in American history from speaking effectively to the challenges of our time."[55] While "traces of bigotry" remained, Reagan contended that these were relics of a bygone era and that America had indeed overcome. Perhaps most significant, he applauded the minister for awakening "something strong and true, a sense that true justice must be colorblind."[56] In doing so, Reagan cast the individualism of the New Right as the true heir to King's political legacy. For Stephen Lawson, this strategy helped to frame King's "dream" as one that "exalted individualism, opposed race-conscious remedies such as affirmative action, and pursued integration as an end in itself."[57]

The president's position was strengthened by the unlikely support of former King aides and colleagues such as Hosea Williams, whose backing was based around the promise of investment in minority enterprise.[58] Despite their vilification by progressive black intellectuals, Williams and other black Reaganites were able to reconcile their call for a radical interpretation of King's legacy with Reagan's promise for new business opportunities to help inner-city black communities "break free" from dependency on the welfare state.[59] Reagan could also point to black conservatives such as Thomas Sowell and Clarence Thomas, who reiterated the president's distrust for race-based social welfare and argued for a greater degree of "personal responsibility" within black communities.[60] Although the black majority overwhelmingly rejected Reagan's candidacy, the bootstraps rhetoric of Sowell and other conservative intellectuals confirmed the reemergence of black conservatism as "a small yet powerful current within the African American middle class," and bolstered the president's efforts to appropriate King's legacy in support of his own political agenda.[61]

A Hero to Be Remembered

Against this backdrop, Bennett sought to explain King's memory and the significance of the holiday movement through the lens of critical memory. The editor used *Ebony* as a platform to warn that the emergence of the New Right during the 1970s paralleled the racist backlash to Reconstruction during the 1870s.[62] Whereas Reagan saw the civil rights years as a triumphant flood that signaled the full entry of black citizens into a colorblind society, Bennett envisioned the movements "golden decade" as just one wave in a much longer struggle for racial justice that "started with the first revolt on the first slave ship and will not end until America deals with the revolutionary mandate of its birth." Similarly, while Bennett recognized King's importance to post–World War II black activism, he emphasized the minister's place within a broader activist tradition that continued to rise and fall with the "ebbing and flowing of the energies of the people."[63]

Bennett's contributions to *Ebony* were complemented by his activities outside of Johnson Publishing Company. Through speaking engagements at black historical organizations and historically black colleges, Bennett repeatedly asserted that a new generation of activists must fight to keep the flame of civil rights pro-test alive.[64] While conservatives argued that liberal government programs were responsible for black poverty, Bennett contended that "the problem is not the poor. The problem is power. The problem is not the black ghetto. The problem is the system which created it."[65] In doing so, Bennett reiterated the sentiments of activists such as Julian Bond, who warned King's legacy had been imperiled by black leaders who, through their willingness to enter into the political main-stream, "postured for attention, competed for loyalties and money, but could not inspire mass action or allegiance."[66] For figures such as Bennett and Bond, younger generations were required to take up the "baton of the black spirit" handed down by King and other black pioneers, while also ensuring that their activism would not become blunted by the weight of public commemoration.[67]

Bennett would develop this position further through a trilogy of articles pub-lished in *Ebony* between 1981 and 1985. In a February 1981 article titled "Listen to the Blood," he reinforced his understanding of black history as an organic and cyclical process in order to explicitly situate King's legacy within a broader living history of black America.[68] Bennett rejected a triumphalist interpreta-tion of the modern civil rights movement to argue that "black history is a part of nature and revolves in cycles, endlessly, birth, growth and death, progression and retrogression."[69] Critically, Bennett argued that it was not enough for black Americans to symbolically commemorate the dead, and that a full commit-ment to the ongoing struggle was the only way to honor past heroes: "We are responsible, totally responsible, not only for ourselves but for the whole of the black experience . . . it is only through us that Martin Luther King, Jr. can finally reach the peak of the mountaintop."[70]

This sentiment rejected the transcendent image of King endorsed by politi-cians such as Reagan, and it reiterated Bennett's belief that an "honest" inter-pretation of black history relied on an understanding that black Americans lived in a "different reality" from whites.[71] Accordingly, while an appreciation of King's memory was vital to understanding the American condition, it could not be divorced from his racial and regional identity.[72] Readers applauded Bennett for discarding the "myth of objectivity" that had "hamstrung our historians and journalists" and for recognizing the unique implications of black history, and the King holiday, for black Americans.[73] The following year, in an article titled "Why Black History Is Important to You," Bennett pushed this idea further, reiterating the need for black history to be "functional, pragmatic, and this-worldly in orientation."[74] He argued that King's elevation should not obscure the fact that black history was "and has always been the absolute ground of black resistance." Echoing the sentiments expressed in earlier work such as "Of Time,

Space and Revolution," Bennett contended that "history is knowledge because it is a practical perspective and a practical orientation. It orders and organizes our world and valorizes our projects."[75]

As Pero Dagbovie has noted, Bennett's formulation of black history emphasized its multiple functions as "an ideology, a scholarly discipline, and a source of pride and energy."[76] From this perspective, an understanding of King's political radicalism was not enough to cast black history as the faculty of revolution—it was only by pursuing radical action in the present that African Americans could "give meaning to the strivings of Martin Luther King, Jr."[77] Arguably the most forceful articulation of this belief can be found in Bennett's February 1985 article, "A Living History," which contended that "in and through black history, the voices of the past speak to us personally, calling us by name, asking us what have we done, what are we doing and what are we prepared to do" to ensure that the radical tradition of Nat Turner, Harriet Tubman, Martin Luther King Jr. and Malcolm X would be maintained.[78]

Bennett's voice joined a larger chorus that was calling for a more critical engagement with King's memory. Black periodicals such as *The Crisis* and the *Los Angeles Sentinel* remained openly suspicious of efforts to appropriate King's legacy, highlighting Reagan's previous opposition to King alongside his continued attacks on civil rights.[79] The connection between King's activism and the "principle of race neutrality" advanced by the Reagan administration was also harshly criticized by members of the U.S Civil Rights Commission.[80] However, *Ebony*'s enormous popularity positioned the magazine as a key influencer of black public opinion.[81] By the mid-1980s its monthly circulation had breached 1.7 million, dwarfing the circulation of every other black periodical in the country.[82] Marketing research companies suggested that when accounting for pass-on readership, the magazine reached more than 40 percent of all black adults.[83]

Yet even as this market penetration meant that Bennett's politically engaged reading of black history and the King holiday reached millions of households across the country, this work was complicated by *Ebony*'s broader coverage, which often chose to frame King's legacy through a nostalgic and consumerist lens. This was most readily apparent through the magazine's continued emphasis on the development of the King Center as a tourist attraction, with its multi-million-dollar shrines, visitor center, and gift shop helping to "keep the dream alive."[84] A focus on the great cost of the center's construction and on its impressive physical stature further shifted attention away from grassroots activism and toward expensive public monuments as an "appropriate" way to commemorate King.[85] The magazine's willingness to celebrate the King Center as a "monument to a martyr" was indicative of its efforts to use King's legacy as a rallying point for black America—something that reflected widespread anxieties over the state of black America during the years following his death.

As noted in chapter 5, the black middle class emerged as one of the great beneficiaries of the civil right era, making significant gains in the cultural, economic, and political spheres during the 1970s and 1980s. By contrast, working-class African Americans remained culturally ostracized and economically marginalized.[86] The disproportionate effects of trickle-down economics, deindustrialization, and urban decay on inner-city black communities made it increasingly difficult for *Ebony* to offer its readers a unified image of black life and culture. Similarly, black publications and leaders fretted that the pursuit of "identity politics" by queer African Americans and black feminists had hastened the fragmentation of collective black activism—as evidenced by a series of controversial *Ebony* specials on divisive subjects such as "black on black crime," economic inequality, and matters of gender and sexuality within the black community. Journalist Eugene Robinson has contended that by the 1980s, "symbolism, history and old-fashioned racism" were just about the only things many African Americans appeared to have in common.[87]

From this perspective, adopting a big-tent approach to the King Holiday maximized its potential impact as a historical panacea for the contemporary of black America and helped to celebrate King as "a hero to be remembered." Choosing to downplay criticisms of King from within the black community prior to his death, *Ebony* prioritized the importance of remembering his contributions, arguing that "black people cannot forget their heroes and remain a great people."[88] By framing the holiday in this way, *Ebony* intimated that widening divisions within the black community were not only the result of ongoing racial discrimination and economic inequities but also a failure of individual black citizens to maintain "the spirit of sacrifice and struggle that enabled our forefathers to survive."[89] This tension was clear within Bennett's own conceptualizations of black history, with the editor repeatedly chastising younger African Americans for failing to develop "any community of interest with the past."[90] While Bennett envisioned this argument as a rallying cry for grassroots action, it also suggested that historical illiteracy was linked to generational malaise, and it echoed the sentiments of black conservatives such as Sowell who cast "ignorance and inadequate training" as the root cause of black unemployment.[91]

More problematic still were the tensions created by *Ebony*'s continuing editorial prerogative to "mirror the happier side of Negro life." Even as Bennett highlighted King's position alongside militant black activists and abolitionists such as Malcolm X, the magazine's content, one could argue, provided compelling "evidence" of the move toward a colorblind society. As cultural critic Herman

Gray has noted, *Ebony*'s celebration of black triumphs maintained a politics of representation that saw black visibility become the "basis for claims to racial equality, the elimination of social and economic injustice, and the arrival of a time for racial invisibility."[92] In turn, the magazine's premise as a proudly race-conscious enterprise appeared to chime dissonantly with its coverage of crossover stars such as Diana Ross, who cheerfully informed readers, "I don't think in terms of race."[93] From this perspective, King's ability to "transcend" blackness was comparable to entertainers such as Ross and Bill Cosby, who were celebrated by television and advertising executives as a colorblind entertainers and brand ambassadors.[94]

Successes on an individual and organizational level during the 1980s also helped to supplement this narrative. While scholars such as Kinohi Nishikawa have suggested that Johnson Publishing reached its height during the 1970s, *Ebony*'s circulation actually stagnated during this decade.[95] By contrast, the Reagan era saw a dramatic uptick in circulation, helping Johnson Publishing supplant Motown as the largest black-owned company in America and seeing Johnson himself become the first black person named to the Forbes 400 list.[96] *Ebony*'s fortieth-anniversary issue in November 1985 offered a salute to "four decades of black progress" that championed minority entrepreneurship as a route to racial equality.[97] Yet this narrative helped to disguise the decline of black legacy newspapers, which went out of business at an alarming rate during the 1970s and 1980s.[98] Furthermore, while black magazines such as *Black Enterprise* and *The Crisis* became increasingly critical of Reagan's economic policies and commitment to minority enterprise, Johnson's belief that "politics was something we should cover in an impartial way" meant that *Ebony* largely avoided direct criticism of the political establishment.[99]

The Living King

In the buildup to the first formal celebration of the King holiday in January 1986, Reagan continued to utilize King's rhetoric to advocate for a dismantling of hiring quotas and affirmative action.[100] In a radio address to the nation on civil rights, the president reiterated his opposition to hiring quotas, asserting that they were unconstitutional and denied jobs "to many who would have gotten them otherwise, but who weren't born a specific race or sex." Seeking to justify his remarks, Reagan recalled King's dream of a society where "people would be judged on the content of their character, not by the color of their skin."[101] By appropriating King's words, the president was able to position regressive social and economic policies as the true fulfilment of civil rights legislation.[102] This sentiment was reiterated by Attorney General Edwin Meese, who argued that by eliminating minority hiring quotas for government contractors, the Reagan administration was "trying to carry out the original intent of the civil rights movement."[103]

By contrast, Bennett reminded readers of King's unique place within a black radical tradition and warned his audience that mere acts of remembrance were not enough to fulfil King's dream of a democratic society. He contended that "before confronting us as a spectacle or celebration, black history is a challenge and a call."[104] This point was particularly relevant for younger generations of black Americans, who were tasked with the challenge of picking up the baton left by King and the civil rights generation and pushing on with the relay race that began "with the first revolt on the first slave ships and will not end until America deals with the total challenge of blackness." It was only by taking their place in the "perpetual conversation" of voices that stretched across black communities and geographies that the "new generation" could fulfill the historical legacy of their forefathers.[105]

The generational tensions that underscored the commemoration of King's legacy were articulated more clearly in an article by Patrice Gaines-Carter in September 1985, titled "Is My 'Post-Integration' Daughter Black Enough?" The author described her daughter's ambivalence toward the King holiday—an occasion seen as little more than an opportunity to sleep in—as evidence of the "post-integration blues" suffered by large swaths of young African Americans during the 1980s.[106] Gaines-Carter bemoaned that she came from a "generation of marchers" and could not understand the lethargy of black youths. Her words resonated with older readers such as Alphonso Galloway, who expressed disgust that younger African Americans "know more about Michael Jackson, Prince and Eddie Murphy than Dr. Martin Luther King."[107] By highlighting the apparent "inaction" of their children, Gaines-Carter and some of her readers intimated that the problems facing black youth coming of age in the 1980s were small fry compared to their own struggles during the Jim Crow era.

Perhaps more important, such commentary provides an example of what Michelle Boyd has described as "Jim Crow nostalgia"—a rose-tinted remembering of the Jim Crow period as a "golden era" for black community cohesion and intraracial solidarity.[108] Even as readers such as Ondria Thompson recalled this period in black history as "disgusting, sad and downright frightening," they confessed to "an exciting feeling of nostalgia" for the ways in which racial discrimination and segregation had fostered vibrant black business and political cultures.[109] In some ways, this reading of black America under Jim Crow segregation is understandable, offering an important corrective to hegemonic narratives of black pathology and victimhood that dominated postwar social science. However, it also downplays the diversity and complexity of black identity formation, frames intercommunal discord and disagreement as a purely negative force, and minimizes "the unevenness of African Americans' experience across class and gender."[110]

Not all members of the magazine's audience supported such criticisms of "post-integration" black youth. Californian reader Yvonne Birge professed to find Gaines-Carter's policing of black identity politics and her equation of racial authenticity with black oppression "disturbing." While she appreciated Gaines-Carter's desire for her daughter to "never forget where we are and how we got here," Birge suggested that this desire could be expressed without enforcing ethnocentric identity boundaries and "expecting our children to stay within these boundaries in order to prove they are black."[111] Such comments highlighted the limitations of holding up participation in arbitrary events such as the King holiday as a model of black collective activism. When readers such as Pamela Dunn positioned marches in support of the holiday as evidence that "we still have the power—Black Power," they risked reducing the demand for revolutionary change and radical black activism to the commercially mediated commemoration of an individual figure.[112]

Paralleling the first formal celebration of the King Holiday in January 1986, *Ebony*'s coverage of the event climaxed with a special issue on "The Living King." The special was fronted by an article from Bennett that sought to educate readers about the "real meaning" of birthday celebration. Whereas Reagan and other Republican strategists looked to claim the holiday as a moment of political largesse in support of an individual movement icon, Bennett argued that the holiday's first formal celebration was a moment that had been taken, not given. The pressure brought to bear by movement activists had meant that Americans of all backgrounds and political persuasions would be forced to reckon with "not only of Martin Luther King, Jr. but also of the maids, the sharecroppers, the students and the Rosa Parkses who made him what he was." Subverting the language of race and criminality that had come to underpin debates into the war on drugs and the "urban crisis," Bennett declared that King and other agitators for racial equality had broken into American history "like beneficent burglars, bringing with them the gifts of vision, passion, and truth."[113]

Critically, whereas Reagan's address to the nation for the first official observance of Martin Luther King Jr. Day on January 18 promoted the holiday as a time for reflecting on the movement's victories, Bennett argued that "this is *not* a holiday for rest and frivolity . . . this is a day for study, struggle, and preparation."[114] Highlighting the radical implications of King's opposition to racism, militarism, and economic injustice, Bennett argued that "it is on this deep level, and in the context of personal responsibilities, that the King Holiday assumes its true meaning." Through such rhetoric, Bennett pushed back against an uncritical commemoration of King to frame the "real meaning" of the King holiday as a recommitment to black activism and militant protest. By doing so, Bennett was able to situate an "appropriate" observance of the Holiday within the broader responsibility of black Americans to utilize their history as a tool in the ongoing struggle for racial justice.

This sentiment was reinforced through another section of "The Living King" special, which printed quotations from King that "speak to contemporary problems and struggles." Many of the selected quotations provide a direct critique of Reagan's efforts to appropriate King's rhetoric in support of "colorblind" social and economic policies. For example, *Ebony* posited that "no amount of gold could provide an adequate compensation for the exploitation and humiliation of the Negro in America . . . the payment should be in the form of a massive program by the government of special, compensatory measures."[115] Numerous scholars have pointed to this quotation as an acknowledgement of King's support for racial reparations, and the decision to print it echoed the sentiments of Adam Fairclough and other left-wing historians who had emphasized King's "deep political radicalism" in the lead-up to the holiday.[116] Further quotations underscored the need for economic justice and class solidarity, with one extract asserting that the "salvation of the Negro middle class is ultimately dependent on the salvation of the Negro masses."[117]

However, other segments of *Ebony*'s January 1986 issue reinforced a less critical memorialization of King that reflected pervasive currents of black conservative nostalgia and the "memorial" style of commemoration identified by Daynes.[118] Physical memorials to King—ranging from a forest in Israel to a church in Hungary—were held up as evidence that his memory "is as much alive as the Eternal Flame that burns in front of his crypt" at the King Center.[119] In turn, a photo-editorial reflecting on "poignant moments" in King's life was striking in its individualistic portrayal of the minister, as it was heavily populated by closeup shots of King elevated above his fellow activists or alone with his family. Images of King alongside militant activists such as Malcolm X or Stokely Carmichael were avoided, and the bulk of the feature focused on his funeral, reinforcing his position as a martyr for the movement.[120]

The special also highlighted *Ebony*'s reluctance to address the generational biases that shaped its coverage of the holiday and mediated its role as an outlet for popular black history and as a voice for black America during the 1980s. An illustrative example can be seen in a feature titled "What Martin Luther King Jr. Means To Me," which relayed the opinions of ten prominent African Americans regarding King's legacy.[121] Olympic gold medalist Evelyn Ashford was the only contributor to the article younger than age forty-five, and her earnest description of King as a "symbol of hope" was hardly representative of the fears that the "new generation" were ambivalent to King's legacy expressed by figures such as Bennett and Gaines-Carter. Rather than use the holiday as an opportunity to address why many younger African Americans appeared unconcerned by its commemoration, *Ebony* chose instead to celebrate those who were strong public advocates of the holiday, such as Stevie Wonder. Similarly, for all its emphasis on King's empathy with the "Negro masses," the magazine provided little space for working-class African American responses to the holiday.[122]

This multivalent engagement with King's life and the significance of the King holiday reflected both the challenge of effectively melding the diverse black historical and political perspectives on King's death into a cohesive public narrative, and the complex relationship between the search for a usable black past and the racial realities of the American present. Through the work of Bennett and other contributors, *Ebony* attempted to walk the line between the "twin rhetorics of nostalgia and critical memory"—an approach not only guided by Bennett's enduring belief in black history as "the very faculty of revolution" but also influenced by the magazine's efforts to utilize King's memory as a bridge between different subsections of the African American community.[123] However, as the biases and blind spots in *Ebony*'s coverage made clear, it was often difficult to reconcile the memory of the movement years or an emphasis on the "reciprocal relationship between the past and the future" with the lived experiences of black communities during the 1980s.[124]

At the same time, the magazine's special on "The Living King" provided an important insight into Bennett's changing yet enduring role as a popular black historian. Pero Dagbovie has characterized the 1980s as the "golden age" of African American history—not necessarily due to the importance of the decade in shaping black America, but because it marked a pivotal moment in the maturation of African American historiography and of black history as an academic discipline.[125] A significant increase in articles focused on black history in journals such as the *American Historical Review* was one feature of this trend; another was the growing influence of a new wave of professional black historians.[126] Echoing the tensions that underpinned the early black history movement during the first decade of the twentieth century, this trend threatened to marginalize black scholars working outside of the academy. By the early 1980s Daryl Michael Scott was just one member of this new generation who had come to see Bennett's work as "useful only as a motivational tool or as a means of counting grievances."[127]

In turn, "The Living King" revealed broader tensions affecting *Ebony*'s efforts to deal with the consequences of black history's increasing visibility. As Linda Symcox has noted, by the second half of the 1980s black history had become "central [not only] to mainstream historiography but also to mainstream popular culture."[128] However, this shift served to position public debates about black history at the heart of the developing culture wars. Reagan's efforts to politicize King's memory were just one example of how black history had become a key battleground in the struggle for "the soul of America."[129] For much of its history *Ebony*'s value as a black history text had been predicated on the absence of black historical representation in American culture, just as the broader role of black periodicals had been defined by the failure of mainstream media outlets to cover black demands and concerns. Conversely, if the civil rights revolution had helped to hasten a "brain drain" of black journalists from African American media and the decline of many black print institutions, so too did black history's "coming of age" raise questions over the continued relevance of black periodicals as an outlet for black history education.[130]

And yet, despite the limitations of its coverage and the challenges posed by the growing popularity and politicization of black history, the response of *Ebony*'s readers to "The Living King" special reconfirmed its continued importance as a black history text. Baltimore resident Sherri Barker informed *Ebony*'s editors that "not at any time during my years of schooling did I learn anything pertaining to Dr. King . . . everything I know about Dr. King I've learned from publications such as yours."[131] Correspondent Vanessa Mobley of North Carolina reported that she would preserve the issue as "a momento [*sic*] and a black history reference."[132] Arkansas native N. H. Hilliard echoed such thoughts, declaring that the special issue should be "kept in every home for future generations because it is, in itself, a history book on the life of one of the greatest Americans."[133]

Such statements suggested that the fight for the King holiday and the mainstreaming of black history had not in fact reduced *Ebony*'s value as a black history text among the magazine's extensive audience. Rather, these developments appeared to have reinforced the desire and demand for "authentic" black historical perspectives in American popular and political culture that were accessible to a mass audience. While black professional historians were carving out a new era of scholarship within the academy, white politicians, public spokesmen, and business interests had arguably taken control of black popular history in the public sphere. Faced with this development, Bennett's efforts to advocate for a radical reading of King's legacy, as well as his continued attempts to promote black history for a popular audience, remained one of the most compelling and important features of *Ebony*'s content.[134]

Conclusion

Ebony's coverage of the King holiday movement during the mid-1980s over-lapped with another significant historical milestone: its own fortieth anniversary. The magazine marked the occasion with a blockbuster special issue in November 1985 that ran to more than 250 pages. Its size and scope provided an emphatic reminder of *Ebony*'s unprecedented growth, from an initial print run of twenty-five thousand copies to an estimated pass-on readership of more than eight million per issue by the dawn of its fifth decade.[1] Market research suggested that *Ebony* held the "highest market penetration of any general interest magazine in the nation'"[2] The anniversary was even written into the Congressional Record, with Illinois Representative Cardiss Collins rising to honor the magazine's tremendous success and its "celebration of the best of Black America."[3] Johnson offered his own perspective in an extended interview published in the anniversary special. When asked how he would like to be remembered by future generations, the publisher emphasized *Ebony*'s role in bringing black history to a popular audience.

> I hope they will say that we gave black people faith and confidence in themselves and that we told them about their great heritage . . . that we brought to life, through the historical articles and the books we published, the great black leaders of the past, and that we gave young people the feeling that if our ancestors could do it, during those difficult times, then we can do it today.[4]

It is striking that Johnson would single out *Ebony*'s historical content as a measure of his own place in history, and his decision to do so provides further evidence of how the publisher came to value its role as a "history book." As this book has documented, the previous four decades had seen *Ebony* emerge as a vital outlet for and participant in the "modern black history revival."[5] It had provided new historical perspectives to a vast readership, rebuffed white misrepresentation and underrepresentation of black history, and drawn connections between the black past and the ongoing struggle for racial equality. As an intermediary location between black intellectual and academic circles and the cultural mainstream, *Ebony* provided a unique and important space in which diverse and frequently dynamic depictions of popular black history could be recovered, revised, and rearticulated. In this regard, the magazine's content should be celebrated as part of an inclusive rather than exclusive reading of black history work that acknowledges the important contributions of popular black historians, bibliophiles, and black print institutions.[6]

While Johnson deserves recognition for helping to facilitate the magazine's expanding coverage of black history, he played little part in its editorial production.[7] Two years before the magazine's 1985 special, its senior editor and inhouse historian Lerone Bennett Jr. had marked his own thirtieth anniversary at Johnson Publishing. In a letter to Bennett, Johnson declared that working with him had proved to be "one of the most rewarding experiences" of his professional career.[8] The unusual degree of editorial and intellectual independence afforded by his publisher had facilitated Bennett's rise from relative obscurity to scholarly prominence and had underpinned his emergence as arguably the most influential historian within the black community and the most widely read black historian in the United States.[9] Building on the influence of earlier black historians and black history popularizers who had utilized the black press as a tool for historical education, Bennett's writing lay at the core of *Ebony*'s role as a "history book" for millions of readers.[10]

This sentiment was reflected through the responses of *Ebony*'s audience to its fortieth anniversary special, which applauded its historical significance and the magazine's enduring influence as an outlet for popular black history. Ernestine Foster, a reader from Florida, declared that she would treasure the issue as "a black history reference book."[11] Otis Hollingsworth echoed this statement, praising *Ebony* for documenting "the history of our great people and our struggle for freedom." Louisiana native Ollie White stressed its educational value, asserting that *Ebony* was "the best history book" black children could read to "see where we have come from and how we got here."[12] Michigan reader Ruth McDowell went even further, contending that the anniversary issue was "a witness, a revelation, a history and a prophecy to the world."[13] Through such statements, these letters echoed the praise levied by scores of earlier readers, who had repeatedly lauded *Ebony*'s educational and historical value and aimed to place its content within the broader parameters of black historical scholarship.

From both an ideological and philosophical perspective, *Ebony*'s coverage of black history appeared to have evolved significantly since it was first published in 1945. Initially wedded to its editorial prerogative to "mirror the happier side of Negro life," the magazine's history content had become more substantive throughout the 1950s and increasingly radical during the 1960s. On an individual level, Bennett had moved away from the more "objective" or "detached" approach presented in 1961 and 1962 through his first "Negro History" series, and toward a "more subjective and interpretative" understanding of black history by the end of the decade.[14] The editor would continue to advocate for an activist-oriented interpretation of black history during the so-called "post–civil rights" years, using moments such as the American bicentennial and the King holiday movement to reiterate his belief in the power of black history to function as a pragmatic tool for black liberation.[15] Similarly, whereas earlier readers had looked to reinforce Bennett's scholarly credentials through appeals to historical objectivity or professional creditability, articles such as "Listen to the Blood" were applauded for "crushing the myth" of objectivity to approach history unapologetically from a "black perspective."[16]

Yet if Bennett's writing appeared to continue this trajectory, other aspects of the magazine's engagement with black history can be seen to have adopted a less politically incisive and more commemorative position during the 1970s and 1980s. As *Ebony* was forced to contend with shifts in the nation's political and cultural climate, as well as significant changes and enduring challenges within and between black communities across the country, radical editorial perspectives on either past or present became less commercially attractive to both Johnson and his advertisers. Bennett would repeatedly defend *Ebony* against accusations of petty bourgeoisie ideals and middle-class bias during the 1960s, pointing to, among other things, "its contributions in the area of Negro history and Black consciousness."[17] However, as black radical periodicals and organizations struggled to remain politically relevant, much of *Ebony*'s editorial content, including some aspects of its black history content, retreated to the center.

It was unrealistic to expect, as some Black Power advocates appeared to do, that *Ebony* would become a consistent outlet for black radical perspectives and ideologies. Michael Hanson has argued that criticisms faced by popular black entertainers such as James Brown and periodicals such as *Ebony*—criticisms that stimulated and were partially satiated by the release of songs such as "Say

It Loud (I'm Black and I'm Proud)" and special issues such as "The Black Revolution"—reflected frustrations at black nationalism's "inability to appeal to and enlist the political potential of the mass black public that it so valorized."[18] Yet even at the height of *Ebony*'s engagement with Black Power during the late 1960s, the desire for black critical perspectives emanating from many of its readers could only push back so far against its consumerist orientation and its dependence on corporate advertisers. This reality makes Bennett's writing even more important, offering a tantalizing glimpse of the magazine's radical potential and confirming his characterization by Howard Zinn as an editor who "was far more militant than the magazine he edited."[19]

Such frustrations were not limited to commentators from outside Johnson Publishing Company. In private correspondence, fellow *Ebony* editor Charles Sanders implored Bennett to use his good standing with Johnson to help push the magazine toward a more radical position in order to develop "some truly significant analyses of the black condition."[20] While Bennett played a prominent role in a "small band of left-leaning JPC journalists" who pushed the boundaries of *Ebony*'s editorial content during the 1960s and early 1970s, figures such as Sanders expressed disappointment over his "reluctance" to exert a greater influence.[21] For other editors, Bennett was part of an institution that was beyond saving. When John Woodford quit the publication in 1968, he provided a litany of concerns regarding *Ebony*'s content that he took "as insults to the Afro American community and myself."[22]

In hindsight, Bennett's ill-fated foray into academia during the early 1970s may have helped to crystallize the benefits of his position at *Ebony*. Despite the magazine's clear limitations as a mouthpiece for black radicalism, Bennett was less accountable to the types of administrative and institutional restrictions that had undermined his short tenure as the chair of Northwestern's Afro-American Studies Department. In the aftermath of his departure from Northwestern, Bennett clarified these sentiments in an interview with the *Black Books Bulletin*. He noted that *Ebony*'s commercial thrust and the limitations of its format meant that it was hardly the "ideal atmosphere for the presentation of . . . serious work." However, he also recognized the magazine's role in facilitating his work and allowing him to press black history's form and function "to a wider audience than is normally available to a historian on a continuous basis . . . [as] it is possible, month by month, to talk to two million, perhaps five million black people about their history."[23]

During the 1970s, Bennett was able to utilize this position to critique the mainstream embrace of "black heritage" and to attack nostalgia-driven commemorations of the bicentennial. His continued prominence within Johnson

Publishing Company stands in contrast to the fate of other radical editors such as Hoyt Fuller, who was forced out of the organization following the cancellation of *Black World* in 1976.[24] However, the frequency of original content from Bennett's pen dramatically slowed, as he was unable to keep up with his prodigious output during the first decade following his first "Negro History" series. His five-part "Chronicles of Black Courage" series, published between 1982 and 1983, marked Bennett's last original black history series for *Ebony*, while the publication of *Wade in the Water* in 1979 would be his last original history book for more than twenty years.[25] This decline in productivity was compounded by Bennett's promotion to executive editor in 1987, which effectively ended his submission of new historical content.[26]

As Carolyn Kitch has noted, *Ebony* continued to publish a "significant amount of historical material" during the years following its fortieth anniversary.[27] Yet it is critical to note that much of this content was recycled from Bennett's earlier work. Similarly, whereas many of Bennett's earlier black history series had been published throughout the year, during the 1980s *Ebony*'s historical content became more restricted to the months of January and February, coinciding with the national commemoration of the King holiday and the celebration of Black History Month. At the same time, new features such as "Memorable Photos from the *Ebony* Files" continued to celebrate the magazine's own past and move it toward a more self-reverential and depoliticized representation of black history.[28] Indeed, from the mid-1980s onward, it can be argued that the bulk of original historical content in *Ebony* came not through its editorial features but in the contributions of its advertisers.

While there is much that remains to be said about the role of corporate advertisers in shaping public attitudes toward and engagement with popular black history, presenting *Ebony* as merely a gateway to such material by the end of the 1980s is a simplistic and overly cynical reading of its enduring significance as a black history text. Long before American politicians, business and media interests decided to jump on the "Negro history bandwagon," *Ebony* and other black periodicals were laying the groundwork for the postwar black history revival.[29] If Bennett's frustrations over the commercial and political cooptation of "black heritage" had become acute by the first formal celebration of the King holiday, they also provide a telling reminder as to the continuing impact of his own writing and of *Ebony*'s importance as a history book. Through its production and dissemination of historical content, the magazine played a key role in black history's relocation from the margins of American historiography, politics, and popular culture to "center stage" in analyses of the nation's past and future development.[30]

Notes

Introduction

1. "Backstage," *Ebony*, June 1969, 27.

2. In *Ebony*'s statement of circulation for 1969, the average paid subscription circulation over the previous twelve months was 939,717, and the magazine's paid newsstand readership was 207,079. This did not include freely distributed copies or account for the magazine's substantial pass-on readership. "Statement of Ownership, Management and Circulation," *Ebony*, November 1969, 22.

3. Arthur Schomburg, "The Negro Digs Up His Past," *Survey Graphic*, March 1965, 670.

4. "Backstage," *Ebony*, June 1969, 27.

5. By only its second issue, *Ebony* was arguably the largest black magazine in the world in both size and circulation. By the early 1970s, the magazine had "broken every circulation and financial record ever set by a black publication." "Backstage," *Ebony*, December 1945, 1; "Backstage," *Ebony*, October 1972, 32.

6. Johnson, "Publisher's Statement," *Ebony*, August 1968, 29.

7. By the early 1990s *Before the Mayflower* had sold more than a million copies. Bennett, *Challenge of Blackness*; Bennett, *Before the Mayflower*, "*Ebony* Book Shelf," *Ebony*, February 1988, 26; Ken Ringle, "Against the Drift of History," *Washington Post*, August 27, 1993; Painter, "Our Kind of Historian," box 12, Bennett Papers.

8. Salley, *Black 100*, 260.

9. Adelaide Gulliver, "The Shaping of Black America," *Black Times*, August 1975, 36.

10. Harris, "Coming of Age," 107.

11. Dagbovie, *What Is African American History?* 6.

12. "Backstage," *Ebony*, December 1945, 2.

13. "Backstage," *Ebony*, October 1946, 4.

14. "Backstage," *Ebony*, November 1945, 2.

15. Frazier, *Black Bourgeoisie*.

16. Chambers, *Madison Avenue*, 45; Green, *Selling the Race*.

17. Cohen, *A Consumers' Republic*; Glickman, *Buying Power*; Weems, *Desegregating the Dollar*; Wright, *Sharing the Prize*.

18. Green, *Selling the Race*, 15.

19. Carter-David, "Fashioning Essence Women and Ebony Men"; Fenderson, *Building the Black Arts Movement*.

20. Harding, "Power from Our People," 48.

21. Quarles, *Black Mosaic*, 181.

22. Henderson, *Ebony Jr!*; Christian, "John H. Johnson."

23. Kitch, *Pages from the Past*, 208.

24. Ibid., 93–94.

25. "Backstage," *Ebony*, March 1985, 24.

26. Wilson, *Whither the Black Press?*

27. Harding, "Power from Our People," 40.

28. Harris, "Coming of Age," 107.

29. Dagbovie, *African American History Reconsidered*, 39.

30. Painter, "Our Kind of Historian," box 12, Bennett Papers; Tinson, "Held in Trust by History"; West, "Lerone Bennett, Jr."

31. For more information about the African American Intellectual History Society, visit https://www.aaihs.org.

32. A. Peter Bailey, "Remembering Lerone Bennett, Jr.," *New Pittsburgh Courier*, March 5, 2018.

33. Ayana Jones, "Lerone Bennett, Jr., 89, Former *Ebony* Editor," *Philadelphia Tribune*, February 16, 2018, 10B; Neil Genzlinger, "Lerone Bennett, Jr., Historian of Black America, Dies at 89," *New York Times*, February 16, 2018.

34. Berger, "Professional and Popular Historians," 16.

35. Scott, "Following in the Footsteps," 40.

36. Meier and Rudwick, *Black History*.

37. "Lerone Bennett, Jr." tape 4, The History Makers.

38. Hall, *Faithful Account of the Race*; Snyder, *Making Black History*; Rocksborough-Smith, *Black Public History in Chicago*.

39. Painter, "Our Kind of Historian," box 12, Bennett Papers.

40. Hall, *Faithful Account of the Race*, 10.

41. Snyder, *Making Black History*, 2.

42. Bennett, "An Adamant 'No,'" *Ebony*, August 1975, 40.

43. Bennett, "Why Black History Is Important to You," *Ebony*, February 1982, 61.

44. I am unable to comment more on this collection at time of press. For more information, please contact Chicago State University Archives and Special Collections, or the Bennett estate.

45. "Publisher of Iconic Black Magazines Files for Bankruptcy," *New York Times*, April 11, 2019.

46. "Lerone Bennett, Jr.," tapes 1–6, The History Makers; "Opening Remarks to Sixth Pan-African Congress," box 16, Bennett Papers; "FESTAC Taskforce, 18 October 1976," box 12, Bennett Papers.

47. My own brief attempt to address this need can be seen in an essay for *The Black Scholar*. West, "Lerone Bennett, Jr."

48. "Lynn Norment," tape 6, The History Makers.

49. "John H. Johnson," tape 7, The History Makers.

50. Bennett, "A Living History," *Ebony*, February 1985, 28.

Chapter 1. An Abundance of Outright Untruths

1. Ernest, *Nation within a Nation*, 167; Vogel, "Introduction," 1; Hughes, quoted in De Santis, *Langston Hughes*, 13.

2. Frazier, *Black Bourgeoisie*, 185–86; "Why Negroes Buy Cadillacs," *Ebony*, September 1949, 34.

3. Holloway, *Jim Crow Wisdom*, 64.

4. Wilson, *Whither the Black Press?* 28.

5. Harding, "Power from Our People," 48; Thompson, "Booker T. Washington," 1.

6. "Ebony Hall of Fame," *Ebony*, November 1955, 149.

7. Bacon, *Freedom's Journal*, 38; Todd Steven Burroughs, "Publish or Perish," *The Crisis*, March 2002, 39.

8. "To Our Patrons," *Freedom's Journal*, March 16, 1827, 1.

9. Ibid.

10. Hines, "Learning Freedom," 618.

11. Gardner, *Black Print Unbound*; McHenry, *Forgotten Readers*, 108.

12. Green, *Educational Reconstruction*, 2.

13. Grant, *Multiculturalism*, 8; Moreau, *Schoolbook Nation*, 58.

14. Johnson, *A School History*, preface.

15. Foner, *Reconstruction*; "Teaching the History of Negro Americans," box W40, John Hope Franklin Papers.

16. Doreski, *Writing America Black*, xv.

17. McHenry, *Forgotten Readers*, 188.

18. Des Jardins, *Women*, 120.

19. Hall, *Faithful Account*, 188; Kilson, *Transformation*, 4.

20. Franklin, *George Washington Williams*, 25.

21. Franklin, "Evolution of Scholarship," xxiii.

22. Washington, *Up from Slavery*; Washington, *Story of the Negro*.

23. Franklin, "Evolution of Scholarship," xxiii.

24. "Editorial," *The Crisis*, November 1910, 10; Lewis, *W. E. B Du Bois*, 267.

25. Andrew Burt, "The Negro as a Soldier," *The Crisis*, February 1911, 23; M. D. Maclean, "African Civilization," *The Crisis*, March 1911, 23; Maclean, "The First Bloodshed of the Civil War," *The Crisis*, October 1911, 246; Michael Lomax, "Tapping Two Educational Roots," *The Crisis*, September–October 1998, 24.

26. Stein, *World of Marcus Garvey*, 80.

27. Hall, *Faithful Account*, 8.

28. Stewart and Ruffins, "Faithful Witness," 312–16.

29. "Joel Augustus Rogers," *The Crisis*, April 1966, 201.

30. Van Deburg, *Modern Black Nationalism*, 64.

31. Hall, *Faithful Account*, 226.

32. Asukile, "Joel Augustus Rogers," 330.

33. Morris, *Carter G. Woodson*, preface.

34. Houston, "Negro History Bulletin," 492.

35. Thuesen, *Greater than Equal*, 69–70.

36. "Double V Campaign," *Pittsburgh Courier*, February 7, 1942.

37. Washburn, *Question of Sedition*.

38. "The Black Magazine," box 11, folder 1, Saunders Papers.

39. "I. J. K Wells to W. E. B Du Bois, 3 December 1946," MS 312, Du Bois Papers.

40. "Negro Story," box 9, folders 1–3, Browning Papers; Reed, *Chicago NAACP*, 108; "The Black Magazine," Saunders Papers.

41. Johnson and Bennett, *Succeeding against the Odds*, 119–21; "New Magazine out This Month," box 150, folder 1, Barnett Papers.

42. Green, *Selling the Race*, 137.

43. "Editorial Statement," *Negro Digest*, November 1942, 2.

44. Holloway, *Jim Crow Wisdom*, 43.

45. Grant, "Negro Digest"; Green, *Selling the Race*, 138.

46. Brown, "Souled Out," 31.

47. This function became more pronounced in the magazine's second iteration, which ran from 1961 until 1976. Dagbovie, *African American History Reconsidered*, 32.

48. Eslanda Goode Robeson, "Old Country for Thirteen Million," *Negro Digest*, January 1945, 3.

49. "*Ebony* Magazine, 1945–1965," box 2, Ben Burns Papers.

50. "White Man Turns Negro," *Life*, June 9, 1947, 131.

51. Chambers, *Madison Avenue*, 41; Wald, *Crossing the Line*, 125–26.

52. Regester, "Robert S. Abbott," 23–24.

53. Burns, *Nitty Gritty*, 88.

54. "John H. Johnson," tape 1, The History Makers.

55. Burt, "Vivian Harsh," 68–69; Rocksborough-Smith, *Black Public History in Chicago*, 46.

56. Johnson and Bennett, *Succeeding against the Odds*, 69; "The Black Magazine," box 11, folder 1, Saunders Papers.

57. "Great Negro Thinkers," *Ebony*, October 1946, 38.

58. The article mentioned a dozen black men by name, but no black women.

59. "Great Negro Thinkers," 38.

60. Rickford, *We Are an African People*, 49.

61. "California Centennial," *Ebony*, November 1949, 28–29.

62. "Early State Pioneers," *Ebony*, November 1949, 30–31.

63. "Was Lincoln Anti-Negro?" *Ebony*, February 1948, 48.

64. "Time to Count Our Blessings," *Ebony*, November 1947, 44.

65. "Backstage," *Ebony*, August 1947, 8.

66. "Letters to the Editor," *Ebony*, May 1948, 10.

67. "Biography," box 1, folder 1, Morrison Papers; "New York Urban League Journalism Award," box 1, folder 1, Morrison Papers.

68. "JET-EBONY Editor Allan Morrison Dies in N.Y.," *Jet*, June 5, 1968, 51.

69. Conrad, *Harriet Tubman*; Conrad, "A Great Leader—Harriet Tubman," *Negro World Digest*, August 1940, 46–59; Conrad, "General Tubman on the Combahee," *Negro World Digest*, December 1940, 13–16.

70. Humez, *Harriet Tubman*, 7.

71. "Allan Morrison to John H. Johnson, January 3, 1947," box 1, folder 1, Morrison Papers; Johnson and Bennett, *Succeeding against the Odds*, 164.

72. "Biography," box 1, folder 1, Morrison Papers.

73. "Richard Giles to Allan Morrison, August 29, 1946," box 1, folder 1, Morrison Papers.

74. Burns, *Nitty Gritty*, 76.

75. Johnson and Bennett, *Succeeding against the Odds*, 164; Hutson, "Schomburg Center," 76.

76. Thompson, "What Africans Think about Us," *Ebony*, February 1954, 37.

77. "Bibliography of Era Bell Thompson," box 2, Burns Papers.

78. Thompson, *American Daughter*, 7–8.

79. Burns, *Nitty Gritty*, 101; Broussard and Cooley, "*Ebony*'s Era Bell Thompson," 15.

80. "John H. Johnson to Era Bell Thompson, 4 August 1969," box 1, Thompson Papers; "John H. Johnson to Era Bell Thompson, 24 May 1984," box 1, Thompson Papers.

81. "Backstage," *Ebony*, June 1953, 12.

82. "Book of the Week," *Jet*, September 30, 1954, 52; "*Ebony* Editor Completes Book on Africa," *Jet*, June 3, 1954, 53; "Bibliography," box 2, Burns Papers; Thompson, "What Africans Think about Us," 37; Thompson, *Africa*.

83. Johnson and Bennett, *Succeeding against the Odds*, 173.

84. "Backstage," *Ebony*, November 1947, 6; Chambers, *Succeeding against the Odds*, 42.

85. While Henson's expedition was widely celebrated for reaching the Pole, later explorers and scholars have disputed the claim. Bryant and Cones, *Dangerous Crossings*.

86. Johnson and Bennett, *Succeeding against the Odds*, 186; Henson, *Negro Explorer*.

87. "Matt Henson," *Ebony*, July 1947, 20.

88. Johnson and Bennett, *Succeeding against the Odds*, 188; "John H. Johnson," tape 4, The History Makers.

89. Dingle, *Black Enterprise Titans*; Christian, *Empire*.

90. "Backstage," *Ebony*, April 1946, 1.

91. Dingle, *Black Enterprise Titans*, 16.

92. Johnson and Bennett, *Succeeding against the Odds*, 180.

93. Ibid., 187.

94. Green, *Selling Black History*.

95. "Henry H. Brown," tapes 5–8, The History Makers; "Black Guardians," box OP2, Brown Papers; "Black Treasures," box OP3, Brown Papers.

96. For example, see John Hope Franklin's role as an advisor on the Pepsi-Cola "Adventures in Negro History" series. "Calvert," *Ebony*, December 1951, 67; "John Hope Franklin to William Payne, 22 December 1964," box W25, John Hope Franklin Papers; "To Introduce 'Adventures in Negro History,'" box W25, John Hope Franklin Papers.

97. "The 15 Outstanding Events in Negro History," *Ebony*, February 1950, 44; "America's Oldest Negro Community," *Ebony*, February 1952, 42–43.

98. "Woodson Wins Long Fight for an Idea," *Ebony*, February 1950, 47.

99. "This Week in Negro History," *Jet*, November 1, 1961, 13; "Jet Press Release, 1951," box 150, folder 1, Barnett Papers.

100. "Famous Negro Sons of White Fathers," *Ebony*, October 1950, 96; Roi Ottley, "5 Million U.S White Negroes," *Ebony*, March 1948, 20–21; "Passing," *Ebony*, May 1949, 27–29.

101. Rooks, *Ladies' Pages*, 125.

102. Johnson and Bennett, *Succeeding against the Odds*, 235.

103. Ibid, 235.

104. Green, *Selling the Race*, 138; Nishikawa, "Race, Respectability."

105. Burns, *Nitty Gritty*, 189; Johnson and Bennett, *Succeeding against the Odds*, 236; "John H. Johnson," tape 5, The History Makers.

106. Burns, *Nitty Gritty*, 190; "Ben Burns to Earl Conrad, 2 March 1971," box 4, Burns Papers; "Letter to Fortune, 2 January 1968," box 2, Burns Papers.

107. "Is the Negro Happy?" *Ebony*, December 1953, 132.

108. Booker, *Shocking the Conscience*.

109. Ibid., 84.

110. "The New Fighting South," *Ebony*, August 1955, 69–71.

111. Roberts and Klibanoff, *Race Beat*, 79.

112. "Lerone Bennett, Jr.," tapes 1–2, The History Makers.

113. "Birth Certificate," box 1, Bennett Papers; "Biographical Sketch," box 1, Bennett Papers.

114. Wayne Dawkins, "Black America's Popular Historian," *Black Issues Book Review*, January 2004, 13; "Black History as a Lifework," box 1, Bennett Papers; "Lerone Bennett, Jr.," tape 1, The History Makers.

115. Williams, "Lerone Bennett, Jr.," 29.

116. "Benjamin Mays Memorial Lecture, 1993," box 1, Bennett Papers.

117. "Biographical Sketch," box 1, Bennett Papers; "Torch Yearbook," box 1, Bennett Papers; "Student Council," box 1, Bennett Papers.

118. "Certificate of Acceptance," box 1, Bennett Papers.

119. "John H. Johnson," tape 7, The History Makers.

120. "Biographical Sketch," box 1, Bennett Papers; "Current Biography Yearbook 2001," box 1, Bennett Papers; "Read the *Atlanta Daily World*," box 1, Bennett Papers.

121. "*Ebony* Staff material," box 9, Burns Papers.

122. "The Legacy of Our Negro Greats," *Ebony*, February 1953, 88.

123. Burns, *Nitty Gritty*, 139; Green, *Selling the Race*, 191; Booker, *Shocking the Conscience*, 102–4; "Southern Trip," box 4, Burns Papers; Bennett, "The South and the Negro," Ebony, April 1957, 77–81.

124. "Dred Scott's Children," *Ebony*, April 1954, 83.

125. "Famous Negro Sons," 96.

126. Bennett, "Thomas Jefferson's Negro Grandchildren," *Ebony*, November 1954, 78,

127. "Negro Senators from Mississippi," *Ebony*, May 1956, 65; "Alabama's Negro Congressman," *Ebony*, June 1958, 81.

128. "*Ebony* Hall of Fame," *Ebony*, November 1955, 149.

129. Johnson with Bennett, *Succeeding against the Odds*, 198–199; "*Ebony* Opens Its New Building," *Ebony*, October 1949, 34; "The Story of *Ebony*," *Ebony*, November 1955, 122.

130. "First Ten Years Are the Happiest," *Ebony*, November 1955, 98–99.

131. "*Ebony* Hall of Fame," *Ebony*, February 1956, 25.

132. Regester, "Robert Abbott," 26; Trodd, "Black Press," 458.

133. Hines, "Blackboard and the Color Line," 2.

134. Rocksborough-Smith, *Black Public History in Chicago*, 2.

135. "*Ebony* Hall of Fame," *Ebony*, February 1957, 25.

136. "*Ebony* Hall of Fame," *Ebony*, February 1958, 27.

137. Dagbovie, *Carter G. Woodson in Washington*, 20.

138. "*Ebony* Hall of Fame," *Ebony*, February 1959, 61.

139. Pochmara, *Making of the New Negro*, 10.

140. Matelski, *Reducing Bodies*, 113.

141. Tinson, *Radical Intellect*, 97; Spencer, *Revolution Has Come*; Farmer, *Remaking Black Power*.

142. White "Introduction," 42.

143. Hine, *Hine Sight*, xx.

144. "Backstage," *Ebony*, December 1959, 25; "*Ebony* Hall of Fame," *Ebony*, February 1959, 61–63; "Negro History," *Jet*, February 23, 1961; "Back to School, Stay in School Kit," box 263, folder 2623, Chicago Urban League Papers.

145. "A Message from the Publisher," *Ebony*, November 1955, 121.

146. "Era Bell Thompson to John H. Johnson, June 26, 1959," box 1, Thompson Papers.

147. Johnson with Bennett, *Succeeding against the Odds*, 287.

Chapter 2. Tell Us of Our Past

1. "Backstage," *Ebony*, January 1963, 20.

2. "Biographical Sketch," box 1, Bennett Papers.

3. "Backstage," *Ebony*, July 1960, 24.

4. "Backstage," *Ebony*, May 1960, 24.

5. "Ebony's Fifteenth Birthday," *Ebony*, November 1960, 159.

6. Chambers, *Madison Avenue*, 120; Thernstrom and Thernstrom, *America in Black and White*, 80–82.

7. "Ebony's Fifteenth Birthday," 159.

8. Tyson, *Radio Free Dixie*.

9. Carson, *In Struggle*; Sellers, *River of No Return*.

10. Bennett, "The Ghost of Marcus Garvey," Ebony, March 1960, 21.

11. No editorial byline was attached to this article, but it bears all the hallmarks of Bennett's writing. "The Revolt of Negro Youth," *Ebony*, May 1960, 38.

12. "Backstage," *Ebony*, July 1960, 24.

13. Bennett, "South Africa: The Handwriting on the Wall," *Ebony*, July 1960, 27.

14. Burns, *Nitty Gritty*, 95–96.

15. Grant, *We Shall Win*.

16. Johnson and Bennett, *Succeeding against the Odds,* 259.

17. Thompson, "Freedom Comes to 83 Million Africans," *Ebony*, December 1960, 144; Morrison, "His Toughest Assignment," *Ebony*, November 1960, 29; "Nigeria Unshackled," *Ebony*, October 1960, 25.

18. Ahmann, *New Negro*, 34.

19. James Baldwin, "A Negro Assays the Negro Mood," *New York Times*, March 12, 1961.

20. Marc Crawford, "The Scholar Nobody Knows," *Ebony*, February 1961, 59.

21. Du Bois, *The Negro*.

22. Crawford, "Scholar Nobody Knows," 65.

23. "Letters to the Editor," *Ebony*, May 1961, 16.

24. Ibid., 16.

25. "Africa's Golden Past," *Ebony*, October 1964, 28.

26. "Backstage," *Ebony*, July 1961, 22.

27. Ibid.

28. Semmes, *Roots of Afrocentric Thought*, xii; Fenderson, "Journey toward a Black Aesthetic."

29. "The United States and Neo-Colonialism," *Liberator*, May 1961, 1; Tinson, *Radical Intellect*.

30. Stange, "Photographs," 208.

31. Bennett, "The African Past," *Ebony*, July 1961, 40–44.

32. "Ebony Pictures," *Ebony*, September 1961, 18.

33. "Slave Reunion," *Ebony*, March 1955, 61–64.

34. Bennett, "Behind the Cotton Curtain," *Ebony*, January 1962, 82; Elkins, *Slavery*.

35. Bennett, "Behind the Cotton Curtain," 90.

36. Bennett, "Slave Revolts and Insurrections," *Ebony*, February 1962, 90.

37. A total of fifty-one letters or partial letters focusing on Bennett's series were published across seventeen issues between September 1961 and February 1963.

38. "Letters to the Editor," *Ebony*, September 1961, 12.

39. DuRocher, *Raising Racists*, 39.

40. Weiner, *Power, Protest, and Public Schools*, 114–15.

41. "Letters to the Editor," *Ebony*, September 1961, 13; Putnam, *Race and Reason*; Wolters, *Race and Education*, 92.

42. "Letters to the Editor," *Ebony*, September 1961, 13.

43. "Letters to the Editor," *Ebony*, November 1961, 20.

44. "Contribution of *Ebony*," 141.

45. "Masthead," *Ebony*, March 1965, 4.

46. "Contribution of *Ebony*," 141.

47. Emphasis added.

48. "Contribution of *Ebony*," 142.

49. "Perspectives," *Negro Digest*, November 1962, 98.

50. "Letters to the Editor," *Ebony*, July 1962, 12.

51. "Books," *Jet*, January 3, 1963, 48.

52. Bennett, "Extract from *Before the Mayflower*," *Negro Digest*, March 1963, 83.

53. "Before the Mayflower Advertising Pamphlet," box 7, folder 9, Fuller Papers.

54. "Jet's 1963 Calendar Pin-Ups," *Jet*, January 10, 1963, 28.

55. Johnson with Bennett, *Succeeding against the Odds*, 287; "Book Division Inventory," box 23, folder 3, Saunders Papers; West, "Books You've Waited For."

56. "Backstage," *Ebony*, October 1962, 22.

57. Bennett, *Before the Mayflower*, preface to first edition.

58. Archie Jones, "Jefferson Said 'All Men,'" *Chicago Sun-Times*, January 27, 1963.

59. Half a century later, this same comparison would underpin Daryl Michael Scott's assessment of Franklin and Bennett's work. Scott, "Following in the Footsteps," 40–41.

60. Henrietta Buckmaster, "Moving Record of Human Passion, Coolly Put Down," *Chicago Tribune*, February 3, 1963.

61. Buckmaster, *Let My People Go*.

62. "A Fine New Treatment," *Chicago Daily News*, February 20, 1963; Marion Jackson, "Before the Mayflower," *Atlanta Daily World*, March 23, 1963.

63. Robert Johnson, "Book of the Week," *Jet*, February 7, 1963, 50.

64. "History of Negro in America," *Boston Globe*, February 10, 1965.

65. Gannon, "Before the Mayflower," 197.

66. At the time of Gannon's review, the narrator of "Death Valley Days" was Ronald Reagan, whose later attempts to utilize black history as a frame for colorblind nostalgia would clash with Bennett's writing during the 1980s.

67. Gannon, "Before the Mayflower," 198.

68. Dagbovie, *African American History Reconsidered*, 27.

69. Franklin, *Mirror to America*, 134.

70. Dagbovie, *African American History Reconsidered*, 27.

71. Kenneth Reich, "Some Still Unhappy with History Book," *Tuscaloosa News*, February 23, 1971.

72. "Letters to the Editor," *Ebony*, April 1962, 16.

73. "Backstage," *Ebony*, March 1963, 23.

74. "Backstage," *Ebony*, July 1963, 25.

75. "Backstage," *Ebony*, September 1963, 18.

76. Medgar Evers, "Why I Live in Mississippi," *Ebony*, September 1963, 143.

77. Johnson, "Publisher's Statement," *Ebony*, September 1963, 19.

78. "Negro Progress in 1953," *Ebony*, January 1954, 17.

79. Bennett, "Ten Most Dramatic Moments in Negro History," *Ebony*, September 1963, 30.

80. "Proclaimed . . . Promised . . . Still Deferred," *Freedomways*, Winter 1965, 5.

81. Tinson, *Radical Intellect*, 124.

82. Dagbovie, *African American History Reconsidered*, 30.

83. Quarles, *Negro in the Civil War*; Quarles; Quarles, *Lincoln and the Negro*.

84. Cook, "Unfinished Business," 52.

85. Bodnar, *Remaking America*, 207.

86. Cook, "Unfinished Business," 51.

87. Bodnar, *Remaking America*, 220.

88. "Gov. Kerner Names 3 to Illinois Centennial Unit," *Jet*, February 15, 1962, 7.

89. Glymph, "Liberty Dearly Bought," 138.

90. Cook, "Unfinished Business," 51; "JDK Aides Act in Negro Centennial Snub," *Jet*, September 27, 1962, 3.

91. Blight, *Race and Reunion*, 15.

92. Cook, "Unfinished Business," 49.

93. Sundquist, "From Antislavery to Civil Rights," 417.

94. Bennett, "Frederick Douglass," 51.

95. Ibid., 52.

96. Carby, *Race Men*.

97. In the final three months of 1963 and the first month of 1964, Ebony published in excess of fifty letters from readers relating either to specific articles in the Emancipation Proclamation special or to the issue more generally.

98. "Letters to the Editor," *Ebony*, November 1963, 12–14; "Letters to the Editor," *Ebony*, December 1963, 20–22; "Letters to the Editor," *Ebony*, January 1964, 16.

Chapter 3. White Problems and the Roots of Black Power

1. *"Ebony* Magazine, 1945–1965," box 2, Burns Papers.

2. "Backstage," *Ebony*, November 1964, 28.

3. "Letters to the Editor," *Ebony*, January 1964, 16; Johnson and Johnson, *Propaganda and Aesthetics*, 167.

4. "Ten Negroes," box 150, folder 1, Barnett Papers.

5. Horne, *Fire This Time*; Jacobs, *Race, Media and the Crisis of Civil Society*.

6. Reed, *Black Chicago's First Century*, 28.

7. Bennett, "Negro Who Founded Chicago," *Ebony*, December 1963, 172.

8. Morrison, "Negroes Who Fought at Bunker Hill," *Ebony*, February 1964, 44–53.

9. "Research Notes," Foster Papers, University of Southern Mississippi.

10. "John Scobell—Union Spy in Civil War," *Ebony*, December 1963, 135–45.

11. "Letters to the Editor," *Ebony*, February 1964, 17.

12. "Africa's Golden Past," *Ebony*, October 1964, 28.

13. Jesse Zimmerman, "A Secretary of Peace," *The Crisis*, April 1950, 214.

14. Bennett, "Pioneers in Protest," *Ebony*, March 1964, 51.

15. Bennett, "Pioneers in Protest," *Ebony*, October 1964, 64.

16. Bennett, "Pioneer in Protest," 148–49.

17. "Letters to the Editor," *Ebony*, June 1964, 16; "Letters to the Editor," *Ebony*, July 1964, 16.

18. Bennett, "Pioneers in Protest," *Ebony*, June 1964, 76.

19. "Letters to the Editor," *Ebony*, June 1965, 18.

20. Alex Poinsett, "School Segregation Up North," *Ebony*, June 1962, 89–98; Fuller, "Earl B. Dickerson: Warrior and Statesman," *Ebony*, December 1961, 150–54; Bennett, "North's Hottest Fight For Integration," *Ebony*, March 1962, 31–38; "Civil Rights Battle: Northern Style," *Ebony*, March 1963, 96–102; Morrison, "Top Woman Civil Rights Lawyer," *Ebony*, January 1963, 50–58.

21. Bennett, "The Mood of the Negro," *Ebony*, July 1963, 27.

22. "Editor of Ebony Reproves Churches and Militants," *The Sun*, September 16, 1963, 17.

23. "'Before the Mayflower' Author in Panel Talk," *Jet*, June 6, 1963, 41.

24. Cohen, *Howard Zinn's Southern Diary*, 162.

25. Bennett, *Confrontation*; Bennett, *Negro Mood*; Sewell and Dwight, *Mississippi Black History Makers*, 279; Hurt, "Fruit of Little Meanness," 41.

26. "The Confrontation," *Chicago Daily Defender*, August 26, 1965, 17.

27. "Books Noted," *Negro Digest*, January 1965, 79.

28. Clarke, "Lerone Bennett," 489.

29. Josh MacPhee, "Power, Fists, Guns, Books: Black Power and Book Cover Design," *Paper*, June 13, 2016; Nat Hentoff, "Message for Whitey," *New York Times*, February 27, 1966.

30. Bennett, "Mood of the Negro," 27.

31. Lumpkins, *American Pogrom*; Godshalk, *Veiled Visions*.

32. Thernstrom and Thernstrom, *America in Black and White*; Hirsch, *Making the Second Ghetto*.

33. Flamm, *In the Heat of the Summer*, 10–11.

34. Ron Grossman, "The Gin Bottle Race Riot," *Chicago Tribune*, November 25, 2014.

35. "Racial Demonstrations Take Heavy Toll on Juke Boxes," *Billboard*, August 15, 1964, 41.

36. Quoted in Flamm, *In the Heat of the Summer*, 2.

37. Bennett, *Negro Mood*, 45.

38. "*Ebony*'s Bennett Predicts Unrest in Chapel Speech," *Daily Orange*, March 3, 1965, JPC Clippings Collection.

39. Horne, *Fire This Time*, 54–58; Stevens, *Radical L.A.*, 307.

40. Jacobs, *Race, Media*, 54–56.

41. Art Berman, "Looting Spreads! City Block Afire," *Los Angeles Times*, August 14, 1965.

42. "Out of a Cauldron of Hate—Arson and Death," *Life*, August 27, 1965, 20.

43. Don Moser, "There's No Easy Place to Pin the Blame," *Life*, August 27, 1965, 31.

44. Jacobs, *Race, Media*, 56.

45. Johnson, "Publisher's Statement," *Ebony*, August 1965, 27.

46. Ibid., 27.

47. Almena Lomax, "Political What-Not," *Los Angeles Tribune*, October 30, 1959.

48. Scott, *Contempt and Pity*, 1.

49. Myrdal, *American Dilemma*.

50. Nakayama and Martin, "White Problem," 111.

51. Killens, "The Black Man's Burden," *Ebony*, August 1965, 173.

52. Bennett, "The WHITE Problem in America," *Ebony*, August 1965, 29.

53. "Ten Best Cities for Negro Employment," *Ebony*, March 1965, 118.

54. Dallek, *Right Moment*, 137.

55. May, *Golden State, Golden Youth*, 158; Don Moser, "There's No Easy Place to Pin the Blame," *Life*, August 27, 1965, 31.

56. Gilyard, *John Oliver Killens*, 211.

57. Ponchitta Pierce, "Crime in the Suburbs" *Ebony*, August 1965, 167–69.

58. Atwater, "Editorial Policy of *Ebony*," 90.

59. Eddie Ellis, "Is *Ebony* a Negro Magazine?" *Liberator*, October 1965, 4–5, and November 1965, 18–19.

60. "Letters to the Editor," *Ebony*, October 1965, 10–18; "Letters to the Editor," *Ebony*, November 1965, 16–18.

61. Johnson, "Publisher's Statement," *Ebony*, November 1965, 27.

62. "From Materialism to Militancy," *Philadelphia Tribune*, December 4, 1965; "*Ebony* Magazine, 1945–1965," box 2, folder 2, Burns Papers.

63. "Felicitations to *Ebony*," *The Crisis*, December 1965, 621.

64. "*Ebony* Magazine, 1945–1965," box 2, folder 2, Burns Papers.

65. Bennett, "SNCC: Rebels with a Cause," *Ebony*, July 1965, 146.

66. Hamilton Bims, "CORE: Wild Child of Civil Rights," *Ebony*, October 1965, 35.

67. Bennett, "SNCC: Rebels with a Cause," 146.

68. Joseph, *Stokely*, 101.

69. Jeffries, *Bloody Lowndes*, 103–4.

70. Bennett, "Black Power, Part I," *Ebony*, November 1965, 28.

71. Ibid., 38.

72. Bennett, "Black Part, Part III," *Ebony*, January 1966, 119.

73. Du Bois, *Black Reconstruction in America*.

74. Foner, *Reconstruction*, xviii.

75. Ibid., xix.

76. Bennett, "Black Power, Part II," *Ebony*, December 1965, 51.

77. Van Deburg, *New Day in Babylon*, 2.

78. X, *End of White World Supremacy*, 26.

79. Harding, "Power from Our People," 46.

80. Thorpe, *Black Historians*, 18.

81. Bennett, "Black Power, Part III," 122.

82. Bennett, "Black Power, Part V," *Ebony*, April 1966, 121.

83. Bennett, "Black Power, Part II," *Ebony*, December 1965, 59.

84. "Backstage," *Ebony*, May 1966, 26.

85. Joseph, *Waiting 'til the Midnight Hour*, 132–41.

86. Ogbar, *Black Power*, 61–62.

87. Goudsouzian, *Down to the Crossroads*, 143.

88. Joseph, *Waiting 'til the Midnight Hour*, 137.

89. Joseph, *Stokely*, 116.

90. Ogbar, *Black Power*, 75.

91. "An Ominous Cloud Shadows the March towards Equality," *Courier-Journal*, July 7, 1966; "Black Power Issue Splits Civil Righters," *Columbus Dispatch*, July 10, 1966; "Negro Chief Assails Call for 'Black Power,'" *New York Post*, July 6, 1966; "Negro Cry: 'Black Power!'—What Does It Mean?" *U.S News and World Report*, July 11, 1966; "Power Militants Blacken a Hot Summer," *Miami Herald*, July 17, 1966, JPC Clippings Collection.

92. "Black Power," *New York Times*, July 10, 1966.

93. "Panther on the Prowl," *Chicago Sun-Times*, July 24 1966, JPC Clippings Collection.

94. Dennis Hevesi, "Claude Sitton, 89, Acclaimed Civil Rights Reporter," *New York Times*, March 10, 2015.

95. Roberts and Klibanoff, *Race Beat*, 395–407.

96. Roy Wilkins, "Wilkins Speaks," *Afro-American*, June 11, 1966, 4; Nicholas von Hoffman, "Black Power Called Racism By Humphrey," *Washington Post*, July 7, 1966.

97. Joseph, *Waiting 'til the Midnight Hour*, 146–47.

98. Carmichael, *Ready for Revolution*, 507.

99. Williams, *Concrete Demands*, 2–3.

100. Ibid., 59.

101. Carl Rowan, "Has Paul Robeson Betrayed the Negro?" *Ebony*, October 1957, 33.

102. Bennett, "Black Power, Part VI," *Ebony*, July 1966, 58.

103. "McKissick Defines Black Power," *Chicago Daily Defender*, July 11, 1966, 5.

104. Bennett, "Stokely Carmichael: Architect of Black Power," *Ebony*, September 1966, 25.

105. Ibid., 25–26.

106. "Letters to the Editor," *Ebony*, December 1966, 16; Young, "The Big Beat," *Los Angeles Sentinel*, December 1, 1966.

107. Bennett, "Stokely Carmichael," 26.

108. "Black Power Must Be Defined," *Life*, July 22, 1966, 4.

109. Joseph, *Stokely*, 126.

110. Goudsouzian, *Down to the Crossroads*, 156.

111. Bennett, "Stokely Carmichael," 27.

112. Ibid.

113. Joseph, *Stokely*, 126.

114. Bennett, "Black Power, Part V," *Ebony*, April 1966, 121.

115. Bennett, "Stokely Carmichael," 25.

116. Ibid., 26.

117. King, "Nonviolence: The Only Road to Freedom," *Ebony*, October 1966, 27; Rowan, "Crisis in Civil Rights Leadership," *Ebony*, November 1966, 27.

118. King's radicalization during the later years of his life will be discussed more in chapter 6. Harding, *Martin Luther King*, vii–ix.

119. King, "Nonviolence," 28.

120. Rowan, "Crisis in Civil Rights Leadership," 27.

121. Bennett, "Black Power Part VII," 152.

122. Bennett, "Black Power Part III," 122.

123. William Price, "Negroes Division over Black Power Widens," National Guardian, October 22, 1955, 5.

124. Bennett, "Black Power, Part VIII," *Ebony*, December 1966, 146.

125. "Letters to the Editor," *Ebony*, January 1967, 10.

126. Brown, "Souled Out," 108.

127. Howard Meyer, "One Jew Looks at Black Power," *The Negro* 41 (1966); "Negro Editor Blames Whites for Racism," *Boston Globe*, November 13, 1966.

128. Bennett, "Stokely Carmichael," 28.

129. Bennett, "The Rise of Black Power," *Ebony*, February 1969, 36; Carmichael and Hamilton, *Black Power*, 219; "Lerone Bennett, Jr. to Josephine Baker, 14 October 1970," box 5, Bennett Jr. Papers.

130. Pohlmann, *African American Political Thought*, 165.

131. Carmichael, "Speech at Garfield High School, Seattle, Washington, 1967."

132. Rodgers, "Is Ebony Killing Black Women?" *Liberator*, May 1966, 12–13; Stone, *Black Political Power in America*, 9.

133. "White Power," *Washington Post*, October 27, 1966; "Rowan Calls 'Black Power' Phony Cry," *Chicago Daily Defender*, November 7, 1966; Averill, "Drop in White Backing Jolts Negroes." *Boston Globe*, October 12, 1966, 1, 3; Young, "The Big Beat," *Los Angeles Sentinel*, December 1 1966; "Carl T. Rowan Claims Black Power Is Hoax," *Philadelphia Tribune*, November 5, 1966.

134. "Carl T. Rowan Claims 'Black Power' Is a Hoax."

135. "Letters to the Editor," *Ebony*, June 1966, 12.

136. "Letters to the Editor," *Ebony*, March 1966, 14.

137. "Letters to the Editor," *Ebony*, November 1966, 13; "Letters to the Editor," *Ebony*, December 1966, 18.

138. "Letters to the Editor," *Ebony*, June 1966, 12.

139. "Letters to the Editor," *Ebony*, December 1966, 16.

140. "Letters to the Editor," *Ebony*, November 1966, 13.

141. Bennett, "Black Power, Part IX," *Ebony*, January 1967, 114.

142. "BLACK POWER," *Ebony*, December 1967, 117.

Chapter 4. Learning Is an All-Black Thing

1. Burroughs, "Ebony," 119.

2. West, "Power Is 100 Years Old."

3. Johnson, "Publisher's Statement," *Ebony*, August 1968, 29.

4. "*Ebony* 1945–1965," box 2, folder 2, Burns Papers; "*Ebony* in the Classroom," *Ebony*, February 1971, 92.

5. "A Matter of Pride," *Ebony*, January 1972, 121.

6. Van Deburg, *New Day in Babylon*, 280.

7. Rickford, *We Are an African People*, 35; Biondi, *Black Revolution on Campus*.

8. Fenderson, "Journey toward a Black Aesthetic," 44.

9. "John H. Johnson," tape 7, The History Makers.

10. "Top Leaders, Writers, and Editors," box 150, folder 1, Barnett Papers; Dagbovie, "History as a Core Subject Area," 602; Tinson, "Held in Trust," 182.

11. "What Is the Institute of the Black World?" box 36, Bennett, Jr. Papers.

12. "Ruby Lawson to Lerone Bennett, October 9, 1968," box 4, Bennett Papers.

13. "Lerone Bennett, Jr.," box 36, Bennett, Jr. Papers.

14. Duberman, *Howard Zinn*, 73.

15. "Great Negro Thinkers of History," *Ebony*, October 1946, 38.

16. Zimmerman, *Whose America?* 113.

17. Ibid., 114.

18. "NAACP to Launch Drive against Biased Textbooks," *Jet*, July 28, 1966, 55.

19. "JPC Book Division," *Ebony*, February 1967, 41.

20. Hubert Humphrey, "Closing America's History Gap," *Negro Digest*, February 1967, 7.

21. Zimmerman, *Whose America?* 115.

22. Bennett, "The Negro in Textbooks," *Ebony*, March 1967, 130.

23. Charles Harrison, "Black History and the Schools," *Ebony*, December 1968, 111.

24. "Wilmington Finds an Answer," *Ebony*, July 1965, 57–68; "That They Might Learn," *Ebony*, March 1965, 93–98; Poinsett, "Thirteen Years after 1954," *Ebony*, April 1967, 76.

25. Poinsett, "School Segregation Up North," *Ebony*, July 1962, 89; Charles Sanders, "Playing Hooky for Freedom," *Ebony*, April 1964, 153.

26. Poinsett, "Ghetto Schools: An Educational Wasteland," *Ebony*, August 1967, 52.

27. Johnson, "Publisher's Statement," *Ebony*, August 1967, 21.

28. "Letters to the Editor," *Ebony*, May 1967; "Letters to the Editor," *Ebony*, June 1967, 19.

29. "*Ebony*, 1945–1965," box 2, folder 2, Burns Papers.

30. "Backstage," *Ebony*, October 1970, 30.

31. "Letters to the Editor," *Ebony*, October 1972, 19.

32. "Backstage," *Ebony*, May 1975, 30.

33. "*Ebony* in the Classroom," *Ebony*, October 1974, 177.

34. "*Ebony* in the Classroom," *Ebony*, February 1971, 92; Garvey, *Writing with Scissors*, 131.

35. Larry Finley, "Teacher Helped Neediest Kids," *Chicago Sun-Times*, March 7, 2007.

36. "Teacher Authors Children's Textbook," *Jet*, November 15, 1973, 25.

37. "Editor's Note," *Ebony*, July 1967, 15; "Famous Negroes of the Past," MSS 1040, box 3, Woodson Papers.

38. "Publisher's Statement," *Ebony Jr.*, May 1973, 4; Henderson, *Ebony Jr!* 3–4.

39. "Backstage," *Ebony*, June 1969, 27.

40. "The Negro Handbook," *Ebony*, May 1967, 105.

41. "Pictorial History of Black America," *Ebony*, June 1975, 49.

42. "Pictorial History," *Ebony*, November 1971, 45.

43. "The *Ebony* Bookshop," *Ebony*, June 1970, 101.

44. "Are You Reading Him?" *Ebony*, October 1967, 110.

45. Johnson, "Publisher's Statement," *Ebony*, August 1968, 29.

46. "John H. Johnson," tape 7, The History Makers.

47. "Was Lincoln Anti-Negro?" *Ebony*, February 1948, 48.

48. Bennett, "Ten Most Dramatic Events in Negro History," 31; Quarles, *Lincoln and the Negro*; Mike Quigley, "Carl Sandburg," *Ebony*, September 1963, 158.

49. Bennett, "Was Abe Lincoln a White Supremacist?" 37.

50. Ibid., 42.

51. Bennett, *Before the Mayflower*; Bennett, *What Manner of Man*.

52. Bennett, *Forced Into Glory*; Schaub, "Learning to Love Lincoln," 97–98; Painter, "Our Kind of Historian," box 12, Bennett Papers; James McPherson, "Lincoln the Devil," *New York Times*, August 27, 2000.

53. Fredrickson, *Big Enough to Be Inconsistent*, 2–3.

54. Barr, "Holding Up," 44.

55. "Backstage," *Ebony*, February 1968, 22; Schwartz, *Abraham Lincoln*, 166.

56. Herbert Mitgang, "Was Lincoln Just a Honkie?" *New York Times*, February 11, 1968.

57. Carson, *In Struggle*, 256.

58. Mitgang, "Was Abraham Lincoln Just a Honkie?"

59. Painter, "Our Kind of Historian," box 12, Bennett Papers.

60. Bennett, "In Search of the Real Lincoln," *New York Times*, March 3, 1968.

61. Ibid.

62. Mitgang, "The Time, the Place, the Man," *New York Times*, March 17, 1968.

63. Zilversmit, "Lincoln," 5; Barr, "Holding Up," 48.

64. Guelzo, *Lincoln's Emancipation Proclamation*, 247.

65. Lester, *Look Out Whitey!* 58.

66. Fehrenbacher, *Lincoln*, 100.

67. Styron, *Confessions of Nat Turner*.

68. Quoted in Thelwell, "Mr. William Styron," 391.

69. Jess Row, "Styron's Choice," *New York Times*, September 5, 2008.

70. Clarke, *William Styron's Nat Turner*.

71. Williams, "William Styron," 189.

72. "John Henrik Clarke to Lerone Bennett, 26 July 1968," box 2, Bennett Papers.

73. Bennett, "The Case against Styron's *Nat Turner*," *Ebony*, October 1968, 148.

74. Ibid., 149.

75. Eugene Genovese, "The Nat Turner Case," *New York Review of Books*, September 12, 1968.

76. Black nationalist outrage at this suggestion was not dissimilar to the response of some activists to Manning Marable's portrayal of Malcolm X in his 2011 study *Malcolm X: A Life of Reinvention*. Ball and Burroughs, *A Lie of Reinvention*; Williams, "William Styron," 191.

77. Washington, "Lerone Bennett, Jr.," Bennett, Jr. Papers.

78. Jess Row, "Styron's Choice," *New York Times*, September 5, 2008.

79. "Letters to the Editor," *Ebony*, April 1968, 14.

80. Danns, *Something Better*, 96.

81. Rickford, *We Are an African People*, 3.

82. Poinsett, "Battle over Control of Ghetto Schools," *Ebony*, May 1969, 44; Jack Slater, "Learning Is an All-Black Thing," *Ebony*, September 1971, 88.

83. Franklin, *Mirror to America*, 167.

84. Robert Malson, "The Black Power Rebellion at Howard," *Negro Digest*, December 1967, 22.

85. Nathan Hare, "The Black College Revolt," *Ebony*, August 1967, 60.

86. Bennett, "What's In a Name?" *Ebony*, November 1967, 47.

87. Rogers, *Black Campus Movement*, 29.

88. Biondi, *Black Revolution on Campus*, 1.

89. Bennett, "Confrontation on Campus," *Ebony*, May 1968, 27.

90. Ibid., 28.

91. "State-Wide Battle on Illinois Jim Crow," *The Crisis*, February 1937, 43.

92. Pridmore, *Northwestern University*, 213.

93. Biondi, *Black Revolution on Campus*, 82.

94. Pridmore, *Northwestern University*, 217.

95. Biondi, *Black Revolution on Campus*, 82–84.

96. Pridmore, *Northwestern University*, 217.

97. Ibid., 222.

98. Biondi, *Black Revolution on Campus*, 94.

99. "Robert Strotz to Lerone Bennett, 7 November 1968," box 6, Bennett Papers.

100. "Lerone Bennett," box 1, Bennett Papers.

101. Fredrickson, *Black Image*.

102. "Directory," box 6, Bennett Papers.

103. "Lerone Bennett to John Johnson, 7 October 1968," box 6, Bennett Papers.

104. "History CO1–1 Book List," box 6, Bennett Papers; "History Co1-1 Syllabus," box 6, Bennett Papers.

105. Biondi, *Black Revolution on Campus*, 94.

106. "Making Black Power Work," box 6, Bennett Papers.

107. "C. Eric Lincoln to Lerone Bennett, 13 March 1969," box 6, Lerone Papers.

108. For a concise history of the Institute see White, *Challenge of Blackness*.

109. "Bennett Sees Our Saviors," *Afro-American*, October 25, 1969, 9.

110. Bennett, "The First Generation," *Ebony*, June 1969, 31.

111. Bennett, "Of Time, Space, and Revolution," *Ebony*, August 1969, 31.

112. Ibid., 31.

113. Schmidtz and Goodin, *Social Welfare*, 103–4.

114. "Ten Negroes," box 150, folder 1, Barnett Papers.

115. Kasisi Jitu Weusi, "Around Our Way," *Black News*, January 1, 1973, 13.

116. "John Woodford to JPC," box 15, Fuller Papers.

117. Brown, "Souled Out," 4.

118. Fenderson, "Journey toward a Black Aesthetic," 44.

119. Fuller, "Editor's Notes," *Black World*, May 1970, 4.

120. Smethurst, *Black Arts Movement*, 208.

121. "Backstage," *Ebony*, August 1969, 26.

122. Brown, "Souled Out," 115–16; Collins, *Seventh Child*, 177; "Backstage," *Ebony*, February 1974, 32.

123. "Backstage," *Ebony*, August 1969, 26.

124. Johnson, "Publishers Statement," *Ebony*, August 1969, 29.

125. Ibid.

126. David Llorens, "Amiri (LeRoi Jones) Baraka," *Ebony*, August 1969, 75; Huey P. Newton, "The Black Panthers," *Ebony*, August 1969, 107; Larry Neal, "Any Day Now," *Ebony*, August 1969, 54.

127. Brown, "Souled Out," 118.

128. James Turner, "Black Students and their Changing Perspective," *Ebony*, August 1969, 135.

129. Harding, "Black Students and the 'Impossible' Revolution," *Ebony*, August 1969, 143.

130. Ogbar, *Black Power*, 241.

131. White, *Challenge of Blackness*, xiv

132. Turner, "Africana Studies and Epistemology, 92.

133. White, *Challenge of Blackness*, 20.

134. "Black Paper No. 1," box 2, Bennett Papers; McClendon, "Act Your Age," 281.

135. "The Challenge of Blackness," box 2, Bennett Papers; "Institute of the Black World Memo, 8 December 1969," box 2, Bennett Papers.

136. Poinsett, "Think Tank for Black Scholars," *Ebony*, February 1970, 46.

137. Harding, "Toward the Black University, Part I," *Ebony*, August 1970, 156.

138. Bennett, "Liberation," *Ebony*, August 1970, 36.

139. Henderson, "Toward the Black University, Part II," *Ebony*, September 1970, 108.

140. "Hoyt Fuller to John Johnson, 15 April 1970," box 21, folder 17, Hoyt Fuller Papers; "Hoyt Fuller to John Johnson, 30 April 1970," box 21, folder 17, Hoyt Fuller Papers; "John Johnson to Hoyt Fuller, 30 April 1970," box 21, folder 17, Hoyt Fuller Papers.

141. "Hoyt Fuller to IBW Staff, 1 August 1970," box 21, folder 17, Fuller Papers; Vincent Harding to Hoyt Fuller and Lerone Bennett, 16 September 1970," box 21, folder 17, Fuller Papers.

142. "Hoyt Fuller to John Johnson, 9 July 1971," box 16, folder 22, Fuller Papers.

143. "Editor's Note," *Negro Digest*, March 1969, 4.

144. "Roosevelt Adams to Lerone Bennett, 25 October 1973," box 1, Bennett Papers; "The Black University, Pt. 1," *Negro Digest*, March 1968; "The Black University, Pt. 2," *Negro Digest*, March 1968; "The Black University, Pt. 3," *Negro Digest*, March 1970.

145. Sellers with Terrell, *River of No Return*, 260.

146. Downs, *Cornell '69*, 100.

147. David Llorens, "Black Don Lee," *Ebony*, March 1969, 74; Downs, *Cornell '69*, 129.

148. "Editor's Notes," *Negro Digest*, March 1969, 4.

149. "Vincent Harding to Lerone Bennett, 5 March 1972," box 5, Bennett, Jr. Papers; "Visitor Turns To Boss," box 6, Bennett Papers.

150. Biondi, *Black Revolution on Campus*, 97.

151. "Raymond Mack to Lerone Bennett, 9 December 1971," box 6, Bennett Papers.

152. Biondi, *Black Revolution on Campus*, 94.

153. "Lerone Bennett to Raymond Mack, 20 January 1972," box 6, Bennett, Jr. Papers.

154. Ibid.

155. "Backstage," *Ebony*, April 1972, 28.

156. Johnson, "Publishers Statement," *Ebony*, August 1968, 29.

157. "Chair at NU to Bennett," *Chicago Defender*, March 2, 1972, 10.

158. "NU Blacks Like Choice of Bennett," box 6, Bennett Papers.

159. Biondi, *Black Revolution on Campus*, 99.

160. "Resignation Letter, Undated," box 6, Bennett Papers.

161. Biondi, *Black Revolution on Campus*, 100.

162. "NW Students to Lerone Bennett, undated," box 5, Bennett, Jr. Papers.

163. Biondi, *Black Revolution on Campus*, 100; "NW Students to Lerone Bennett, 17 November 1972," box 5, Bennett, Jr. Papers.

164. "Bennett Leaves NU Post," *Chicago Defender*, November 30, 1972, 3; "NU Afro Dept. Torn by Open Controversy," December 28, 1972, 9.

165. "BU Afro-Center Director, 12 Aides Quite in Dispute," *Boston Globe*, April 6, 1971.

166. Asante, *African American People*, 367.

167. Werner, *A Change Is Gonna Come*, 116.

Chapter 5. We Can Seize the Opportunity

1. Vincent Harding, "Toward the Black University," *Ebony*, August 1970, 108.

2. "A Matter of Pride," *Ebony*, December 1961, 83.

3. "Letters to the Editor," *Ebony*, April 1971, 16.

4. Dagbovie, *What Is African American History?* 1; Rooks, *White Money/Black Power*; Rojas, *From Black Power*.

5. Gibson, *The $30 Billion Negro*, 221.

6. Ford, "Message."

7. Harding, "Power from Our People," 45.

8. John Hope Franklin, "The New Negro History," *The Crisis*, February 1957, 74.

9. Zimmerman, *Whose America?* 113.

10. Rocksborough-Smith, *Black Public History in Chicago*, 69.

11. Cook, "Unfinished Business," 49.

12. Harris, "Coming of Age," 108.

13. Meier and Rudwick, *Black History*, 161.

14. "To Establish a National Commission on Negro History and Culture," Ninetieth Congress, Second Session, March 18, 1968.

15. Wilson, *Negro Building*, 270.

16. Hubert H. Humphrey, "Closing America's History Gap," *Negro Digest*, February 1967, 5.

17. "To Establish a National Commission," 2.

18. Zelizer, *Kerner Report*, 384.

19. "Lerone Bennett Testimony to Kerner Commission," box 6, Bennett Papers.

20. Rickford, *We Are An African People*, 1–2.

21. Valerie Jo Bradley, "New Surge in Afro-American History," *Jet*, February 20, 1969, 46.

22. Biondi, *Black Revolution on Campus*, 211–13.

23. Delmont, *Making Roots*.

24. Bradley, "New Surge."

25. "Acknowledgements," *Life*, December 13, 1968, 93; Roger Butterfield, "Search for a Black Past," *Life*, November 22, 1968, 90; "Scholar, Traveler, Orchidologist," *Life*, November 22, 1968, 3.

26. "Backstage," *Ebony*, July 1961, 22.

27. Chambers, *Madison Avenue*, 74.

28. "Leading Firms Getting on Negro History Bandwagon," *Chicago Defender*, December 31, 1966, 21; Gibson, *$30 Billion Negro*, 221.

29. "John Hope Franklin to William Payne, 22 December 1964," box W25, Franklin Papers; "To Introduce 'Adventures in Negro History,'" box W25, Franklin Papers; Marable, *How Capitalism*, 160.

30. "Chicago Premiere," box W25, Franklin Papers.

31. "To Introduce 'Adventures in Negro History,'" box W25, Franklin Papers.

32. Weems, *Desegregating the Dollar*, 53.

33. "Clarence Holte's Search into the Past," *Ebony*, April 1970, 95.

34. The spread of "Soul" advertising is one example of how corporate efforts to woo black consumers were often fraught with cultural assumptions and racial biases. Chambers, *Madison Avenue*, 93.

35. Gibson, *$30 Billion Negro*, 227.

36. "Ingenious Americans," *Ebony*, March 1967, 133.

37. "Seagram," *Ebony*, February 1969, 11.

38. "Seagram," *Ebony*, November 1969, 122.

39. "*Seagram Spotlight*, Fall 1968," Seagram Collection; "*Seagram Spotlight*, Fall 1970," Seagram Collection.

40. "Seagram Press Release, 1972," Seagram Collection; "Seagram," *Ebony*, December 1971, 135.

41. Wright, *Critical Reflections*, 17.

42. Harris, "Coming of Age," 108.

43. Rooks, *Ladies' Pages*, 140–41; Walker, *Style and Status*, 93–94.

44. Lewis, *Man from Essence*, 104.

45. Gross, *Forbes*, 154.

46. Johnson, "Publishers Statement," *Ebony*, August 1970, 33.

47. Fischer, *America*, 349.

48. Springer, *Living for The Revolution*; Spencer, *Revolution Has Come*; Farmer, *Remaking Black Power*.

49. Baraka, quoted in Marable, *How Capitalism*, 97.

50. Tinson, *Radical Intellect*, 97.

51. Angela Davis, "Rhetoric vs. Reality," *Ebony*, July 1971, 115.

52. "Cover," *Ebony*, August 1969, 4.

53. Helen King, "The Black Woman and Women's Lib," *Ebony*, March 1971, 68; Carol Morton, "Mistakes Black Men Make Relating to Black Women," *Ebony*, December 1975, 170; "Black Women/Black Men: Has Something Gone Wrong between Them?" *Ebony*, August 1977, 160; "The War between the Sexes," *Ebony*, June 1979, 33

54. "Letters to the Editor," *Ebony*, May 1971, 20.

55. Russell, "Color of Discipline," 113.

56. Johnson and Henderson, "Introduction," 4.

57. "Amiri Baraka to Eunice Johnson cc. John H. Johnson, 7 March 1973," box 15, folder 20, Fuller Papers; West, "I See Enough Queers."

58. Wiese, *Places of Their Own*, 2.

59. Mark Lowery, "The Rise of the Black Professional Class," *Black Enterprise*, August 1995, 44.

60. Toliver, *Black Families*, 7–8.

61. Poinsett, "Computer Tutors for Ghetto Pupils," *Ebony*, December 1967, 91.

62. "A Challenge to Youth," *Ebony*, August 1967, 144.

63. Ibid.

64. Gordon, "Take Amtrak," 55.

65. The term "post–civil rights" has been used widely (and with various degrees of critical engagement) in reference to the period following the passage of major federal civil rights legislation during the 1960s. Smith, *Racism*; Iton, *Black Fantastic*; Bonilla-Silva, *White Supremacy*.

66. "Annual Vacation Guide," *Ebony*, June 1966, 39; "Annual Vacation Guide," *Ebony*, June 1968, 186.

67. "Annual Vacation Guide," *Ebony,* June 1969, 148

68. "Go Back Home for Your 1974 Vacation," *Ebony*, May 1974, 142.

69. "Annual Vacation Guide," *Ebony*, June 1972, 176.

70. Wu, *Frederick Douglass*, 4.

71. "A Share in the Life of Frederick Douglass," *Ebony*, June 1972, 76.

72. "Exploring the Past," box 36, Bennett, Jr. Papers.

73. "Harding to Bennett, 5 March 1972," box 5, Bennett, Jr. Papers.

74. "On the Conference Beat," *Negro Digest*, July 1967, 91.

75. "Exploring the Past," box 36, Bennett, Jr. Papers.

76. Clarke, "Shapes of the Black American Past," 213.

77. Bennett, *Shaping of Black America*, preface.

78. Bennett, "The First Generation," *Ebony*, June 1969, 32.

79. Bennett, "White Servitude in America," *Ebony*, November 1969, 31.

80. Carmichael and Hamilton, *Black Power*, 5.

81. Watkins, *Black Power, Yellow Power*, 6–7.

82. "William Taylor to Lerone Bennett, Jr., 5 October 1971," box 5, Bennett, Jr. Papers.

83. Johnson and Johnson, *Propaganda and Aesthetics*, 167; Tinson, *Radical Intellect*.

84. Robinson, *Black Marxism*.

85. Bennett, "System," *Ebony*, April 1972, 33; Bennett, "The Black Worker," *Ebony*, July 1972, 110; Bennett, "Black Bourgeoisie Reconsidered," *Ebony*, August 1973, 53.

86. "It's Good to Be Home Again," *Ebony*, August 1971, 66; Garland, "Atlanta—Mecca of the South," *Ebony*, August 1971, 152.

87. "Voices of the South," *Ebony*, August 1971, 1965.

88. Bennett, "Old Illusions and New Souths," *Ebony*, August 1971, 37.

89. Churchill and Wall, *Agents of Repression*; Joseph, *Stokely*.

90. Haas, *Assassination of Fred Hampton*.

91. Poinsett, "Black Power in State Governments," *Ebony*, April 1972, 94.

92. "Vice Pres., EBONY Editor Help Pres. Nixon Launch 45th Negro History Week," *Jet*, February 25, 1971.

93. Zimmerman, *Whose America?* 126.

94. Quoted in Mattson, *What the Heck Are You Up To?* x.

95. Hixson, *Historical Memory*, 306–7.

96. Rymsza-Pawlowska, *History Comes Alive*, 39; Weems, *Business in Black and White*.

97. Zaretsky, *No Direction Home*, 144.

98. Bodnar, *Remaking America*, 228.

99. "Black Bicentennial Exhibit," *New York Times*, September 30, 1973; "Black Museum Backed for Bicentennial," *New York Times*, March 19, 1975; "Philadelphia 76 Board, 9 April 1976," box 5, Bennett, Jr. Papers.

100. Margot Hornblower, "No Frills at this Party," *Washington Post*, May 8, 1975.

101. Sugrue, *Origins of the Urban Crisis*, 269.

102. "Black Woman to Head Detroit Bicentennial," *Jet*, April 4, 1974, 30; Longo, "Remembering the Renaissance City," 89.

103. "Urban League Pays Bicentennial Tribute to Black Americans," *New York Times*, May 17, 1976. Nunn linked these concerns to the tiny percentage of black park superintendents. "Bicentennial Unit To Be Increased," *Afro-American*, September 23, 1972, 17; "Park Service Bicentennial Plans Lagging on Minority Involvement," *Afro-American*, July 19, 1975, 1.

104. Donald Janson, "Black Dissent and High Cost Snag Philadelphia Bicentennial Plans," *New York Times*, November 14, 1970; "Minorities Fight Plan for 1976 Bicentennial Fair," *New York Times*, January 10, 1971.

105. Linda Charlton, "Getting a Jump on D.C's Bicentennial," *New York Times*, June 29, 1975.

106. Ford, "Message"; Mayes, *Kwanzaa*, 249.

107. "1976 Black History Week Expanded to Month-Long Bicentennial Celebration," *Jet*, February 5, 1976, 25.

108. Ford, "Message."

109. Zaretsky, *No Direction Home*, 154.

110. Ford, "Message."

111. Ryan, "Re-enacting Independence," 26.

112. "*Ebony* Planning Bicentennial Issue," *Chicago Defender*, August 2, 1975, 7.

113. "Cover," *Ebony*, August 1975, 4.

114. Fowler, *Nikki Giovanni*, 85; Pochmara, *Making of the New Negro*, 9–10.

115. "Letters to the Editor," *Ebony*, December 1975, 20.

116. "Cover," *Ebony*, August 1975, 4.

117. Johnson, "Publisher's Statement," *Ebony*, August 1975, 32.

118. Joseph Jackson, "A Resounding 'Yes!'," *Ebony*, August 1975, 36.

119. Jordan, "A Qualified 'Maybe'," *Ebony*, August 1975, 37.

120. Bennett, "An Adamant 'No'," *Ebony*, August 1975, 40.

121. Ibid., 38.

122. Ibid., 40.

123. Mayes, *Kwanzaa*, 190.

124. "Backstage," *Ebony*, October 1975, 22.

125. "Letters to the Editor," *Ebony*, October 1975, 12–17.

126. Bennett, "An Adamant 'No,'" 40.

127. John S. Johnson, "Why Negroes Buy Cadillacs," *Ebony*, September 1949, 34; Pattillo-McCoy, *Black Picket Fences*, 147.

128. Bims, "Annual Vacation Guide," *Ebony*, May 1976, 80.

129. "National Urban League Address, 1 August 1976," Johnson Publishing Company Clipping Files; "Howard University, 13 October 1975," box 5, Bennett, Jr. Papers; "Bloomsburg State College, 6 January 1976," box 5, Bennett, Jr. Papers; "Chicago Urban League, 11 March 1976," box 5, Bennett, Jr. Papers; "Chicago Black Caucus, 20 March 1976," box 5, Bennett, Jr. Papers; "WNET, 20 November 1975," box 5, Bennett, Jr. Papers; "Black Journal," *Milwaukee Star*, February 26, 1976; "George Mason University, 25 September 1975," box 5, Bennett, Jr. Papers; "Atlanta University Center, 22 September 1975," box 5, Bennett, Jr. Papers.

130. This remark was in response to an invitation to appear in a radio series for Chicago Public Library. Bennett would eventually reverse his decision not to appear, based on reassurances that the series was in no way "conceived to sugar-coat or gloss over historic fact." "Barbara Moro to Lerone Bennett, 4 June 1975," box 5, Bennett, Jr. Papers; "Barbara Moro to Lerone Bennett, 25 August 1975," box 5, Bennett, Jr. Papers.

131. "Speech to ASNLH, 1976," box 2, Bennett Papers.

132. "Photo Standalone 7," *Chicago Defender*, May 8, 1975, 11; "Illinois Bell Telephone Company, 14 May 1975," box 5, Bennett, Jr. Papers.

133. "Bell System," *Ebony*, August 1975, 12.

134. "WNET, 20 November 1975," box 5, Bennett, Jr. Papers; "Black Journal to PBS," box 5, Bennett, Jr. Papers.

135. "American," *Ebony*, February 1976, 101.

136. "United," *Ebony*, June 1975, 107.

137. "Amtrak," *Ebony*, August 1975, 13.

138. Gibson, *$30 Billion Negro*; Gibson, *$70 Billion in the Black*.

139. Gordon, "Take Amtrak," 57.

140. Poinsett, "Where Are the Revolutionaries?" *Ebony*, February 1976, 84.

141. Ibid., 84.

142. "Letters to the Editor," *Ebony*, April 1976, 15; "Letters to the Editor," *Ebony*, May 1976, 16.

143. Fenderson, *Building the Black Arts Movement*; "Ben Burns to John Johnson, 4 December 1970," box 18, Folder 7, Burns Papers.

144. Fenderson, "Journey towards a Black Aesthetic," 218.

145. "Backstage," *Ebony*, May 1976, 22.

146. Fenderson, "Journey Towards A Black Aesthetic," 220–1.

147. B. J. Mason, "A Shift to the Middle," *Ebony*, August 1973, 80.

148. Ellis Cose, "Another Voice Silenced," *Chicago Sun-Times*, March 29, 1976.

149. "Time to Help Black World?" box 2, folder 2, Burns Papers.

Chapter 6. A Hero to Be Remembered

1. Bennett, "Why Black History Is Important to You," *Ebony*, February 1982, 61.

2. Baker, "Critical Memory," 3.

3. "Congressman Conyers Predicts Passage of King Holiday Bill," *Jet*, January 29, 1981, 13.

4. Chappell, *Waking from the Dream.*

5. Hartman, *War for the Soul of America*, 107.

6. "Birthday Celebration for M.L.K.," *Ebony*, March 1981, 126–29.

7. Bennett, "The King Plan for Freedom," *Ebony*, July 1957, 66–67; Ling, *Martin Luther King, Jr.*, 59; Lentz, *Symbols*, 34.

8. "Lerone Bennett to Martin Luther King, Jr., 30 January 1957," box 1, Bennett Papers.

9. Bennett, "The King Plan for Freedom," *Ebony*, July 1956, 66–67; "The Revolt of the Negro Youth," *Ebony*, May 1960, 39; "What Sit-Downs Mean to America," *Ebony*, June 1960, 35; "A Tribune to the Rev. Martin Luther King Jr.," *Ebony*, April 1961, 91.

10. "Lerone Bennett to Maude Ballou, 21 October 1957," box 1, Bennett Papers; "Lerone Bennett to Maude Ballou, 6 December 1957," box 1, Bennett Papers; "Martin Luther King, Jr. to Lerone Bennett, 13 February 1961," box 1, Bennett Papers.

11. "To A. Philip Randolph, 8 November 1958" in *The Papers of Martin Luther King, Jr.: Symbol of the Movement*, 527.

12. Atwater, "Editorial Policy of *Ebony*," 88; King, "My Trip to the Land of Gandhi," *Ebony*, July 1959, 84; King, "A Letter From Birmingham Jail," *Ebony*, August 1963, 23.

13. King, "Advice for Living," *Ebony*, September 1957, 53; "M. L. King Begins New Column in Ebony," box 2, Bennett Papers.

14. "Assorted King columns, undated," box 2, Bennett Papers; Jackson, *From Civil Rights*, 80.

15. Bennett, "From Booker T. to Martin L.," *Ebony*, November 1962, 153, 160.

16. "Current Biography, 2001," box 1, Bennett Papers.

17. Bennett, *What Manner of Man.*

18. "Telegram, 6 May 1965," box 1, Bennett Papers.

19. Johnson and Johnson, *Propaganda and Aesthetics*, 165

20. Joseph, *Waiting 'til the Midnight Hour*, 68; Tinson, *Radical Intellect*, 147–48.

21. "Nobel Prize Winner's Triumph in Europe," *Ebony*, November 1964, 41; "Violence Versus Non-Violence," *Ebony*, April 1965, 168.

22. "A Tribute to Martin Luther King, Jr.," *Ebony*, December 1964, 126.

23. "Letters to the Editor," *Ebony*, February 1967, 15–17.

24. King, "The Un-Christian Christian," *Ebony*, August 1965, 77.

25. King, "Nonviolence: The Only Road to Freedom," *Ebony*, October 1966, 28.

26. "Should Negroes Boycott the Olympics?" *Ebony*, March 1968, 111.

27. West, "The Radical King We Don't Know," xvi.

28. Sokol, *Heavens Might Crack*, 89.

29. Dyson, *I May Not Get There*, 60–62.

30. Mays, *Born to Rebel*, 360.

31. Hartnett and Libby, "Agreement"; Blauner, *Still the Big News*, 34–35.

32. Lentz, *Symbols*, 281.

33. Heitner, *Black Power TV*, 2–4.

34. "New Surge in Afro-American History," 46–48.

35. Roscoe Brown, "The White University Must Respond," *Negro Digest*, March 1969, 29; Harding, "Black Students and the 'Impossible' Revolution," 143.

36. Daynes, *Making Villains*, 51.

37. Garrow, *Bearing the Cross*, 625.

38. Bennett, *The Challenge of Blackness*, 84.

39. White, *The Challenge of Blackness*, 16; "A Monument to a Martyr," *Ebony*, April 1974, 127.

40. Mayes, *Kwanzaa*, 32.

41. Leroy Aarons, "Abernathy Declares King Day," *Washington Post*, January 9, 1970.

42. "What Has Mr. Nixon Ever Really Done for You?" *Ebony*, November 1972, 29; Rhea, *Race Pride*, 114.

43. Edward Walsh, "President Urges King Birthday," *Washington Post*, January 15, 1979.

44. Seay, "A Prophet with Honor?" 242–44.

45. Daynes, *Making Villains*, 135.

46. Broussard, *Ronald Reagan*, 151; Courtwright, *No Right Turn*, 13; Francis Clines, "Reagan's Doubts on Dr. King Disclosed," *New York Times*, October 21, 1983.

47. Chappell, *Waking from the Dream*, 114.

48. Dyson, *I May Not Get There*, 225.

49. "A National Holiday for a King," *Black Enterprise*, January 1984, 21; Robert Pear, "President, Signing Bill, Praises Dr. King," *New York Times*, November 3, 1983.

50. David Hoffman, "King Is Saluted as President Signs Holiday into Law," *Washington Post*, November 3, 1983; "NAACP Hails Passage of King Holiday Bill," *The Crisis*, November 1983, 16.

51. "Backstage," *Ebony*, November 1983, 24; Bebe Moore Campbell, "A National Holiday for King," *Black Enterprise,* January 1984, 21.

52. Reagan, "Remarks," November 2, 1983.

53. Delmont, *Why Busing Failed*; Parker, *Black Votes Count*.

54. Seay, "A Prophet with Honor?" 244.

55. Hall, "Long Civil Rights Movement," 1234.

56. Reagan, "Remarks."

57. Lawson, "Long Origins," 27; Laham, *Reagan Presidency*, 11.

58. "Reagan's Supporters Tried to Woo Blacks Into Fold," *Jet*, November 20, 1980, 8.

59. Marable, "The Black Elite vs. Reaganism," *Afro-American*, October 9, 1982, 5; Ondaatje, *Black Conservative Intellectuals*, 101.

60. "Black America under the Reagan Administration," 27; Lee May, "U.S. Aide's 'Colorblind' Remark Draws Rebuke," *Hartford Courant*, September 13, 1983; Ondaatje, *Black Conservative Intellectuals*, 9; Wolters, *Right Turn*, 218–19.

61. Marable, *How Capitalism*, xxxvi.

62. Bennett, "Have We Overcome?" *Ebony*, November 1979, 33–42; Bennett, "The Second Time Around," *Ebony*, October 1981, 32.

63. Bennett, "Have We Overcome?" 40.

64. "Bennett Addresses Convocation Honoring King at Lincoln University," *Philadelphia Tribune*, January 29, 1980; "Lerone Bennett, Jr., Addresses ASALH's 51st Anniversary Luncheon," *Philadelphia Tribune*, October 24, 1980.

65. Daynes, *Making Villains*, 135; "Bennett Addresses Convocation."

66. Julian Bond, "Martin Luther King: Again a Victim—This Time of History Revised," *Los Angeles Times*, January 14, 1979.

67. "The Passing of the Black Spirit, Dillard University, 14 May 1980," box 2, Bennett Papers.

68. Bennett, "Listen to the Blood," *Ebony*, February 1981, 33.

69. Ibid., 33–34.

70. Ibid., 42.

71. "The Shaping of Black America," box 34, Bennett, Jr. Papers.

72. Bennett, "Listen to the Blood," 38.

73. "Larry Coleman to Lerone Bennett, February 3, 1981," box 34, Bennett, Jr. Papers.

74. Dagbovie, *African American History Reconsidered*, 41.

75. Bennett, "Why Black History Is Important to You," *Ebony*, February 1982, 61.

76. Dagbovie, *African American History Reconsidered*, 40.

77. Bennett, "Why Black History Is Important to You," 66.

78. Bennett, "A Living History," *Ebony*, February 1985, 27.

79. Betty Pleasant, "Reagan MLK Mimicry Invokes Anger, Rebuff," *Los Angeles Sentinel*, July 12, 1984; Althea Simmons, "The Civil Rights Act of 1964 Revisited," *The Crisis*, November 1984, 31; "NAACP Report Card on Reagan Administration Policies," *The Crisis*, April 1984, 167.

80. May, "U.S. Aide's 'Colorblind' Remark Draws Rebuke."

81. "Literary Giants Pay Tribute to Historian-Author Bennett," *Jet*, July 10, 1980, 7.

82. "Statement of Circulation," *Ebony*, December 1986, 23; "Statement of Circulation," *The Crisis*, March 1986, 145; "Statement of Circulation," *Black Enterprise*, January 1986, 18.

83. "Backstage," *Ebony*, March 1985, 24.

84. "Coretta Scott King: Keeping the Dream Alive," *Ebony*, January 1980, 60.

85. Walter Leavy, "A Living Memorial to the Drum Major for Justice," *Ebony*, February 1983, 120.

86. Chappell, *Waking from the Dream*, 62.

87. Robinson, *Disintegration*, 4; "Black on Black Crime," *Ebony*, August 1979; "Blacks and the Money Crunch," *Ebony*, August 1980; "Black Love," *Ebony*, August 1981; "The Black Woman of the '80s," *Ebony*, August 1982; "The Crisis of the Black Male," *Ebony*, August 1983.

88. "Hero to be Remembered," 134.

89. Bennett, "The Crisis of the Black Spirit," *Ebony*, October 1977, 142.

90. Bennett, "The Lost/Found Generation," *Ebony*, August 1978, 35.

91. Marable, "Black Elite vs. Reaganism," 5.

92. Gray, *Cultural Moves*, 186.

93. "*Ebony* interview with Diana Ross," *Ebony*, November 1981, 39.

94. Stephen Gayle, "Commercial Success," *Black Enterprise*, December 1981, 53.

95. Rachel Siegel, "Johnson Publishing Company, the Ex-Publisher of *Ebony* and *Jet* Magazines, Files for Bankruptcy," *Washington Post*, April 10, 2019.

96. "Statement of Ownership," *Ebony*, January 1981, 20; "Statement of Ownership," *Ebony*, December 1990, 145; Earl Graves, "Publisher's Page," *Black Enterprise*, June 1984, 13.

97. "Publishers Statement," *Ebony*, November 1985, 37.

98. Pride and Wilson, *History of the Black Press*, 246.

99. Johnson was less reticent away from the magazine's pages, echoing Bennett's warning that Reagan's policies represented the biggest threat to black civil liberties since Reconstruction. "Are the Promises Being Kept?" *Black Enterprise*, October 1983, 117; "Paving the Way," *Black Enterprise*, February 1985, 119; Thomas Atkins and Michael Sussman, "Reaganisms, Reaganauts and the NAACP," *The Crisis*, Jan. 1982, 4; Alison Muscatine, "UDC Graduates Told to Preserve Civil Rights," *Washington Post*, May 12, 1985; "John H. Johnson," tape 10, The History Makers.

100. Reagan, "Radio Address."

101. Reagan, "Radio Address."

102. Laham, *Reagan Presidency*, 74–75.

103. Howard Kutz, "King Cited in Defense of End to Hiring Goals," *Washington Post*, January 16, 1986.

104. Bennett, "A Living History," *Ebony*, February 1985, 27.

105. Ibid., 28.

106. Patrice Gaines-Carter, "Is My 'Post-Integration' Daughter Black Enough?" *Ebony*, September 1985, 54.

107. "Letters to the Editor," *Ebony*, December 1985, 17.

108. Boyd, *Jim Crow Nostalgia*, 2.

109. "Letters to the Editor," *Ebony*, December 1985, 17.

110. Boyd, *Jim Crow Nostalgia*, 2–3.

111. "Letters to the Editor," *Ebony*, December 1985, 17.

112. "Letters to the Editor," *Ebony*, May 1981, 12.

113. Bennett, "The Real Meaning of the King Holiday," *Ebony*, January 1986, 31.

114. Reagan, "Proclamation 5431—Martin Luther King, Jr. Day, 1986," Reagan Library, January 18, 1986.

115. "The Living King," *Ebony*, January 1986, 62.

116. Dyson, *I May Not Get There*, 28; Fairclough, "Was Martin Luther King a Marxist?" 184.

117. "The Living King," *Ebony*, January 1986, 62.

118. Daynes, *Making Villains*, 51.

119. "In Memory of Martin Luther King, Jr." *Ebony*, January 1986, 64; "The World Honors MLK through Stamps," *Ebony*, January 1986, 82.

120. "Memorable Photos from the King Years," *Ebony*, January 1986, 86.

121. "What Martin Luther King Jr. Means to Me," *Ebony*, January 1986, 74.

122. "The Crusade for a King Holiday," *Ebony*, January 1986, 36.

123. Baker, "Critical Memory," 3.

124. Bennett, "Why Black History," 61.

125. Dagbovie, *African American History Reconsidered*, 203.

126. Ibid., 204.

127. Scott, "Following in the Footsteps," 40.

128. Symcox, *Whose History?* 31.

129. Hartman, *War for the Soul of America*.

130. Craig, *African Americans and Mass Media*, 85; Wilson, *Whither the Black Press?*

131. "Letters to the Editor," *Ebony*, April 1986, 16.

132. "Letters to the Editor," *Ebony*, May 1986, 5.

133. "Letters to the Editor," *Ebony*, April 1986, 18.

134. Dagbovie, *African American History Reconsidered*, 39.

Conclusion

1. "Backstage," *Ebony*, April 1983, 28; "Statement of Ownership, Management and Circulation," *Ebony*, December 1985, 23.

2. "Backstage," *Ebony*, March 1985, 24.

3. "EBONY magazine's 40th Anniversary," E5480.

4. "The *Ebony* interview with John H. Johnson," *Ebony*, November 1985, 58.

5. Harding, "Power from Our People," 49.

6. Snyder, *Making Black History*, 2; Painter, "Our Kind of Historian," box 12, Bennett Papers.

7. "John H. Johnson," tape 7, The History Makers.

8. "John Johnson to Lerone Bennett, Jr., 23 December 1983," box 1, Bennett Papers.

9. Asante, *African American People*, 367; Tinson, "Held in Trust."

10. Dagbovie, *Reconsidering African American History*, 39; Kitch, *Pages from the Past*, 208.

11. "Letters to the Editor," *Ebony*, January 1986, 12.

12. "Letters to the Editor," *Ebony*, February 1986, 17.

13. "Letters to the Editor," *Ebony*, January 1986, 12.

14. Washington, "Lerone Bennett, Jr.," Bennett Jr. Papers.

15. Iton, *Black Fantastic*.

16. "Larry Coleman to Lerone Bennett, 3 February 1981," box 34, Bennett Jr. Papers.

17. "On the Conference Beat," 91.

18. Hanson, "Suppose James Brown," 341.

19. Duberman, *Howard Zinn*, 73.

20. "Charles Sanders to Lerone Bennett, 1971," box 5, Bennett Jr. Papers.

21. Fenderson, "Journey," 44.

22. "John Woodford to JPC," box 15, Fuller Papers.

23. "Exploring the Past/Creating a Future," box 36, Bennett Jr. Papers.

24. Fenderson, *Building the Black Arts Movement*.

25. Bennett, "Chronicles of Black Courage Part I," *Ebony*, November 1982, 44; Bennett, *Wade in the Water*.

26. "Backstage," *Ebony*, October 1987, 29.

27. Kitch, *Pages from the Past*, 91–92.

28. "Memorable Photos from the *Ebony* Files," *Ebony*, December 1984, 122.

29. "Leading Firms Getting on Negro History Bandwagon," *Chicago Defender*, December 31, 1966.

30. Dagbovie, *What Is African American History?* 7; Walker, *Deromanticizing Black History*, xi; Quarles, *Black Mosaic*, 181.

Bibliography

Archival Collections

A. Peter Bailey Collection, Manuscripts, Archives and Rare Book Library, Emory University, Atlanta, Ga.

Alice Browning Papers, Vivian G. Harsh Research Collection, Chicago Public Library, Chicago, Ill.

Allan Morrison Papers, Schomburg Center for Research in Black Culture, New York Public Library, New York, N.Y.

Barbara E. Allen Papers, Vivian G. Harsh Research Collection, Chicago Public Library, Ill.

Ben Burns Papers, Vivian G. Harsh Research Collection, Chicago Public Library, Ill.

Carter G. Woodson Papers, Manuscripts, Archives, and Rare Book Library, Emory University, Atlanta, Ga.

Chicago Urban League Papers, Archives and Special Collections, University of Illinois-Chicago, Chicago, Ill. .

Claude Barnett Papers, Archives and Research Center, Chicago History Museum, Chicago, Ill.

Doris Saunders Papers, Vivian G. Harsh Research Collection, Chicago Public Library, Chicago, Ill.

Era Bell Thompson Papers, Vivian G. Harsh Research Collection, Chicago Public Library, Chicago, Ill.

G. Allen Foster Papers, McCain Library and Archives, University of Southern Mississippi, Hattiesburg, Miss. .

Gerri Major Papers, Schomburg Center for Research in Black Culture, New York Public Library, New York, N.Y.

Henry H. Brown, tapes 1–8, August 9–12, 2007, History Makers Digital Archive, Library of Congress, Washington, D.C.

Hoyt W. Fuller Collection, Robert W. Woodruff Library, Atlanta University Center, Atlanta, Ga.

Institute of the Black World Records, Schomburg Center for Research in Black Culture, New York Public Library, New York, N.Y.

John H. Johnson, tapes 1–10, November 11, 2004, History Makers Digital Archive, Library of Congress, Washington, D.C.

John Hope Franklin Papers, David M. Rubenstein Rare Book and Manuscript Library, Duke University, Durham, N.C.

Johnson Publishing Company Clipping Files Collection, Robert W. Woodruff Library, Atlanta University Center, Atlanta, Ga.

Lerone Bennett Papers, Stuart A. Rose Manuscript, Archives, and Rare Book Library, Emory University, Atlanta, Ga.

Lerone Bennett Jr. Papers, Archives and Special Collections, Chicago State University, Chicago, Ill.

Lerone Bennett Jr., tapes 1–6, August 29, 2002. History Makers Digital Archive, Library of Congress, Washington, D.C.

Lynn Norment, tapes 1–9, February 6, 2008, and January 20, 2012. History Makers Digital Archive, Library of Congress, Washington, D.C.

Northwestern University African American Publications Collection, Shorefront Legacy Center, Evanston, Ill.

Paul E. X. Brown, Stuart A. Rose Manuscript, Archives, and Rare Book Library, Emory University, Atlanta, Ga.

Phyl Garland Collection, Archives of African American Music and Culture, Indiana University, Bloomington, Ind.

Robert E. Johnson Papers, Stuart A. Rose Manuscript, Archives, and Rare Book Library, Emory University, Atlanta, Ga.

Timuel Black Papers, Vivian G. Harsh Research Collection, Chicago Public Library, Chicago, Ill.

Vincent Harding Papers, Stuart A. Rose Manuscript, Archives, and Rare Book Library, Emory University, Atlanta, Ga.

W. E. B Du Bois Papers, Special Collections and University Archives, University of Massachusetts, Amherst, Mass.

Periodicals

Advertising Age
Afro-American
Atlanta Daily World
Black Books Bulletin

Black Enterprise
Black Stars
Black Times
Boston Globe
Chicago Defender
Chicago Daily Defender
Chicago Daily News
Chicago Guide
Chicago Sun-Times
Chicago Tribune
The Crisis
Dissent
Ebony
Ebony, Jr!
Ebony Man: EM
Essence
Freedom's Journal
Freedomways
Fortune
Jet
Liberator
Life
Los Angeles Sentinel
Los Angeles Times
Look
Miami Herald
Negro Digest/Black World
Negro History Bulletin
Negro Story
New York Amsterdam News
New York Times
Our World
Philadelphia Tribune
Sacramento Observer
Survey Graphic
Washington Post
Washington Times

Other Resources

Ahmann, Matthew. *The New Negro*. New York: Biblo and Tannen, 1969.
Alexander, Leslie. *African or American? Black Identity and Political Activism in New York City, 1784–1861*. Urbana: University of Illinois Press, 2008.

Appleton, Sheldon. "Martin Luther King in Life . . . and Memory." *Public Perspective* 6 (1995): 11–13, 47–8.

Asante, Molefi Kete. *The African American People: A Global History*. New York: Routledge, 2012.

Asukile, Thabiti. "Joel August Rogers: Black International Journalism, Archival Research, and Black Print Culture." *Journal of African American History* 95 (2010): 322–47.

Atwater, Tony. "Editorial Policy of *Ebony* before and after the Civil Rights Act of 1964." *Journalism and Mass Communication Quarterly* 59 (1982): 87–91.

Bacon, Jacqueline. *Freedom's Journal: The First African-American Newspaper*. Lanham, Md.: Lexington, 2007.

Baker, Houston A. "Critical Memory and the Black Public Sphere." *Public Culture* 7 (1994): 3–33.

Baldwin, Davarian. *Chicago's New Negroes: Modernity, the Great Migration, and Black Urban Life*. Chapel Hill: University of North Carolina Press, 2007.

Ball, Jared, and Todd Steven Burroughs. *A Lie of Reinvention: Correcting Manning Marable's Malcolm X*. Baltimore: Black Classic, 2013.

Barr, John M. "Holding Up a Flawed Mirror to the American Soul: Abraham Lincoln in the Writing of Lerone Bennett, Jr." *Journal of the Abraham Lincoln Association* 35 (2014): 43–65.

Bennett, Lerone, Jr. *Before the Mayflower: A History of Black America*. 7th Edition. Chicago: Johnson Publishing Company, 2007.

———. *Black Power, U.S.A.: The Human Side of Reconstruction, 1867–1877*. Chicago: Johnson Publishing Company, 1967.

———. *The Challenge of Blackness*. Chicago: Johnson Publishing Company, 1972.

———. *Confrontation: Black and White*. Chicago: Johnson Publishing Company, 1965.

———. *Forced into Glory: Abraham Lincoln's White Dream*. Chicago: Johnson Publishing Company, 2000.

———. *The Making of Black America*. Chicago: Johnson Publishing Company, 1975.

———. "Nat's Last White Man." In *The Second Crucifixion of Nat Turner*, edited by John Henrik Clarke, 3–16. Baltimore, Md.: Black Classic, 1997.

———. *The Negro Mood and Other Essays*. Chicago: Johnson Publishing Company, 1964.

———. *Pioneers in Protest*. Chicago: Johnson Publishing Company, 1968

———. *Wade in the Water: Great Moments in Black History*. Chicago: Johnson Publishing Company, 1979.

———. *What Manner of Man: A Biography of Martin Luther King, Jr*. Chicago: Johnson Publishing Company, 1964.

Berger, Stefan. "Professional and Popular Historians." In *Popular History Now and Then: International Perspectives*, edited by Barbara Korte and Sylvia Paletschek, 13–30. New Brunswick, N.J.: Transaction, 2012.

Biondi, Martha. *The Black Revolution on Campus*. Berkeley: University of California Press, 2012.

"Black America under the Reagan Administration: A Symposium of Black Conservatives." *Policy Review* 34 (1985): 27–41.

Blauner, Bob. *Still the Big News: Racial Oppression in America*. Philadelphia: Temple University Press, 2001.

Blight, David. *Race and Reunion: The Civil War in American Memory*. Cambridge, Mass.: Belknap Press of Harvard University, 2001.

Bodnar, John. *Remaking America: Public Memory, Commemoration and Patriotism in the Twentieth Century*. Princeton, N.J.: Princeton University Press, 1992.

Bonilla-Silva, Eduardo. *White Supremacy and Racism in the Post–Civil Rights Era*. Boulder: Rienner, 2001.

Booker, Simeon. With Carole McCabe Booker. *Shocking the Conscience: A Reporter's Account of the Civil Rights Movement*. Jackson: University Press of Mississippi, 2013.

Bostdorff, Denise M., and Steven R. Goldzwig. "History, Collective Memory, and the Appropriation of Martin Luther King, Jr.: Reagan's Rhetorical Legacy." *Presidential Studies Quarterly* 35 (2005): 661–90.

Boyd. Michelle R. *Jim Crow Nostalgia: Reconstructing Race in Bronzeville*. Minneapolis: University of Minnesota Press, 2008.

Broussard, James H. *Ronald Reagan: Champion of Conservative America*. New York: Routledge, 2014.

Broussard, Jinx Coleman, and Sky Chance Cooley. "*Ebony*'s Era Bell Thompson Travels the World to Tell the Story." *American Journalism* 26 (2009): 7–30.

Brown, Korey Bowers. "Souled Out: Ebony Magazine in an Age of Black Power, 1965–1975." PhD diss., Howard University, 2010.

Bryant, John, and Harold Cones. *Dangerous Crossings: The First Modern Polar Expedition*. Annapolis, Md.: Naval Institute Press, 2000.

Buckmaster, Henrietta. *Let My People Go: the Story of the Underground Railroad and the Growth of the Abolition Movement*. Boston: Beacon, 1959.

Burns, Andrea. *From Storefront to Monument: Tracing the Public History of the Black Museum Movement*. Amherst: University of Massachusetts Press, 2013.

Burns, Ben. *Nitty Gritty: A White Editor in Black Journalism*. Jackson: University Press of Mississippi, 1996.

Burroughs, Todd Steven. "Ebony." In *Encyclopedia of African American History*, edited by Paul Finkelman, 119–21. Oxford: Oxford University Press, 2009.

Burt, Laura. "Vivian Harsh, Adult Education, and the Library's Role as Community Center." *Libraries and the Cultural Record* 44 (2009): 234–55.

Carby, Hazel V. *Race Men*. Cambridge, Mass.: Harvard University Press, 1998.

Carmichael, Stokely. With Ekwueme Michael Thelwell. *Ready for Revolution: The Life and Struggles of Stokely Carmichael*. New York: Scribner, 2003.

Carmichael, Stokely, and Charles Hamilton. *Black Power: The Politics of Liberation*. New York: Vintage, 1992.

Carson, Clayborne. *In Struggle: SNCC and the Black Awakening of the 1960s*. Cambridge, Mass.: Harvard University Press, 1981.

Carson, Clayborne, Susan Carson, Susan Englander, Troy Jackson, and Gerald L. Smith. *The Papers of Martin Luther King, Jr.: Volume IV—Symbol of the Movement*. Berkeley: University of California Press, 2000.

Carson, Clayborne, Tenisha Armstrong, Susan Carson, Adrienne Clay, and Kieran Taylor. *The Papers of Martin Luther King, Jr.: Volume V—Threshold of a New Decade*. Berkeley: University of California Press, 2005.

Carter-David, Siobhan. "Fashioning Essence Women and Ebony Men: Sartorial Instruction and the New Politics of Racial Uplift in Print, 1970–1993." PhD diss., Indiana University, 2011.

Chambers, Jason. *Madison Avenue and the Color Line: African Americans in the Advertising Industry*. Philadelphia: University of Pennsylvania Press, 2008.

Chappell, David L. *Waking from the Dream: The Struggle for Civil Rights in the Shadow of Martin Luther King, Jr*. New York: Random House, 2014.

Christian, Margena. *Empire: The House That John H. Johnson Built*. Chicago: DocM.A.C. Write, 2018.

——. "John H. Johnson: A Historical Study on the Re-education of African Americans in Adult Education through the Selfethnic Liberatory Nature of Magazines." PhD diss., National Louis University, 2013.

Churchill, Ward, and Jim Vander Wall. *Agents of Repression: The FBIs Secret Wars against the Black Panther Party and the American Indian Movement*. Cambridge: South End, 1988.

Clarke, John Henrik. *William Styron's Nat Turner: Ten Black Writers Respond*. Boston: Beacon, 1968.

——. "Shapes of the American Past." *Phylon* 38 (1977): 212–5.

Cohen, Lizabeth. *A Consumers' Republic: The Politics of Mass Consumption in Postwar America*. New York: Random House, 2003.

Cohen, Robert. *Howard Zinn's Southern Diary: Sit-Ins, Civil Rights, and Black Women's Student Activism*. Athens: University of Georgia Press, 2018.

Collins, Rodnell. *Seventh Child: A Family Memoir of Malcolm X*. New York: Dafina, 2002.

Collins, Sharon M. *Black Corporate Executives: The Making and Breaking of the Black Middle Class*. Philadelphia: Temple University Press, 1997.

Conrad, Earl. *Harriet Tubman*. Washington, D.C.: Associated, 1943.

Cook, Robert. "Unfinished Business: African Americans and the Civil War Centennial." In *Legacy of Disunion: The Enduring Significance of the American Civil War*, edited by Susan Mary Grant and Peter Parish, 48–64. Baton Rouge: Louisiana State University Press, 2003.

Courtwright, David T. *No Right Turn: Conservative Politics in Liberal America*. Cambridge, Mass.: Harvard University Press, 2010.

Craig, Maxine Leeds. *Ain't I a Beauty Queen? Black Women, Beauty, and the Politics of Race*. Oxford: Oxford University Press, 2002.

Craig, Richard T. *African Americans and Mass Media: A Case for Diversity in Media Ownership*. Lanham, Md.: Lexington, 2015.

Crump, Paul. *Burn, Killer, Burn!* Chicago: Johnson Publishing Company, 1962.

Dagbovie, Pero Gaglo. *African American History Reconsidered*. Urbana: University of Illinois Press, 2010.

———. *Carter G. Woodson in Washington, D.C.: the Father of Black History*. Charleston: The History Press, 2014.

———. *The Early Black History Movement, Carter G. Woodson, and Lorenzo Johnston Greene*. Urbana: University of Illinois Press, 2007.

———. *What is African American History?* Malden: Polity, 2015.

Dallek, Matthew. *The Right Moment: Ronald Reagan's First Victory and the Decisive Turning Point in American Politics*. Oxford: Oxford University Press, 2000.

Danns, Dionne. *Something Better for Our Children: Black Organizing in Chicago Public Schools, 1963–1971*. New York: Routledge, 2003.

Davidson, Basil. *The Lost Cities of Africa*. Boston: Little, Brown, 1959.

Daynes, Gary. *Making Villains, Making Heroes: Joseph R. McCarthy, Martin Luther King, Jr., and the Politics of American Memory*. New York: Garland, 1997.

Delmont, Matthew. *Making Roots: A Nation Captivated*. Berkeley: University of California Press, 2016.

———. *Why Busing Failed: Race, Media, and the National Resistance to School Desegregation*. Berkeley: University of California Press, 2016.

De Santis, Christopher. *Langston Hughes and the Chicago Defender: Essays on Race, Politics, and Culture, 1942–62*. Urbana: University of Illinois Press, 1995.

Des Jardins, Julie. *Women and the Historical Enterprise in America: Gender, Race, and the Politics of Memory, 1880–1945*. Chapel Hill: University of North Carolina Press, 2003.

Dingle, Derek. *Black Enterprise Titans of the B. E. 100s: Black CEOs Who Redefined and Conquered American Business*. New York: Wiley, 1999.

Doreski, C. K. *Writing America Black: Race Rhetoric and the Public Sphere*. Cambridge: University of Cambridge Press, 1998.

Downs, Donald. *Cornell '69: Liberalism and the Crisis of the American University*. Ithaca, N.Y.: Cornell University Press, 1999.

Duberman, Martin. *Howard Zinn: A Life on the Left*. New York: New Press, 2012.

Du Bois, W. E. B. *Black Folk Then and Now*. New York: Holt, 1939.

———. *Black Reconstruction in America*. New York: Harcourt, Brace, 1935.

———. *The Souls of Black Folk*. Reprint. Rockville, Md.: Arc Manor, 2008.

DuRocher, Kristina. *Raising Racists: The Socialization of White Children in the Jim Crow South*. Lexington: University Press of Kentucky, 2011.

Dyson, Michael Eric. *I May Not Get There with You: The True Martin Luther King, Jr.* New York: Free Press, 2000.

Ebony Presents the John H. Johnson Interview. Chicago: Johnson Publishing Company, 2007. DVD.

Elkins, Stanley. *Slavery: A Problem in American Institutional and Intellectual Life*. Chicago: University of Chicago Press, 1963.

Ernest, John. *Liberation Historiography: African American Writers and the Challenge of History, 1794–1861*. Chapel Hill: University of North Carolina Press, 2004.

———. *A Nation within a Nation: Organizing African American Communities before the Civil War*. Chicago: Dee, 2011.

Fairclough, Adam. "Was Martin Luther King a Marxist?" *History Workshop* 15 (1983): 117–25.

Farmer, Ashley. *Remaking Black Power: How Black Women Transformed an Era*. Chapel Hill: University of North Carolina Press, 2017.

Fehrenbacher, Don. *Lincoln in Text and Context: Collected Essays*. Stanford, Calif.: Stanford University Press, 1987.

Fenderson, Jonathan. *Building the Black Arts Movement: Hoyt Fuller and the Cultural Politics of the 1960s*. Urbana: University of Illinois Press, 2019.

———. "Journey toward a Black Aesthetic: Hoyt Fuller, the Black Arts Movement and the Black Intellectual Community." PhD diss., University of Massachusetts, 2011.

Ferguson, Roderick. *Aberrations in Black: Toward a Queer of Color Critique*. Minneapolis: University of Minnesota Press, 2004.

Fischer, Klaus. *America in White, Black, and Gray: A History of the Stormy 1960s*. New York: Continuum, 2006.

Flamm, Michael V. *In the Heat of the Summer: The New York Riots of 1964 and the War on Crime*. Philadelphia: University of Pennsylvania Press, 2017.

Foner, Eric. *Reconstruction: America's Unfinished Revolution, 1863–1877*. New York: Perennial Classics, 2002.

Ford, Gerald. "Message on the Observance of Black History Month." February 10, 1976. https://www.fordlibrarymuseum.gov/library/speeches/760074.htm.

Fowler, Virginia. *Nikki Giovanni: A Biography*. New York: Twayne, 1992.

Franklin, John Hope. *The Emancipation Proclamation*. Garden City, N.J.: Doubleday, 1963.

———. *From Slavery to Freedom: A History of Negro Americans*. New York: Knopf, 1947.

———. *George Washington Williams: A Biography*. Durham, N.C.: Duke University Press, 1998.

———. *Mirror to America: The Autobiography of John Hope Franklin*. New York: Farrar, Straus and Giroux, 2005.

———. "On the Evolution of Scholarship in Afro-American History." In *The Harvard Guide to African American History*, edited by Evelyn Brooks Higginbotham, Leon F. Litwack, and Darlene Clarke Hine, xxiii–xxx. Cambridge, Mass.: Harvard University Press, 2001.

Frazier, E. Franklin. *Black Bourgeoisie*. New York: Free Press, 1957.

Fredrickson, George. *Big Enough to Be Inconsistent: Abraham Lincoln Confronts Slavery and Race*. Cambridge, Mass.: Harvard University Press, 2008.

———. *The Black Image in the White Mind: The Debate on Afro-American Character and Destiny, 1817–1914*. Middletown, Conn.: Wesleyan University Press, 1971.

Gannon, Michael. "Before the Mayflower." *Florida Historical Quarterly* 43 (1964): 197–98.

Gardner, Eric. *Black Print Unbound: The Christian Recorder, African American Literature, and Periodical Culture*. Oxford: Oxford University Press, 2015.

Garrow, David J. *Bearing the Cross: Martin Luther King, Jr., and the Southern Christian Leadership Conference*. New York: Morrow, 1986.

Garvey, Ellen Gruber. *Writing with Scissors: American Scrapbooks from the Civil War to the Harlem Renaissance*. Oxford: Oxford University Press, 2013.

Geary, Daniel. *Beyond Civil Rights: The Moynihan Report and Its Legacy*. Philadelphia: University of Pennsylvania Press, 2015.

Gibson, D. Parke. *The $30 Billion Negro*. London: Macmillan, 1969.

———. *$70 Billion in the Black*. London: Macmillan, 1978.

Gilyard, Keith. *John Oliver Killens: A Life of Black Literary Activism*. Athens: University of Georgia Press, 2010.

Glickman, Lawrence B. *Buying Power: A History of Consumer Activism in America*. Chicago: University of Chicago Press, 2009.

Glymph, Thavolia. "Liberty Dearly Bought: The Making of Civil War Memory in Afro-American Communities in the South." In *Time Longer than Rope: A Century of African American Activism, 1850–1950*, edited by Charles Payne and Adam Green, 111–40. New York: New York University Press, 2003.

Godshalk, David Fort. *Veiled Visions: The 1906 Atlanta Race Riot and the Reshaping of American Race Relations*. Chapel Hill: University of North Carolina Press, 2006.

Gordon, Tammy. "'Take Amtrak to Black History': Marketing Heritage Tourism to African Americans in the 1970s." *Journal of Tourism History* (2015): 1–21.

Goudsouzian, Aram. *Down to the Crossroads: Civil Rights, Black Power, and the Meredith March against Fear*. New York: Farrar, Straus and Giroux, 2014.

Grant, Carl. *Multiculturalism in Education and Teaching*. London: Routledge, 2015.

Grant, Nicholas. "The Negro Digest: Race, Exceptionalism and the Second World War." *Journal of American Studies* 52 (2018): 358–89.

———. *We Shall Win Our Freedoms Together: African Americans and Apartheid, 1945–1960*. Chapel Hill: University of North Carolina Press, 2017.

Green, Adam. *Selling the Race: Culture, Community and Black Chicago, 1940–1955*. Chicago: University of Chicago Press, 2007.

Green, Hilary. *Educational Reconstruction: African American Schools in the Urban South*. New York: Fordham University Press, 2016.

Greene, Lorenzo. *Selling Black History for Carter G. Woodson: A Diary, 1930–1933*. Edited by Arvarh E. Strickland. Columbia: University of Missouri Press, 1996.

Gross, Daniel. *Forbes Greatest Business Stories of All Time*. New York: Wiley, 1996.

Grossman, James. *Land of Hope: Chicago, Black Southerners, and the Great Migration*. Chicago: University of Chicago Press, 1991.

Guelzo, Allen. *Lincoln's Emancipation Proclamation: The End of Slavery in America*. New York: Simon and Schuster, 2004.

Gutman, Herbert. *The Black Family in Slavery and Freedom, 1750–1925*. New York: Pantheon, 1976.

Haas, Jeffrey. *The Assassination of Fred Hampton: How the FBI and the Chicago Police Murdered a Black Panther*. Chicago: Hill, 2010.

Haley, Alex. *Roots: The Saga of an American Family*. Garden City, N.J.: Doubleday, 1976.

Hall, Jacquelyn Dowd. "The Long Civil Rights Movement and the Political Uses of the Past." *Journal of American History* 91 (2005): 1233–63.

Hall, Stephen G. *A Faithful Account of the Race: African American Historical Writing in Nineteenth-Century America*. Chapel Hill: University of North Carolina Press, 2009.

Hanson, Michael. "Suppose James Brown Read Fanon: The Black Arts Movement, Cultural Nationalism and the Failure of Popular Musical Praxis." *Popular Music* 27 (2008): 341.

Harding, Vincent. *Martin Luther King: The Inconvenient Hero*. Maryknoll, N.Y.: Orbis, 2008.

———. "Power from Our People: The Sources of the Modern Revival of Black History." *The Black Scholar* 18 (1987): 40–51.

Harris, Robert. "Coming of Age: The Transformation of Afro-American Historiography." *Journal of Negro History* 67 (1982): 107–21.

Hartman, Andrew. *A War for the Soul of America: A History of the Culture Wars*. Chicago: University of Chicago Press, 2015.

Hartnett, Rodney, and Carol Libby. "Agreement with Views of Martin Luther King, Jr., before and after His Assassination." *Phylon* 33 (1972): 79–87.

Heitner, Devorah. *Black Power TV*. Durham, N.C.: Duke University Press, 2013.

Helgeson, Jeffrey. *Crucibles of Black Empowerment: Chicago's Neighborhood Politics from the New Deal to Harold Washington*. Chicago: University of Chicago Press, 2014.

Henson, Matthew. *Negro Explorer at the North Pole: The Autobiography of Matthew Henson*. Reprint. Montpelier, Vt.: Invisible Cities, 2001.

Herskovits, Melville. *The Myth of the Negro Past*. Boston: Beacon, 1958.

Henderson, Laretta. *Ebony Jr! The Rise, Fall, and Return of a Black Children's Magazine*. Lanham: Scarecrow, 2008.

Higginbotham, Evelyn Brooks. *Righteous Discontent: The Women's Movement in the Black Baptist Church, 1880–1920*. Cambridge, Mass.: Harvard University Press, 1993.

Hill, Lauren Warren, and Julia Rabig. "Toward a History of the Business of Black Power." In *The Business of Black Power: Community Development, Capitalism and Corporate Responsibility in Postwar America*, edited by Lauren Warren Hill and Julia Rabig, 15–44. Rochester, N.Y.: University of Rochester Press, 2012.

Hine, Darlene Clark Hine. *Hine Sight: Black Women and the Re-Construction of American History*. New York: Carlson, 1994.

Hines, Michael. "The Blackboard and the Color Line: Madeline Morgan and the Alternative Black Curriculum in Chicago's Public Schools, 1941–1945." PhD diss., Loyola University Chicago, 2017.

———. "Learning Freedom: Education, Elevation, and New York's African American Community, 1827–1829." *History of Education Quarterly* 56 (2016): 618–45.

Hirsch, Arnold. *Making the Second Ghetto: Race and Housing in Chicago, 1940–1960*. Cambridge: Cambridge University Press, 1983.

Hixson, Walter. *Historical Memory and Representations of the Vietnam War*. New York: Garland, 2000.

Holloway, Jonathan Scott. *Jim Crow Wisdom: Memory and Identity in Black America since 1940*. Chapel Hill: University of North Carolina Press, 2013.

Horne, Gerald. *Fire This Time: The Watts Uprising and the 1960s*. Charlottesville: University of Virginia Press, 1995.

Houston, Helen. "Negro History Bulletin." In *Encyclopedia of African American Education*, edited by Kofi Lomotey, 492. Los Angeles: Sage, 2010.

Humez, Jean. *Harriet Tubman: The Life and Life Stories*. Madison: University of Wisconsin Press, 2003.

Hurt, H. H. "The Fruit of Little Meanness." *North American Review* 250 (1965): 41.

Hutson, Jean Blackwell. "The Schomburg Center for Research in Black Culture." In *Black Bibliophiles and Collectors: Preservers of Black History*, edited by Elinor Des Verney Sinnette, Paul Coates, and Thoma Battle, 69–80. Washington D.C.: Howard University Press, 1990.

Ingham, John, and Lynne Feldman. *African American Business Leaders: A Biographical Dictionary*. Westport, Conn.: Greenwood, 1994.

Iton, Richard. *In Search of the Black Fantastic: Politics and Popular Culture in the Post–Civil Rights Era*. Oxford: Oxford University Press, 2008.

Jackson, Esther Cooper, "Introduction." In *Freedomways Reader: Prophets in their Own Country*, edited by Esther Cooper Jackson and Constance Pohl, xix–xxx. Boulder, Colo.: Westview, 2000.

Jackson, Thomas. *From Civil Rights to Human Rights: Martin Luther King, Jr., and the Struggle for Economic Justice*. Philadelphia: University of Pennsylvania Press, 2007.

Jacobs, Ronald. *Race, Media and the Crisis of Civil Society: From Watts to Rodney King*. Cambridge: Cambridge University Press, 2000.

Jeffries, Hasan Kwame. *Bloody Lowndes: Civil Rights and Black Power in Alabama's Black Belt*. New York: New York University Press, 2009.

Jelks, Randal Maurice. *Benjamin Elijah Mays, Schoolmaster of the Movement: A Biography*. Chapel Hill: University of North Carolina Press, 2012.

Johnson, Abby Arthur, and Ronald Maberry Johnson. *Propaganda and Aesthetics: The Literary Politics of African-American Magazines in the Twentieth Century*. Amherst: University of Massachusetts Press, 1991.

Johnson, Edward A. *A School History of the Negro Race in America*. Raleigh: Edwards and Broughton, 1890.

Johnson, John H., and Lerone Bennett Jr. *Succeeding against the Odds*. New York: Warner, 1989.

Joseph, Peniel. "The Black Power Movement: A State of the Field." *Journal of American History* 96 (2009): 751–76.

———. *Stokely: A Life*. New York: Basic Civitas, 2014.

———. *Waiting 'til the Midnight Hour: A Narrative History of Black Power in America*. New York: Henry Holt and Company, 2007.

Joyce, Donald. *Black Book Publishers in the United States: A Historical Dictionary of the Presses, 1817–1990*. New York: Greenwood, 1991.

Keller, Ron. "Abraham Lincoln in African American Memory." In *Encyclopedia of African American History: Volume II*, edited by Paul Finkelman, 172–73. Oxford: Oxford University Press, 2009.

Kelley, Robin. *Race Rebels: Culture, Politics and the Black Working Class*. New York: Free Press, 1994.

Killens, John Oliver. *Black Man's Burden*. New York: Simon and Schuster, 1965.

Kilson, Martin. *Transformation of the African American Intelligentsia, 1880–2012*. Cambridge, Mass.: Harvard University Press, 2014.

King, Toni. "Who's That Lady? *Ebony* Magazine and Black Professional Women." In *Disco Divas: Women, Gender and Popular Culture in the 1970s*, edited by Sherrie A. Inness, 87–102. Philadelphia: University of Pennsylvania Press, 2003.

Kirk, John A. *Martin Luther King, Jr*. London: Routledge, 2014.

Kitch, Carolyn L. *Pages from the Past: History and Memory in American Magazines*. Chapel Hill: University of North Carolina Press, 2005.

Kotlowski, Dean J. *Nixon's Civil Rights: Politics, Principle and Policy*. Cambridge, Mass.: Harvard University Press, 2001.

Kruse, Kevin M. *White Flight: Atlanta and the Making of Modern Conservatism*. Princeton, N.J.: Princeton University Press, 2006.

Kusmer, Kenneth L., and Joe W. Trotter. "Introduction." In *African American Urban History since World War II*, edited by Kenneth L. Kusmer and Joe W. Trotter, 1–18. Chicago: University of Chicago Press, 2009.

Laham, Nicolas. *The Reagan Presidency and the Politics of Race: In Pursuit of Colorblind Justice and Limited Government*. Westport, Conn.: Praeger, 1998.

Lassiter, Matthew D. *The Silent Majority: Suburban Politics in the Sunbelt South*. Princeton, N.J.: Princeton University Press, 2006.

Lawson, Steven F. "Long Origins of the Short Civil Rights Movement, 1954–1968." In *Freedom Rights: New Perspectives on the Civil Rights Movement*, edited by Danielle L. McGuire and John Dittmer, 9–38. Lexington: University Press of Kentucky, 2011.

Lentz, Richard. *Symbols, the News Media, and Martin Luther King*. Baton Rouge: Louisiana State University Press, 1990.

Leslie, Michael. "Slow Fade To? Advertising in *Ebony* Magazine, 1957–1989." *Journalism and Mass Communication Quarterly* 72 (1995): 426–35.

Lester, Julius. *Look Out Whitey! Black Power's Gon' Get Your Mama*. London: Allison and Busby, 1970.

Lewis, David Levering. *W. E. B. Du Bois: A Biography, 1868–1963*. New York: Holt, 2009.

Lewis, Edward, with Audrey Edwards. *The Man from Essence: Creating a Magazine for Black Women*. New York: Atria, 2014.

Ling, Peter. *Martin Luther King, Jr*. London: Routledge, 2002.

Longo, Julie. "Remembering the Renaissance City: Detroit's Bicentennial Homecoming Festival and Urban Redevelopment." *Michigan Historical Review* 32 (2006): 89–118.

Lubin, Alex. *Romance and Rights: the Politics of Interracial Intimacy, 1945–1954*. Jackson: University Press of Mississippi, 2005.

Lumpkins, Charles L. *American Pogrom: The East St. Louis Riots and Black Politics*. Athens: Ohio University Press, 2008.

Marable, Manning. *How Capitalism Underdeveloped Black America: Problems in Race, Political Economy and Society*. Boston: South End, 1983.

Marcus, Daniel. *Happy Days and Wonder Years: The Fifties and Sixties in Contemporary Cultural Politics*. New Brunswick, N.J.: Rutgers University Press, 2004.

Matelski, Elizabeth M. *Reducing Bodies: Mass Culture and the Female Figure in Postwar America*. New York: Routledge, 2017.

Mattsen, Kevin. *What the Heck Are You Up To, Mr. President? Jimmy Carter, America's 'Malaise,' and the Speech that Should have Changed the Country*. New York: Bloomsbury, 2010.

May, Kirse Granat. *Golden State, Golden Youth: The California Image in Popular Culture, 1955–1966*. Chapel Hill: University of North Carolina Press, 2002.

Mayer, Jeremy. "Reagan and Race: Prophet of Color Blindness, Baiter of the Backlash." In *Deconstructing Reagan: Conservative Mythology and America's Fortieth President*. Edited by Kyle Longley, Jeremy Mayer, Michael Schaller, and John Sloan, 70–89. Armonk, N.Y.: Sharpe, 2007.

Mayes, Keith A. *Kwanzaa: Black Power and the Making of the African American Black Holiday*. New York: Routledge, 2009.

Mays, Benjamin. *Born to Rebel: an Autobiography*. Athens: University of Georgia Press, 2003.

McClendon, John H. "Act Your Age and Not Your Color: Blackness as Material Conditions, Presumptive Context, and Social Category." In *White on White/Black on Black*, edited by George Yancy, 275–96. Oxford: Rowman and Littlefield, 2005.

McHenry, Elizabeth. *Forgotten Readers: Recovering the Lost History of African American Literary Societies*. Durham, N.C.: Duke University Press, 2002.

Meier, August, and Elliott Rudwick. *Black History and the Historical Profession, 1915–1980*. Urbana: University of Illinois Press, 1986.

Minchin, Timothy, and John Salmond. *After the Dream: Black and White Southerners since 1965*. Lexington: University Press of Kentucky, 2011.

Moreau, Joseph. *Schoolbook Nation: Conflicts over American History Textbooks from the Civil War to the Present*. Ann Arbor: University of Michigan Press, 2003.

Morris, Burnis. *Carter G. Woodson: History, the Black Press, and Public Relations*. Jackson: University Press of Mississippi, 2017.

Moses, Wilson Jeremiah, *Afrotopia: The Roots of African American Popular History*. Cambridge: Cambridge University Press, 1998.

Murdock, George. *Africa: Its Peoples and Their Culture History*. New York: McGraw-Hill, 1959.

Myrdal, Gunnar. *An American Dilemma: The Negro Problem and Modern Democracy*. New York: Harper, 1944.

Nakamaya, Thomas K., and Judith N. Martin. "The 'White Problem' in Intercultural Communication Research and Pedagogy." In *Whiteness, Pedagogy, Performance:*

Dis/placing Race, edited by Leda M. Cooks and Jennifer S. Simpson, 111–40. Lanham, Md.: Lexington, 2007.

Nishikawa, Kinohi. "Race, Respectability, and the Short Life of *Duke* Magazine." *Book History* 15 (2012): 152–82.

Ogbar, Jeffrey O. G. *Black Power: Radical Politics and African American Identity*. Baltimore, Md.: John Hopkins University Press, 2004.

Olson, Joel. *The Abolition of White Democracy*. Minneapolis: University of Minnesota Press, 2004.

Ondaatje, Michael. *Black Conservative Intellectuals in Modern America*. Philadelphia: University of Pennsylvania Press, 2010.

Painter, Nell Irvin. *Creating Black Americans: African-American History and Its Meanings, 1619 to the Present*. Oxford: Oxford University Press, 2006.

Parker, Frank. *Black Votes Count: Political Empowerment in Mississippi after 1965*. Chapel Hill: University of North Carolina Press, 1990.

Pattillo-McCoy, Mary. *Black Picket Fences: Privilege and Peril among the Black Middle Class*. Chicago: University of Chicago Press, 1999.

Perlstein, Rick. *The Invisible Bridge: The Fall of Nixon and the Rise of Reagan*. New York: Simon and Schuster, 2014.

Phillips, Ulrich B. *American Negro Slavery: A Survey of the Supply, Employment and Control of Negro Labor as Determined by the Plantation Regime*. New York: Appleton, 1918.

Pochmara, Anna. *The Making of the New Negro: Black Authorship, Masculinity and Sexuality in the Harlem Renaissance*. Amsterdam: Amsterdam University Press, 2011.

Pohlmann, Marcus. *African American Political Thought*. New York: Routledge, 2003.

Pride, Armistead Scott, and Clint C. Wilson. *A History of the Black Press*. Washington, D.C.: Howard University Press, 1997.

Pridmore, Jay. *Northwestern University: Celebrating 150 Years*. Evanston, Ill.: Northwestern University Press, 2000.

Pritchett, Wendell E. "Which Urban Crisis? Regionalism, Race, and Urban Policy, 1960–1974." *Journal of Urban History* 34 (2008): 266–86.

Putnam, Carleton. *Race and Reason: A Yankee View*. Washington, D.C.: Public Affairs, 1961.

Quarles, Benjamin. *Black Mosaic: Essays in Afro-American History and Historiography*. Amherst: University of Massachusetts Press, 1988.

———. *Lincoln and the Negro*. New York: Oxford University Press, 1962.

———. *The Negro in the American Revolution*. Chapel Hill: University of North Carolina Press, 1961.

———. *The Negro in the Civil War*. Boston: Little, Brown, 1953.

Ransby, Barbara. *Ella Baker and the Black Freedom Struggle: A Radical Democratic Vision*. Chapel Hill: University of North Carolina Press, 2003.

Reagan, Ronald. "Radio Address to the Nation on Civil Rights." June 15, 1985. https://www.reaganlibrary.gov/research/speeches/61585a.

———. "Remarks on Signing the Bill Making the Birthday of Martin Luther King, Jr., a National Holiday." November 2, 1983. https://www.reaganlibrary.gov/research/speeches/110283a.

Reed, Christopher. *Black Chicago's First Century, 1833–1900*. Columbia: University of Missouri Press, 2005.

———. *The Chicago NAACP and the Rise of Black Professional Leadership, 1910–1966*. Bloomington: Indiana University Press, 1997.

"Reexamining the Racial Record of Abraham Lincoln." *Journal of Blacks in Higher Education* 29 (2000): 126–31.

Regester, Charlene. "Robert S. Abbott." In *Writers of the Black Chicago Renaissance*, edited by Steven Tracy, 15–29. Urbana: University of Illinois Press, 2011.

Report of the National Advisory Commission on Civil Disorders. New York: Bantam, 1968.

Rhea, Joseph Tilden. *Race Pride and American Identity*. Cambridge, Mass.: Harvard University Press, 1997.

Rickford, Russell. *We Are an African People: Independent Education, Black Power, and the Radical Imagination*. Oxford: Oxford University Press, 2016.

Rieder, Jonathan. *Gospel of Freedom: Martin Luther King Jr.'s Letter from Birmingham Jail and the Struggle that Changed a Nation*. New York: Bloomsbury, 2013.

Roberts, Gene, and Hank Klibanoff. *The Race Beat: The Press, the Civil Rights Struggle, and the Awakening of a Nation*. New York: Knopf, 2006.

Robinson, Cedric. *Black Marxism: The Making of the Black Radical Tradition*. Chapel Hill: University of North Carolina Press, 1983.

Robinson, Eugene. *Disintegration: the Splintering of Black America*. New York: Doubleday, 2010.

Rocksborough-Smith, Ian. *Black Public History in Chicago: Civil Rights Activism from World War II to the Cold War*. Urbana: University of Illinois Press, 2018.

Rogers, Ibram. *The Black Campus Movement: Black Students and the Racial Reconstitution of Higher Education, 1965–1972*. New York: Palgrave Macmillan, 2012.

Rojas, Fabio. *From Black Power to Black Studies: How a Radical Social Movement Became an Academic Discipline*. Baltimore, Md.: John Hopkins University Press, 2007.

Rooks, Noliwe. *Ladies' Pages: African American Women's Magazines and the Culture That Made Them*. New Brunswick, N.J.: Rutgers University Press, 2004.

———. *White Money/Black Power: The Surprising History of African American Studies and the Crisis of Race and Higher Education*. Boston: Beacon, 2006.

Russell, Thaddeus. "The Color of Discipline: Civil Rights and Black Sexuality." *American Quarterly* (2008): 101–28.

Ryan, David. "Re-enacting Independence through Nostalgia: The 1976 US Bicentennial after the Vietnam War.'" *Forum for Inter-American Research* 5 (2012): 26–48.

Rymsza-Pawlowska, M. J. *History Comes Alive: Public History and Popular Culture in the 1970s*. Chapel Hill: University of North Carolina Press, 2017.

Salley, Columbus. *The Black 100: A Ranking of the Most Influential African-Americans, Past and Present*. Secaucus, N.J.: Carol, 1993.

Schwartz, Barry. *Abraham Lincoln in the Post-Heroic Era: History and Memory in Late Twentieth Century America*. Chicago: University of Chicago Press, 2008.

Scott, Daryl Michael. *Contempt and Pity: Social Policy and the Image of the Damaged Black Psyche*. Chapel Hill: University of North Carolina Press, 1997.

———. "Following in the Footsteps of John Hope Franklin." In *Tributes to John Hope Franklin: Scholar, Mentor, Father, Friend*, edited by Beverly Jarrett, 39–44. Columbia: University of Missouri Press, 2003.

Schaub, Diana. "Learning to Love Lincoln: Frederick Douglass's Journey from Grievance to Gratitude." In *Lincoln and Liberty: Wisdom for the Ages*, edited by Lucas Morel. Lexington: University Press of Kentucky, 2014.

Schmidtz, David, and Robert Goodin. *Social Welfare and Personal Responsibility*. Cambridge: Cambridge University Press, 1998.

Seay, George. "A Prophet with Honor? The Martin Luther King Jr. Holiday and the Making of a National Icon." In *The Domestication of Martin Luther King Jr.: Clarence B. Jones, Right-Wing Conservatism, and the Manipulation of the King Legacy*, edited by Lewis V. Baldwin and Rufus Burrow, Jr., 236–60. Eugene, Ore.: Cascade, 2013.

Sellers, Cleveland. With Robert Terrell. *The River of No Return: The Autobiography of a Black Militant and the Life and Death of SNCC*. Jackson: University Press of Mississippi, 1990.

Semmes, Clovis E. *Roots of Afrocentric Thought: A Reference Guide to Negro Digest/Black World, 1961–1976*. Westport, Conn.: Greenwood, 1998.

Sewell, George A., and Margaret L. Dwight, ed. *Mississippi Black History Makers*. Jackson: University Press of Mississippi, 1984.

Sinnette, Elinor Des Verney. *Arthur Alfonso Schomburg, Black Bibliophile and Collector: A Bibliography*. Detroit, Mich.: Wayne State University Press, 1989.

Smethurst, James. *The Black Arts Movement: Literary Nationalism in the 1960s and 1970s*. Chapel Hill: University of North Carolina Press, 2005.

Smith, Robert Charles. *Racism in the Post–Civil Rights Era*. Albany: SUNY Press, 1995.

Snyder, Jeffrey Aaron. *Making Black History: The Color Line, Culture, and Race in the Age of Jim Crow*. Athens: University of Georgia Press, 2018.

Sokol, Jason. *The Heavens Might Crack: The Death and Legacy of Martin Luther King, Jr.* New York: Basic, 2018.

Spencer, Robyn. *The Revolution Has Come: Black Power, Gender and the Black Panther Party in Oakland*. Durham, N.C.: Duke University Press, 2016.

Springer, Kimberley. *Living for the Revolution: Black Feminist Organizations, 1968–1980*. Durham, N.C.: Duke University Press, 2005.

Squires, Caroline. *African Americans and the Media*. Cambridge: Polity, 2009.

Stampp, Kenneth. *The Peculiar Institution: Slavery in the Antebellum South*. New York: Knopf, 1956.

Stange, Maren. "Photographs Taken in Everyday Life: Ebony's Photojournalistic Discourse." In *The Black Press: New Literary and Historical Essays*, edited by Todd Vogel, 207–27. New Brunswick, N.J.: Rutgers University Press, 2001.

Stein, Judith. *The World of Marcus Garvey: Race and Class in Modern Society.* Baton Rouge: Louisiana State University Press, 1986.

Stevens, Errol Wayne. *Radical L.A.: From Coxey's Army to the Watts Riots, 1894–1965.* Norman: University of Oklahoma Press, 2009.

Stewart, Jeffrey C., and Fath Davis Ruffins. "A Faithful Witness: Afro-American Public History in Historical Perspective, 1828–1984." In *Presenting the Past: Essays on History and the Public*, edited by Susan Porter Benson, Stephen Brier, and Roy Rosenzweig, 307–38. Philadelphia: Temple University Press, 1986.

Stone, Chuck. *Black Political Power in America.* Indianapolis: Bobbs-Merrill, 1968.

Strickland, Arvarh. *History of the Chicago Urban League.* Columbia: University of Missouri Press, 2001.

Styron, William. *The Confessions of Nat Turner.* New York: Random House, 1967.

Sugrue, Thomas. *The Origins of the Urban Crisis: Race and Inequality in Postwar Detroit.* Princeton, N.J.: Princeton University Press, 1996.

Sundquist, Eric. "From Antislavery to Civil Rights." In *Frederick Douglass and Herman Melville: Essays in Relation*, edited by Robert S. Levine and Samuel Otter, 416–35. Chapel Hill: University of North Carolina Press, 2008.

Symcox, Lisa. *Whose History? The Struggle for National Standards in American Classrooms.* New York: Teachers College Press, 2002.

Thelwell, Michael. "Mr. William Styron and the Reverend Turner." In *Black and White in American Culture.* Edited by Jules Chametzky and Sidney Kaplan, 391–414. Amherst: University of Massachusetts Press, 1971.

Thernstrom, Stephan, and Abigail Thernstrom. *America in Black and White.* New York: Touchstone, 1997.

Thompson, Charles. "Booker T. Washington Is Elected to the Hall of Fame." *Journal of Negro Education* 15 (1946): 1–3.

Thompson, Era Bell. *Africa: Land of My Fathers.* Garden City, N.Y.: Doubleday, 1954.

———. *American Daughter.* Chicago: University of Chicago Press, 1946.

Thompson, Shirley E. "The Black Press." In *A Companion to African American History*, edited by Alton Hornsby, 332–46. Malden: Blackwell, 2005.

Thorpe, Earl. *Black Historians: A Critique.* New York: William Morrow, 1971.

Thuesen, Sarah Caroline. *Greater than Equal: African American Struggles for Schools and Citizenship in North Carolina, 1919–1965.* Chapel Hill: University of North Carolina Press, 2013.

Tinson, Christopher. "Held in Trust by History: Lerone Bennett, Jr., Intellectual Activism, and the Historical Profession." *Africology: The Journal of Pan African Studies* 12 (2018): 175–91.

———. *Radical Intellect: Liberator Magazine and Black Activism in the 1960s.* Chapel Hill: University of North Carolina Press, 2017.

Toliver, Susan Diane. *Black Families in Corporate America.* Thousand Oaks, Calif.: Sage, 1998.

Trodd, Zoe. "The Black Press and the Black Chicago Renaissance." In *Writers of the Black Chicago Renaissance*, edited by Steven C. Tracey, 448–64. Urbana: University of Illinois Press, 2011.

Turner, James. "Africana Studies and Epistemology: A Discourse in the Sociology of Knowledge." In *Africana Studies: A Disciplinary Quest for Both Theory and Method*, edited by James L. Conyers, 91–107. Jefferson, N.C.: McFarland, 1997.

Tyson, Timothy B. *Radio Free Dixie: Robert F. Williams and the Roots of Black Power*. Chapel Hill: University of North Carolina Press, 1999.

Van Deburg, William. *Modern Black Nationalism: From Marcus Garvey to Louis Farrakhan*. New York: New York University Press, 1997.

———. *New Day in Babylon: The Black Power Movement and American Culture, 1965–1975*. Chicago: University of Chicago Press, 1992.

Vogel, Todd. "Introduction." In *The Black Press: New Literary and Historical Essays*, edited by Todd Vogel, 1–14. New Brunswick, N.J.: Rutgers University Press, 2001.

Wald, Gayle. *Crossing the Line: Racial Passing in Twentieth-Century U.S. Literature and Culture*. Durham, N.C.: Duke University Press, 2000.

Walker, Clarence Earl. *Deromanticizing Black History: Critical Essays and Reappraisals*. Knoxville: University of Tennessee Press, 1991.

Walker, Juliet. "Black Business Development." In *The Columbia Guide to African American History Since 1939*, edited by Robert L. Harris Jr. and Rosalyn Terborg-Penn, 194–210. New York: Columbia University, 2006.

Walker, Susannah. *Style and Status: Selling Beauty to African American Women, 1920–1975*. Lexington: University Press of Kentucky, 2007.

Washburn, Patrick. *A Question of Sedition: The Federal Government's Investigation of the Black Press during World War II*. New York: Oxford University Press, 1986.

Washington, Booker T. *Up From Slavery: an Autobiography*. Garden City, N.Y.: Doubleday, 1901.

———. The Story of the Negro. *New York: Association Press, 1909.*

Watkins, Rychetta. *Black Power, Yellow Power, and the Making of Revolutionary Identities*. Jackson: University Press of Mississippi, 2012.

Watras, Joseph. *Politics, Race, and Schools: Racial Integration, 1954–1994*. New York: Garland, 1997.

Watts, Jerry Gafio. *Amiri Baraka: the Politics and Art of a Black Intellectual*. New York: New York University Press, 2001.

Weems, Robert. *Desegregating the Dollar: African American Consumerism in the Twentieth Century*. New York: New York University Press, 1998.

Weems, Robert. With Lewis Randolph, *Business in Black and White: American Presidents and Black Entrepreneurs in the Twentieth Century*. New York: New York University Press, 2009.

Weiner, Melissa. *Power, Protest and Public Schools*. New Brunswick, N.J.: Rutgers University Press, 2010.

Werner, Craig. *A Change is Gonna Come: Music, Race, and the Soul of America*. New York: Plume, 1999.

West, Cornel. "The Radical King We Don't Know." In *The Radical King*, edited by Cornel West, ix–xvi. Boston: Beacon Press, 2015.

West, E. James. "The Books You've Waited For: *Ebony* Magazine, the Johnson Book Division, and Black History in Print." In *Against a Sharp White Background: Infrastructures of African American Print*, edited by Brigette Fielder and Jonathan Senchyne, 62–81. Madison: University of Wisconsin Press, 2019.

———. "A Hero to Be Remembered: *Ebony* Magazine, Critical Memory and the 'Real Meaning' of the King Holiday." *Journal of American Studies* 52 (2018): 503–27.

———. "'I See Enough Queers Walking the Streets in this City": Homosexuality and Sexual Geographies in Black Consumer Magazines during the 1970s." *Souls: A Critical Journal of Black Politics, Culture and Society* 18 (2016): 283–301.

———. "Lerone Bennett, Jr.: A Life in Popular Black History." *The Black Scholar* 47 (2017): 3–18.

———. "Power Is 100 Years Old: *Ebony* Magazine, Lerone Bennett Jr. and the Roots of Black Power." *The Sixties: A Journal of History, Politics and Culture* 9 (2016): 165–88.

———. "We Were All Pioneers: A Discussion with Simeon Booker." *Southern Quarterly* 52 (2014): 215–23.

White, Deborah Gray. "Introduction." In *Telling Histories: Black Women Historians in the Ivory Tower*, edited by Deborah Gray White, 1–52. Chapel Hill: University of North Carolina Press, 2008.

White, Derrick. *The Challenge of Blackness: The Institute of the Black World and Political Activism in the 1970s*. Gainesville: University of Florida Press, 2011.

Wiese, Andrew. *Places of Their Own: African American Suburbanization in the Twentieth Century*. Chicago: University of Chicago Press, 2004.

Wiggins, William H. *O Freedom! Afro-American Emancipation Celebrations*. Knoxville: University of Tennessee Press, 1987.

Wilkerson, Isabel. *The Warmth of Other Suns: The Epic Story of America's Great Migration*. New York: Random House, 2010.

Wilkins, Roy, and Tom Matthews. *Standing Fast: The Autobiography of Roy Wilkins*. New York: Viking, 1982.

Williams, Ernest. "William Styron and His Ten Black Critics: A Belated Mediation." *Phylon* 37 (1976): 189–95.

Williams, George Washington. *History of the Negro Race in America*. Reprint. New York: Bergman, 1968.

Williams, Jimmy. "Lerone Bennett, Jr." In *Lives of Mississippi Authors, 1817–1967*, edited by James B. Lloyd, 29–32. Jackson: University of Mississippi Press, 1981.

Williams, Rhonda. *Concrete Demands: The Search for Black Power in the 20th Century*. New York: Routledge, 2015.

Wilson, Clint. *Whither the Black Press? Glorious Past, Uncertain Future*. Bloomington, Ind.: Xlibris, 2014.

Wilson, Mabel. *Negro Building: Black Americans in the World of Fairs and Museums*. Berkeley: University of California Press, 2012.

Wilson, William Julius. *The Declining Significance of Race: Blacks and Changing American Institutions*. Chicago: University of Chicago Press, 1978.

Wolseley, Roland E. *The Black Press, U.S.A.* Ames: Iowa State University Press, 1990.

Wolters, Raymond. *Right Turn: William Bradford Reynolds, the Reagan Administration, and Black Civil Rights*. New Brunswick, N.J.: Transaction, 1996.

———. *Race and Education, 1954–2007.* Columbia: University of Missouri Press, 2008.

Woodward, C. Vann. *The Strange Career of Jim Crow*. New York: Oxford University Press, 1955.

Wright, Gavin. *Sharing the Prize: The Economics of the Civil Rights Revolution in the American South.* Cambridge, Mass.: Belknap Press of Harvard University Press, 2013.

Wright, William D. *Critical Reflections on Black History*. Westport, Conn.: Praeger, 2002.

Wu, Jinping. *Frederick Douglass and the Black Liberation Movement: The North Star of Black Americans*. New York: Garland, 2000.

X, Malcolm. *The End of White World Supremacy: Four Speeches*. New York: Monthly Review, 1971.

Zaretsky, Natasha. *No Direction Home: The American Family and the Fear of National Decline, 1968–1980.* Chapel Hill: University of North Carolina Press, 2007.

Zelizer, Julian E. *The Kerner Report: The National Advisory Commission on Civil Disorders*. Princeton, N.J.: Princeton University Press, 2016.

Zilversmit, Arthur. "Lincoln and the Problem of Race: A Decade of Interpretations." In *For the Vast Future Also: Essays from the Journal of the Abraham Lincoln Association*, edited by Thomas Schwartz, 3–20. New York: Fordham University Press, 1999.

Zimmerman, Jonathan. *Whose America? Culture Wars in the Public Schools*. Cambridge, Mass.: Harvard University Press, 2002.

Zinn, Howard. *SNCC: The New Abolitionists*. Cambridge: South End, 2002.

Index

National Baptist Convention, 108
National Commission on Negro History
  and Culture, 94
National Negro Congress, 18
Neal, Larry, 85
Negro Digest: cancellation, 111–12, 135;
  content, 52, 70–71, 87, 94; editorial phi-
  losophy, 18–19, 35, 84; popularity, 18;
  rebranding as *Black World,* 35, 84; rela-
  tionship to *Ebony,* 22, 39
Negro History Bulletin, 5, 17, 23, 38–39
Negro History Week, 24, 27–30, 104
Negro Story, 18
Negro World, 16
Negro World Digest, 21
Newton, Huey P., 84
New York: black community, 14, 52–53;
  education, 78; and Johnson Publishing,
  21, 23, 32; police department, 53; protest
  in, 52–53, 93; public library, 10
New York Times, 6, 33, 60, 75–76
Nipson, Herbert, 27
Nishikawa, Kinohi, 124
Nixon, Richard, 33, 104–5, 118
Nkrumah, Kwame, 103
Norford, George, 21
Northwestern University, 6, 9, 69, 79–81,
  88–90, 134

Ogilvie, Richard, 53
Ogletree, Kathryn, 80
Old Taylor, 96–97
Ottley, Roi, 42
Our World, 18
L'Ouverture, Toussaint, 36

Painter, Nell Irvin, 6, 7
Parks, Rosa, 126
Patterson, Orlando, 15
People's Voice, 21
Pepsi-Cola, 96
Philadelphia, 106
Philadelphia Tribune, 57, 65
Phillips, Ulrich B., 36
Pierce, Ponchitta, 56
Pittsburgh Courier, 6, 8, 17
Pochmara, Anna, 29
Poinsett, Alex, 12, 71, 84, 86, 100, 104, 111

"popular historian," 7
Powell, Adam Clayton, 21
Powell, James, 52
Prince, 125
Prosser, Gabriel, 36
Putnam, Carleton, 37

Quaker Oats, 23
Quarles, Benjamin, 4, 44, 95

race riots, 52–53, 64, 117; Watts, 49, 53–55,
  70
Reader's Digest, 18–19
Reagan, Ronald: administration, 83;
  appropriation of Martin Luther King Jr.,
  114, 118–20, 124–25; black support, 120;
  election of, 118; opposition to Martin
  Luther King Jr., 118–19
respectability politics, 3, 19, 23, 99
Rickford, Russell, 78
Roberts, Gene, 26
Robeson, Eslanda, 19
Robeson, Paul, 61
Robinson, Bradley, 23
Robinson, Cedric, 103
Robinson, Eugene, 123
Robinson, Jackie, 32
Rockefeller, Nelson, 53
Rocksborough-Smith, Ian, 7, 28
Rodgers, Evelyn, 29, 99
Rogers, Joel Augustus, 17, 23, 35, 65
Ross, Diana, 124
Rowan, Carl, 61, 63,
Rudwick, Elliott, 7, 93
Russell, Harvey, 96
Russell, Nipsey, 110
Russell, Thaddeus, 99
Russwurm, John, 14–15, 21
Rustin, Bayard, 62

Sandburg, Carl, 74
Sanders, Charles, 134
Scheuer, Jim, 94
Schomburg, Arthur, 1
Schomburg Center, 22
Scobell, John, 50
Scott, Daryl Michael, 7, 55, 129
Seagram, 23, 97

E. JAMES WEST is a Leverhulme Early Career Fellow in American History at Northumbria University.

The University of Illinois Press
is a founding member of the
Association of University Presses.

—————————————————————

University of Illinois Press
1325 South Oak Street
Champaign, IL 61820-6903
www.press.uillinois.edu